For [illegible]

[illegible] 1986

Controversies in Political Economy

Also by G. C. Harcourt

Economic Activity (with P. H. Karmel and R. H. Wallace), Cambridge University Press, 1967

Readings in the Concept and Measurement of Income (with R. H. Parker, eds.), Cambridge University Press, 1969

Capital and Growth, Selected Readings (with N. F. Laing, eds.), Penguin, 1971, 1973

Some Cambridge Controversies in the Theory of Capital, Cambridge University Press, 1972, 1974, 1977

The Microeconomic Foundations of Macroeconomics (ed.), Macmillan, 1977

The Social Science Imperialists. Selected Essays. G. C. Harcourt. Edited by Prue Kerr, Routledge and Kegan Paul, 1982

Keynes and his Contemporaries. The Sixth and Centennial Keynes Seminar held at the University of Kent at Canterbury 1983, (ed.) Macmillan, 1985

Controversies in Political Economy

Selected Essays of G. C. Harcourt

Edited by

O. F. Hamouda
Glendon College
York University, Toronto

Wheatsheaf Books

DISTRIBUTED BY HARVESTER PRESS

First published in Great Britain in 1986 by
WHEATSHEAF BOOKS LTD
A MEMBER OF THE HARVESTER PRESS PUBLISHING GROUP
Publisher: John Spiers
Director of Publications: Edward Elgar
16 Ship Street, Brighton, Sussex

British Library Cataloguing in Publication Data

Harcourt, G. C.
Controversies in political economy.
1. Economics
I. Title II. Hamouda, Omar
330 HB171

ISBN 0–7450–0105–X

Typeset in 11 on 12 point English Times by
Mathematical Composition Setters Ltd, Salisbury, UK.

Printed and bound in Great Britain by
Robert Hartnoll (1985) Ltd., Bodmin, Cornwall

THE HARVESTER PRESS GROUP
The Harvester Group comprises Harvester Press Limited (chiefly publishing literature, fiction, philosophy, psychology, and science and trade books); Harvester Press Microform Publications Ltd., (publishing in microform previously unpublished archives, scarce printed sources, and indexes to these collections); Wheatsheaf Books Limited (chiefly publishing in economics, international politics, sociology, women's studies and related social sciences); Certain Records Ltd., and John Spiers Music Ltd. (music publishing).

Contents

Introduction

The present volume contains a selection of essays which were written mainly in the 1970s and 1980s. It is complementary to an earlier selection, *The Social Science Imperialists*, edited by Prue Kerr and published in 1982 by Routledge and Kegan Paul. There are four parts: Part I on recent history of thought; Part II on the contributions of Joan Robinson and Piero Sraffa; Part III, the capital theory debate; and Part IV on policy issues.

The first essay in Part I, 'Reflections on the development of economics as a discipline', originated as the 1982 G. L. Wood Memorial Lecture at the University of Melbourne in June 1982. I was delighted to be asked to give this Lecture by my friends at my first university, not only because I was a pupil of Gordon Wood, albeit very marginally, but also because I have great affection for the students and teachers of the Melbourne economics department, who have always been exceptionally kind and welcoming to me. The invitation itself forced me to try to bring into focus a research project on which I had been working spasmodically for several years. In the late 1970s I wrote to a number of economists asking them briefly to jot down who and what had been the significant influences on them when they were undergraduates and graduate students. (Milton Friedman was the only person who did not reply to my letter.) I also read the Nobel Prize essays, both those of the recipients and those of the people who wrote about them, in order to see what trends, issues, controversies and moods emerged from them over the years. The first essay is the result of these endeavours. It stops in 1983 with the award to Gerard Debreu, though I was glad to see that I had referred in the essay to the work of Richard Stone, the 1984 recipient. The essay itself centres around reactions in the profession to the increasing use of mathematical and advanced statistical and econometric techniques in economics; the recurrence of the debate about the self-regulating nature of economic systems, in particular, the strength (or even the existence) of forces which lead to such an outcome; and about the influence of the twentieth-century trinity of great books—*The General Theory, Value and Capital* and *The Foundations.*

As I wrote in the introduction to *The Social Science Imperialists,* I have become interested in recent years in the writing of intellectual biographies. In May 1982 I took advantage of a visit by Kenneth Boulding to Australia to prepare an essay on him which is based in part on notes of a conversation I had with him in Melbourne (Ch. 2). I hope that it does justice to a remarkable person whose wit, compassion and humanity combine to inspire and whose written work contains many original insights and is a model of lucidity. I have also included an essay on Richard Goodwin (Ch. 3). I have always admired his work and so it is a pleasure to be able to record an account of his contributions, now happily brought together in the remarkable book that he and Lionello Punzo are soon to publish (see n. 18, pp. 71, below).

It was my privilege and good fortune to have known and worked with both Joan Robinson and Piero Sraffa, alas no more with us. They died within less than a month of one another in August and September 1983, respectively. I have published elsewhere a personal tribute to them (see Harcourt, 1984). In the two essays in Part II, I attempt to evaluate their contributions to economic theory (Chs. 4 and 5). Prediction is, of course, a risky activity, no more so than in our 'miserable subject', as Keynes called it (see *JMK*, Vol. XIV, p. 190); nevertheless, I would like to put on record my belief that a hundred years on from their death, the contributions of Joan Robinson and Piero Sraffa will be suitably celebrated.

I included in *The Social Science Imperialists* a number of papers on the Cambridge capital theory debate. In Part III, I have decided to include three more. The first is the earliest paper published in this selection, a paper which I prepared for an IEA conference on plans and markets held in Nice in

1966 (Ch. 6). It contains the first results of my interest in investment decision-rules and the choice of techniques by firms in both the Western capitalist economies and the European socialist countries. The second essay is the survey of capital theory which was commissioned in 1968 by Mark Perlman for the newly formed *Journal of Economic Literature* (Ch. 7). It was published in June 1969 in the second issue. I have decided to reprint it, first, because this gives me the opportunity to correct printing errors and minor 'howlers' (it had to be written in a great hurry) and, second, because it may be useful for readers to be reminded of the state of play at the end of the 1960s, when as I said in the conclusion, 'We [broke] off in midstream [with] few issues settled'. I am happy to report, though, that those 'best friends' who were neoclassicals still remain so.

The other essay, Chapter 8, was commissioned for the *Journal of Political Economy* by Robert Gordon (I have often wondered whether it might have been partly responsible for his 'move' to Northwestern). The essay is in part a tribute to the first of the important contributions of Jan Kregel, for it uses his first book as the focal point around which the progress report was written. I was tempted to add an essay in which I set out in general terms what I think of the issues now in the post 'Hahn of the neo-Ricardians' era (see Hahn, 1982). However, I decided that I had little of substance to add to the position that I reached in Harcourt, 1975. Subsequent jousting with Frank Hahn before, for example, the Marshall Society in the Lent Term of 1983 has not considerably modified my views. Still, I am always open to persuasion, for Frank Hahn has not the sole monopoly on the search for truth.

Part IV contains papers which have to do with policy issues, with the application of the implications of the theoretical issues that I have tried to understand and expound in other papers. In the 1970s I became concerned, as we all did, with accelerating inflation, especially in Australia, and very early on I became involved in the debate on the merits of wage indexation. Needless to say, I was roundly abused for advocating it (as part of a package deal), the late Donald Whitehead going so far as to say that my suggestions were 'the silliest way to fight inflation'. (We ended up much nearer agreement—perhaps we were both silly?) A request to talk to the State Convention of the South Australian Division of the Society of Accountants in August 1974 led me to write the first essay in this part (Ch. 9), to which is appended a postscript on what became known as 'The Adelaide Plan'. This was jointly worked out by the late Eric Russell, Barry Hughes, Phillip Bentley and myself—I am sure, though, that we all would agree that Eric was the main inspiration and guide. (I have described Eric's sustained interest in these debates in *The Social Science Imperialists,* Essay 21, and in a memoir of Eric in the *Economic Record,* 1977.)

In 1978 I was asked to join the National Committee of Enquiry, which was set up by the Australian Labor Party to find out why the ALP had fared so badly in the elections of 1975 and 1977 and to suggest what reforms could and should be made. I took a special interest in the discussion of economic issues, and the invitation to give the John Curtain Memorial Lecture at the Australian National University in August 1982 was a suitable opportunity for me to range over the issues which I had considered (Ch. 10). I would like to record my great indebtedness to Prue Kerr for helping me to get my thoughts clear on these issues. Many of the ideas that I report here and which I contributed to the ALP enquiry arose from our joint paper, 'The Mixed Economy', which was published in the North and Weller collection in 1980, though it was written several years earlier.

The last essay (Ch. 11), 'Notes on the Social Limits to Growth', was inspired by the work of the late Fred Hirsch, especially his remarkable book, *Social Limits to Growth,* Hirsch, 1977. I prepared the paper for the conference of labour economists which was held in Brisbane in 1978, and I rewrote it when the editors of *Forum* asked me for an article. I thought that Hirsch's views on the concept of positional goods and the implications that they carry for the processes at work in our economies ought to be considered by people who were thinking about the transition to a more just and equitable society.

The editor of this selection, Omar Hamouda, asked me to record what I think the purpose of economics is. Evidently

I said that the purpose is:

> to make the world a better place for ordinary men and women, to produce a more just and equitable society. In order to do that, you have to understand how particular societies work and where the pockets of power are, and how you can either alter those or work within them and produce desirable results for ordinary people, not just for the people who have the power. I see economics as very much a moral as well as a social science and very much a handmaiden to progressive thought. It is really the study of the processes whereby surpluses are created in economies, how they are extracted, who gets them and what they do with them. All economies have created surpluses in one way or another. Capitalism does it in a particular way and that is the process in which I am most interested because I live in capitalist economies. At the same time, I would like to help to create a society where the surplus is extracted and used in a way quite different from that of a capitalist society.

I hope that the essays are seen to illustrate different aspects of these beliefs.

In closing, may I thank Omar for his great help in preparing the essays for publication, for his ever-ready support and for his encouragement in persuading me that such a project would be worth doing?

G. C. HARCOURT
Cambridge
July 1985

REFERENCES

Hahn, F. H. (1982). 'The Neo-Ricardians', *Cambridge Journal of Economics* 6, no. 4 (Dec.), 353–74

Harcourt, G. C. (1975). 'Revival of Political Economy: A Further Comment', *Economic Record* 48, no. 135 (Sept.) 368–70

—— (1984). 'The End of an Era: Joan Robinson (1903–83) and Piero Sraffa (1898–1983)', *Journal of Post Keynesian Economics* 6, no. 3 (Spring), 466–9

Hirsch, F. (1977). *Social Limits to Growth*. London, Routledge and Kegan Paul, 1977

PART I
Recent history of economic thought

1 Reflections on the Development of Economics as a Discipline[1]

I

1. I am honoured to be asked to deliver the 1982 G. L. Wood Memorial Lecture. I went to his 1950 Economic Geography I lectures and his 1951 Public Finance lectures (which were given at 8 o'clock in the morning) and, as a fourth-year student in 1953, I was at the Funeral Service where the Rev. Irving Benson spoke eloquently about his old friend. I remember Wood illuminating the difficulties of developing the north of Australia, despite the economic incentives of beer, by describing a pub in the north which was completely hidden from sight by the pile of crates of empties which surrounded it. I also went to the first G. L. Wood Memorial Lecture, at which I had my first glimpse of Peter Karmel, who gave the lecture. Perhaps these slight but relevant events justify asking me to talk. In any event, I hope I may honour the memory of a man who played such a significant role in the development of the Melbourne Commerce School.

2. The Nobel Prize for Economics has been given for fifteen years. In that time twenty-one distinguished economists have received it. Clearly, the electors have been faced with a stock-and-flow problem: the need to catch up on those who, had the prize been given before 1969, would have received it long ago, as well as to recognise those whose appointed time has just come. While it would be ill-mannered to quarrel with the awards to those who *have* received the Nobel Prize—although some have managed to do so—there are some scandalous oversights. The most notable is Joan Robinson, about whom, alas, nothing now can be done. That Kenneth Boulding has not been honoured as yet also suggests that we lack imagination.

3. Whatever the merits of awarding a Nobel Prize for

economics—one recipient has argued that as economics is *not* a hard science, there should not be a Nobel Prize for it and that he only accepted his because he was told of his award early in the morning before he was properly awake (see Myrdal 1977, p. 52)—it does have the great advantage that the recipients are required to give a lecture at the ceremony at which they receive the award and that other economists are required to write essays about *them*, in order that the selection committee may judge why the subjects are fit and proper people to become Nobel laureates.[2] These lectures and essays, most of which are published in what is now the *Scandinavian Journal of Economics*, are the source material for sections III to VI of this lecture.

4. Section II is based on letters that I have received from a selection of economists. I asked them to jot down who and what most influenced them in their undergraduate and graduate years. In addition to the people I know personally and who kindly responded with a collection of fascinating letters, the Nobel Prize winners are required to write autobiographical notes, and these also have been sources for Section II. (Possibly the most moving of these is the essay by Sir Arthur Lewis, 1980a.) While these various sources obviously preclude anything approaching a comprehensive coverage, they do allow us to discern trends, cross-currents, crises, controversies about which many of the best minds in our trade have written. Changing moods also may be discerned as we pass from the relatively optimistic days of the late 1960s to the uncertain, anxious and troubled times of the early 1980s. Aspirations, expectations, even hopes have all been considerably dampened, and this is reflected in some of the later essays. Indeed, considering how deep-seated our current problems are, the spate of 'lament for economics' presidential addresses of the early 1970s now seem, with hindsight, to have been decidedly premature. It should be said, though, that Marshall's 'cool heads but warm hearts' are well represented—to date—amongst the Nobel laureates. The compassionate, decent, humane personalities that come through the essays, both their own and those of their sympathetic admirers[3], are admirable. Bent Hansen (1969) and Lloyd Reynolds (1974) think that their subjects—Jan

Tinbergen in 1969 and Gunnar Mydal in 1974—just as appropriately could have received the Nobel Prize for peace.[4]

5. Most of the recipients still see our discipline as the means of analysing the malfunctioning of our economies—the existence of poverty, inequality, unemployment, discrimination and inflation. Sometimes their vision extends to encompass the world: Wassily Leontief, laureate in 1973, prepared an input–output model of the world for his lecture (1974). Their object is to obtain an understanding which will allow the lot of ordinary men and women to be improved.[5] Even those who are opposed to discretionary government intervention nevertheless base their case on the damage which they believe will ensue and has ensued. This is because, on their understanding, the system left to itself—and provided only that economic and political power are widely diffused and competition is strong, including letting the losers fall out, at least economically—will provide the best environment for free persons to fulfil themselves. Hayek (1975) is the most articulate proponent of this view. He stresses the limitations of knowledge and of the gathering of information which the market can supersede, but no one brain, or combination of brains, can. As Hahn (1982) has documented, Hayek argued that while 'economically relevant information was highly decentralised, [the price system] successfully aggregates this information so that the economy behaves as if there had been no specialised knowledge in the first place' (p. 16). Hahn adds that 'Hayek did not prove this to be so and . . . only very recently [have] we . . . understood the circumstances in which the claim made is correct' (p. 16). Nevertheless, Hayek argues his case in a civilised manner, exactly as in *The Road to Serfdom*, of which Schumpeter (1946, p. 2169) said; 'It is . . . a polite book that hardly ever attributes to opponents anything beyond intellectual error'.

II

6. Before we move on to our main theme, the general trends, issues and controversies, it is instructive to look at the great changes that have occurred in the systematic training—early

on, it hardly could be called systematic—that we require of fledgling economists. I shall draw on the letters from the various economists to which I referred above, together with some other writings; for example, Hicks's account of his own training (Hicks 1979) and Samuelson's contribution to the series of great men on themselves (Samuelson, 1972). We start with an Australian example. Wilfred Prest (Professor Emeritus of the University of Melbourne) has outlined his training first as an historian and then as an economist at the University of Leeds, in which, surprise, surprise, Marshall figured prominently:

> I returned to Economics [in 1927] after completing a[n] honours degree in History. The first 'advanced' book I read was one of Cassel's ... purchasing-power parity. Monetary problems were still a matter of major concern ... the recognised authority was Hawtrey rather than Keynes. On the theory side we worked through the two volumes of Taussig's Principles and so on to Marshall, with side references to Wicksteed and Pigou. On the historical side we read Lipson [and] Fay ..., Cannan on the History of Doctrine, with some of the original texts, particularly Adam Smith, Ricardo [and] parts of Marx ... I imagine that this sort of course—primarily literary, historical or philosophical—was fairly typical of British universities in the 1920s.

7. Joe Isaac's training at Melbourne was not *that* dissimilar to my own, though a decade separated us. (Joe was my Queen's tutor in my first year, 1950.) He, too, got the (then) Cambridge orientated Melbourne training, and experienced the first flush of enthusiasm of Keynes's (of *The General Theory*) disciples in Australia, as well as Kalecki's, a name that—properly—recurs. Joe adds: 'there was a strong applied bias in relation to the Australian economy, mostly through articles, in the three years of the course'. Nevertheless, Joe chose to go to the LSE for his PhD on wages, which he did in two years (!) and managed as well to read Lerner on *The Economics of Control*, Hicks on the trade cycle and Harrod on growth.

8. I mentioned that Kalecki is a name which recurs, Robert Solow, for example, writes approvingly of him. 'We read Kalecki' (this is Harvard 1945–47). 'The article on the Distribution of Income [was] on the compulsory reading lists. I was much taken by his peculiar style of producing numbers, and still tend to prefer the back of the envelope to

the computing machine.' Furthermore, Solow denies that there was 'some sort of semi-conspiracy to suppress Kalecki in the US'. Kenneth Arrow has also written in admiration of his work, though he does not mention Kalecki as having been an influence in his undergraduate and postgraduate days.[6]

9. A trend that emerges which to my mind is disquieting is how far we have moved away from our primary sources—the great books in the discipline—to dependence on text-books, at least in the training of undergraduates. At honours and postgraduate level, of course, journal articles are the staple diet. But I am not sure that the undergraduates would have the time now as I had to browse in the Melbourne University Library and read haphazardly but hugely from the collection there. And there cannot be many of today's undergraduates who would have done as Kenneth Arrow did and read without bidding all three volumes of Marx, for example, as part of an HET course. Arrow, in fact, did this as a graduate student at Columbia, but it was 'the only year in which [he] really studied economics'. As a graduate student in the Department of Mathematics—his primary aim then was to study mathematical statistics—he did do a course in mathematical economics with Harold Hotelling. 'We read mostly Hotelling's papers . . . a pretty good statement of the more advanced mathematical versions of neoclassical economics.' Arrow did not study Keynes's *General Theory* until after his military service (from 1942 to 1946). Even then it was as part of 'a vast amount of reading' on his own which also included 'some of the classics of mathematical economics (Cournot, Walras, Pareto) and the then current literature in *Econometrica*.' In the 1941/42 course on business cycles at Columbia given by Arthur Burns, the works of Wesley Mitchell, Haberler and Schumpeter were prominent but those of Keynes 'were not mentioned'. As with most of his generation *Value and Capital* figures prominently—'the most important reading [done] completely on [his] own'. Arrow concludes: 'As you can see, it was a very odd education. I have always been very grateful not to have had a better one, which undoubtedly would have been much more constricting'. We could add that you also may need to be Kenneth Arrow to take advantage of it.

10. Of course, we should note as well the quantum jump that has occurred in staffing—compare, for example, Austin Robinson's description (Robinson, 1977) of the Cambridge Faculty in 1930/31, which numbered eleven (or thirteen if the two 'left-overs' to teach pass students are included), with the typical UK or US or Australian undergraduate and graduate department now. Robinson's little band not only coped with teaching the young, they simultaneously carried on two 'revolutions' in economic theory. First, there was the imperfect competition one under Piero Sraffa's stimulus, in his 1926 article (his 1925 article only now has been translated into English, though the first few pages of his 1926 article are a succinct summary of it) and then in his lectures, unhappily lasting only until the beginning of the 1930s. Robinson (1977, p. 29) describes Sraffa's reaction to the criticism of Marshall which he was spearheading, how he stayed up all night before a lecture and in the end begged to be taken off lecturing altogether. Of course, in those days, this was possible, and Sraffa was released for one of the finest pieces of scholarship in our discipline—the superb editions of Ricardo (with the collaboration of Maurice Dobb)—and ultimately for the most powerful twentieth-century work in the critique of orthodox economics, *Production of Commodities by Means of Commodities*.[7]

11. The Second World War was responsible for some unorthodox introductions to economics. Fred Gruen and Aubrey Silberston both started their studies as guests of the combatants, Fred in Australia, Aubrey in Germany. Fred was admitted as an undergraduate to Melbourne University in August 1941 from an internment camp in Tatura. (He had escaped from Hitler's Europe to the UK before the war. He was locked up as an enemy alien when war broke out and then sent to Australia.) He completed his studies as an external student while in the Australian Army from 1942 to 1944. Kingsly Laffer 'introduced [him] to *The General Theory* ... and A. G. L. Shaw and Eric Russell tutored [him] in various subjects'. He sat a BA (Pass) in November 1944, had a full year at the university under CRTS in 1946, and then became an economics research officer for the NSW Department of Agriculture. 'The only other job going [at

that time] was as Research Assistant to a fellow named Trevor Swan'. In the late 1940s he went to Wisconsin for postgraduate work, and from there, to Chicago in the summer of 1950 through the offices of T. W. Schultz, whom he met at Wisconsin. Chicago was 'the most stimulating university I have ever attended'. He was taught by five subsequent Nobel Prize winners—Arrow, Friedman, Hayek (a few lectures only), Koopmans and Schultz. And from the reserves he had Lloyd Metzler, Gale Johnson, Jacob Marschak and Frank Knight 'in his last year before retirement . . . also good value'. Just for good measure, in his first period at the ANU as a Senior Research Fellow he had Ivor Pearce, Wilf Salter and Swan as colleages.

12. Aubrey Silberston 'started studying economics as a prisoner of war for about a year in 1944–45. Then [he] took Part II Economics in Cambridge in one year in June 1946'. He was supervised by Joan Robinson 'on Keynes, but she also gave [Aubrey] quite a lot of work on industry, labour, etc.' In the POW camp he had 'some guidance from others who studied economics'. The books that stand out for him are Joan Robinson's *Economics of Imperfect Competition*, Benham, Meade's *Economic Analysis and Policy* and Dalton's *Public Finance*. At Cambridge itself he lists Kaldor's Appendix C to Beveridge's *Full Employment in a Free Society*, Austin Robinson's *Structure of Competitive Industry*, Marshall, Pigou and Keynes's *The General Theory*.

13. We come now to the recollections of two recent incumbents of Marshall's Chair of Political Economy at Cambridge—Brian Reddaway and the present incumbent, Robin Matthews. Reddaway thought that he read 'rather little' in the two years that he read Economics (1932–34), yet he remembers *The Treatise* and Keynes's earlier work, Marshall, Pigou, Hicks (*The Theory of Wages*, "*not* 'acceptable'"), the Macmillan Report, Clay on unemployment, Fay (*Great Britain from Adam Smith to the present Day*), Alexander Gray, G. D. H. Cole, Joan Robinson (*Imperfect Competition*) and Chamberlin! He went to Economics from Maths, Part I (and not to Chemistry as he originally had intended to do), because he was 'inevitably much stirred by attempts to explain the world slump and see a way out'. He

became 'a great believer in open market operations as a means of easing the slump—[the] War Loan conversion in 1932 was a classic illustration of the powers of [the] B/E to lower rates'. Reddaway had the priceless experience of being supervised by Keynes and Kahn before *The General Theory* was published so that some of the ideas came to him orally—to what good effect we know now from his perceptive review in the *Economic Record* (Reddaway 1936).

14. R. C. O. Matthews' undergraduate education was in Oxford in between 1945 and 1947:

> reading PPE [which included] four papers on economics—Principles, Economic Organization, Statistics and Economic Theory ... The coverage was extremely uneven, according to whether one had covered a topic in a tutorial essay or not ... there were gaps which in retrospect seem amazing; for example, [he took his] Finals without ever having heard of the elasticity approach to the balance of payments. Benham was the introductory textbook ... [He] read the standard literature of the 1930s (Keynes, Chamberlin, etc.) ... and for the ... Theory paper ... became well acquainted with Marshall, Pigou and Wicksell.

Neither as an undergraduate nor as a graduate did he ever go to a course in Mathematics, or Mathematical Economics. Matthews did go to Hicks and Hitch's Theory Seminar for postgraduates, where they went through 'one notable recent article' per seminar. He concludes:

> By the standards of American graduate courses, or even the Cambridge Tripos, it seems in retrospect an extremely inadequate education. However, it did avoid the tendency to staleness that affects some students nowadays. The gaps had to be filled in by private reading after graduation, not directed towards any examination.

15. Hicks too read PPE—in his case, in its very early years. He describes it (Hicks 1979, p. 195) as 'a course which was perhaps better devised for the training of politicians than of academics'. He though it was very 'social'; he himself did a thesis on skill differentials in the building and engineering trades. From 1928 to 1935 he taught—and learned—at the LSE passing 'from [a] state of appalling ignorance ... to [his] first theoretical achievements: the invention of the

elasticity of substitution ... the distinction of income and substitution effects ... and the liquidity spectrum' (pp. 195–6). Hugh Dalton put Hicks onto Pareto because he 'read Italian', so that he was 'deep in Pareto, before [he] got much out of Marshall'. Pareto took him to Walras and Edgeworth. A spell in South Africa in his second year at the LSE, where he analysed the white trade unions as monopolists, made him into a free-market man, ready to fit into Robbins' circle when Robbins came to the LSE in 1929. Hicks read the Austrians and Wicksell (in German). Hayek came to London 'to tell us about Austrian economics; and he did'. What was to become *Value and Capital* 'began from Pareto and Hayek', not from Keynes. Nevertheless, by 1935 Hicks 'had gone on ... to draw consequences from his new approach [and to realise] that [he] had separated [himself] from the faith in the free market which had been dominant among [his] colleagues' (p. 199).

16. Finally, we move to the United States—first, before the war, with James Tobin, who 'as a Harvard sophomore ... started majoring in economics in 1936'. Tobin came to economics because 'the subject was and is intellectually fascinating and challenging [and] at the same time it offered the hope that improved understanding could better the lot of mankind'. He pays tribute to his parents—his mother, who was a social worker and from whose 'first-hand accounts' he 'learned of the human suffering of unemployment and poverty', and his father, a journalist 'who also happened to be an intellectual'. Born in Champaign, Illinois, in 1918, his parents and Tobin too 'were known for eccentric but well-argued political views' (Tobin, 1982, p. 2). At Harvard, his 'tutor presented [him] with a newly published book at [their] first meeting and suggested it could occupy [them] for a while. It was the *General Theory*'. He 'was hooked' (Tobin, 1982, p. 7). Meanwhile, in the introductory courses, they were reading Taussig's *Principles*; later in Chamberlin's undergraduate theory course, which 'was full of classics', there was 'a great deal of Marshall, and of course Chamberlin and Mrs Robinson'. Alvin Hansen also came to Harvard in 1936, and it was from his course, which was 'shared with John Williams', that they 'got macroeconomics ...

exciting because Hansen was becoming the American Keynesian leader [while] Williams was skeptical'. Tobin also remembers 'fondly' Ed Mason and Paul Sweezy on socialism. Tobin was a graduate student at Harvard until he went to the war in 1941. 'Schumpeter was teaching ... marvellous, although he never taught his own writings. We read them anyway'. He presided over a Theory seminar, 'where R. G. D. Allen and Samuelson sat in and that's where [they] got some .. general equilibrium ... and utility theory. Hicks's *Value and Capital* was very influential for [Tobin]'. As the economics department was 'incredibly weak in statistics and econometrics' he 'took statistics in the math department'. Overall 'the Keynesian debate dominated [his] attention, and with Hansen, Harris, and the younger people on one side and Schumpeter, Haberler, [whose *Business Cycles* book, 'a judicious survey, was ... influential'] and others opposed, it was very exciting'.

17. Robert Solow 'came back to Harvard in 1945, as part of a flood of returning soldiers, with two years of undergraduate work still to do'; he was there until June 1949 by which time he was ABD. The main influence on him was Wassly Leontief 'just about the only person teaching rigorous theory at Harvard ... The key book was *Value and Capital* ... the earlier part ... [they] also studied Mosak's ... *General Equilibrium and International Trade* ... because it was an excellent exposition of Pareto-Hicks ideas'. Oskar Lange, 'another intellectual presence', brought 'a lot of light', not only for his article on welfare economics but also for his 'mathematical' models of Keynesian theory, which together with those of Meade, Modigliani and Reddaway 'really taught us Keynesian economics'.[8] Solow was never taught Keynesian economics formally because Hansen was on leave the year that he did the Hansen/Williams course. He read *The General Theory*, but he does not 'think it is a good book for students'. As for the *Foundations* ..., the other member of the trinity that recurs in the pre-war and post-war literature, Solow 'learned it ..., the great liberation,' by himself.

18. William Baumol also belonged to a 'do it yourself' (with other students) generation. At the end of the Depres-

sion at City College in New York 'where instruction in economics was very poor', Baumol taught the micro-theory course to the other students—*The Economics of Imperfect Competition*, Chamberlin, Marshall, and *Value and Capital*, with which he 'was having a great deal of trouble'. The interested undergraduates also struggled with the ideas of *The General Theory*. In 1946 he went to LSE, a faculty which included Robbins, Hayek, Kaldor and Arthur Lewis, Frank Hahn as a postgraduate student and Ralph Turvey as an undergraduate, and frequent meetings 'with Jan Graaf in a joint Cambridge-Longon-Oxford seminar. Welfare economics was a prime subject of interest and Samuelson's *Foundations* the most exciting new book ... Harrod gave his ... lectures on ... Growth ... considerable excitement'. They 'spent many hours discussing all these views [this included Keynes, 'accepted by everyone except Hayek'] and many of [their] ideas were produced as part of a common effort'.

19. It is appropriate to end this section with Samuelson's memories. He was born in 1915. He writes (Samuelson, 1972, pp. 159–61) that 'Chicago was a good place to learn economics [in 1932] precisely because it was a stronghold of [neo] classical economics [which] reached its culmination thirty years earlier [with] Marshall ... a better place [to mark time waiting for Keynes] ... than Harvard, Columbia, or the London School'. As for 'Cambridge ... never within my ken. [Moreover, as economics was also awaiting] mathematical methods, it would have been a personal tragedy if I had become merely a clever First in the Economics Tripos ... [Samuelson likes] to think [he] might have risen above the tragedy, but as Wellington said of Waterloo, it would have been a 'damned close-run thing'. At Chicago Samuelson had Aaron Director, a strong libertarian of the Knight-Hayek school—he was later to refer to Milton Friedman as his 'radical brother-in-law'; but even if he had had Mr Squeers as a teacher, Samuelson felt he was 'made for economics'. 'To a person of analytical ability, the world of economics was his oyster in 1935 ... a terrain strewn with beautiful theorems begging to be picked up and arranged in unified order'.

20. So from Chicago to:

> the Golden Days of the Harvard Yard ... precisely the right place to be in the next half a dozen years—the age of Hansen—and of Schumpeter, and of Leontief as teachers; of comrades at arms—Alan and Paul Sweezy, Kenneth Galbraith, Aaron ... Gordon, Abram Bergson, Shigeto Tsuru, Richard Musgrave, Wolfgang Stolper, [who were already there,] and ... many yet to come—Lloyd Metzler, Robert Triffin, Joe Bain, James Tobin, Robert Bishop, John Lintner, Richard Goodwin, Henry Wallich, Cary Brown, Emile Despres, Walter and William Salant, Sidney Alexander, [Ben] Higgins ... Harvard made us. Yes. But we made Harvard. [pp. 162–3][9]

'Much of Harvard analysis was crude and unrigorous [but] it had life and lacked closure'—it left mistakes to be rectified, gaps to be filled 'as part of the advancing army of science'. Samuelson's enthusiasm and optimism continue to this day, but, as he says, 'All autobiography loses interest when success arrives' (p. 164).

III

21. A continuing theme that runs through the lectures and essays is that our discipline is a science, evidently a very superior buzz word. Great stress is put on this, though I suspect that the users do not always mean the same thing—which is hardly surprising with a spectrum that spans from Frisch to Friedman. Frisch thought that we are scientists in the service of people and that all our problems should be stated in such a way that the solutions could be set out explicitly. Frisch did not believe in cutting corners in the interest of communicating, of being understood. (He was an excellent expositor but never minimised the difficulties of a problem by ignoring them.) He would range over a number of areas as problems presented themselves in the process of moving towards a solution. His essayist, the late Leif Johansen (1969), illustrates this trait by reference to Frisch's paper on the business cycle, 'Propagation Problems and Impulse Problems in Dynamic Economics' (Frisch 1933):

> This trade cycle model is more refined and comprehensive than several

[others] that have become well known ... Frisch's model results in a mixed difference-differential equation ... more difficult to solve than the pure difference ... or pure differential equations ... found in later trade cycle models ... another typical example of the fact that Frisch never chooses the line of least resistance ... did not select the easy way of reformulating his ... models so as to obtain one of these pure forms. Instead, he worked out (in collaboration with mathematicians) a complete solution of the type of equation which arose ... not previously been solved in mathematical literature. [pp. 314–5]

22. In this respect Frisch differed from Tinbergen, who believes that diminishing returns to complex and refined methods set in very quickly in a social science where the urgency of the problems concerned requires a 'crash through' mentality combined with relatively crude but effective methods. Thus, Bent Hansen (1969) in commenting on Tinbergen's theory of economic policy, says of it that it:

is quite simple but it is concerned with the actual macro-policy targets of politicians in actually existing economies and has proved powerful and applicable to current policy problems ... a characteristic feature of all the scientific work of Tinbergen ... never much interested in esoteric theorizing for theory's own sake. His preoccupation has always been quantification and empirical application ... as soon as a method 'works' empirically he does not waste time on further theoretical refinements. [p. 331] [10]

23. Of course, there has long been a debate about whether social sciences can be regarded as akin to natural sciences or whether our problems and data are such as to preclude this, especially the problem that the subjects of analysis can find out what the observers have found out about them—and change their behaviour accordingly. (This is an insight which the rational expectations school are currently stressing.)[11] Keynes, it will be remembered, thought that economics was a moral science in which intuition and ethics, 'introspection and values', played as important roles as so-called scientific methodology. The latter 'leads directly counter to the habit of mind which is most important for an economist proper to acquire'. He further argued that economics:

deals with motives, expectations, psychological uncertainties. One has to be constantly on guard against treating the material as constant and homogeneous. It is as though the fall of the apple to the ground depended on the apple's motives, on whether it is worth while falling to the ground, and whether the ground wanted the apple to fall, and on mistaken calculations on the part of the apple as to how far it was from the centre of the earth. [Keynes, 1973, p. 300]

24. Myrdal's view (1977, p. 51) is that we are a 'soft' science as opposed to the 'hard' natural sciences. He gives two reasons. First, that we can only observe and record at first hand how people actually behave; why they do so is rooted in attitudes and in political and other institutions, all of which may differ as between groups and change over time. We have, therefore, no 'constants', no 'laws of nature' to discover. Second, 'a view is only possible from a viewpoint' so that economic research is of necessity 'political economy'—to call it 'economics' is naively to dodge the problem, to believe that we 'are simply seeking and finding the truth about facts'. Not surprisingly, Friedman (1977) has some different and challenging views on this issue. He says that he has never accepted that there are fundamental qualitative differences as between social sciences and natural sciences:

In both there is no 'certain' substantive knowledge, only tentative hypotheses that can never be 'proved' but can only fail to be rejected, hypotheses in which we may have more or less confidence ... positive knowledge grows by reaction to failure ... to predict ... by patching up until someone suggests a new hypothesis that more simply or elegantly embodies the troublesome phenomena ... In both ... no way to have a self-contained closed system or to avoid interaction between the observer and the observed. [p. 425]

Even the indissoluble mix of analysis and ideology is *not* unique to us—Friedman relates how at dinner in Cambridge, R. A. Fisher told 'one story after another about how accurately he could infer views in genetics from political views' (p. 453). These reflections, of course, lead to Friedman's account of his triumph over (what he takes to be) Keynesianism—the relation between inflation and unemployment, 'an admirable illustration because it has been a powerful political issue ... yet the drastic change ... in accepted professional views was produced primarily by the scientific response to experience that contradicted a tentatively accepted hypothesis ... the classical process for the revision of a scientific hypothesis' (p. 453).

25. In fact both Friedman and Hayek considerably oversimplify the positions of those they are criticising. To Hayek, Keynes's theory 'consists in the assertion that there exists a simple positive correlation between total employment and the size of the aggregate demand for goods and services' (see Hayek, 1975, p. 433). To Friedman, the battles with Keynes—superficially anyway—are empirical arguments over the stability and values of the parameters of certain key functions of IS/LM models. This, of course, is extraordinary, since Keynes's own work was not meant to be confined within the context of a general-equilibrium model. His essential methodology, partly derived from Marshall, partly from the classical economists, partly due to his own insights, was meant to escape from a general-equilibrium methodology; that is, from a notion of self-correction both in the system itself and in models of it, from simultaneity in the interrelationships of the important functions of the system, from including time in the analysis only insofar as it had the characteristics of space.[12] Hayek's characterisation is also quite at odds with the evidence of *The General Theory* itself, especially the discussions of the nature of the aggregate supply function (Ch. 3), the employment function (Ch. 20) and the theory of prices (Ch. 21), and with the evidence of Kahn's multiplier article of 1931.

26. It is interesting to reflect on how many of the Nobel laureates have been either natural scientists or greatly influenced by them. Thus Tinbergen and Koopmans were physicists, Kantorovich was an applied mathematician,[13] and Samuelson was greatly influenced by the Harvard mathematical physicist Edwin Bidwell Wilson, whom he couples with Hansen, Schumpeter and Leontief to make an Age—so much so that Samuelson has kept up his interest in physics ever since. Certainly Koopmans' and Samuelson's contributions reflect their early training and influence—elegance, rigour, preciseness of statement of the problem, belief that they *will* make a breakthrough in the end as they move from simple cases to more complex ones. Thus Koopmans (1977)

in his paper at the 1975 S'Agaro Conference wrote that the acceptance of the shadowy notion of perfect allocation 'is adopted on the hunch that aggregation is simpler with it than without it, while what is learned in this way may still be a worthwhile starting point for the study of more complicated situations' (p. 144). This optimism contrasts with Kaldor's well-known attack on neoclassical economics:

It is the hallmark of the neoclassical economist to believe that however severe the abstractions from which he is forced to start, he will 'win through' by the end of the day—bit by bit, if he only carries the analysis far enough, the scaffolding can be removed, leaving the basic structure intact. In fact, these props are never removed; the removal of any one of a number of them—as for example, allowing for increasing returns or learning-by-doing—is sufficient to cause the whole structure to collapse like a pack of cards. [Kaldor, 1966, p. 310].

27. Leontief's essayist Robert Dorfman (1973) has also praised him as a scientist, especially as an applied one who cut through the practical difficulties of applying a theoretical idea—his great contribution:

There is a dominant theme that runs through Leontief's four decades of professional work ... that economics is an empirical and applied science ... The only valid test of economic research is its empirical significance and its practical implications ... the clue to his discovery of input–output economics ... It was Leontief who first saw the practical potentiality of an input–output *table* and who learned how to really put one together. [pp. 430–1]

Dorfman contrasts Leontief's achievement with what he describes as Sraffa's 'very elegant independent discovery of the theoretical basis of input–output analysis' (p. 440). 'Sraffa,' he says, 'was content to present some interesting and important logical relationships', whereas Leontief kicked on to show 'how they could be measured ... confirmed ... and applied' (p. 440). This is an extraordinary howler, since Sraffa's object was entirely different to that of Leontief. Sraffa provides a critique of the supply and demand theories and points the way forward for a reemergence of the surplus theories of the classicals and Marx as applicable to modern problems,[14] in the process solving some logical puzzles. Sraffa has made quite clear his understanding of the distinction between theory and measurement and has stressed that the former must be logically watertight, not only in order to be consistent but also in order to be able to survive (see Sraffa 1961). Theory is as important for sorting out conceptual issues and approaches as for providing theorems. This quibble apart, though, I certainly agree with Dorfman and applaud Leontief's philosophy, which is very similar to those of the late Eric Russell and the late Wilfred Salter, to whose work I have always tried to pay tribute (see Harcourt, 1972, Ch. 2; 1982b, Parts III and VI). Stigler's essayists, Mincer (1983) and Schmalensee (1983), also argue that their person has a similar philosophy:

> One can see Stigler's approach to economic theory quite clearly in his elegant and influential text, *The Theory of Price*. In it, Stigler emphasizes the development of analytical tools and styles of thought useful in applications. He is clearly willing to sacrifice theoretical generality and mathematical rigor in order to stress the development of empirically relevant, testable propositions. [Schmalensee, 1983, p. 78]

28. Associated also with the nature of the scientific procedures of economics, we recently have had the absorbing essay by Melvin Reder (1982) on Chicago then and now and the unique characteristics of Chicago methodology. Reder sums this up in one proposition and four assumptions which must form the basis of any hypothesis used to tackle a specific problem—if it is to be acceptable to Chicago. (The pages of the *JPE* in recent years record how well this describes what is likely to get through their refereeing sieve. Except for a brief interlude in the late 1960s and early 1970s, under the more liberal and open-minded editorship of Robert Gordon, now safely moved away to Northwestern, the Chicago model as described by Reder is repeated over and over again.)

29. The Chicago view—'Tight Prior Equilibrium' in Reder's terms—

> is rooted in the hypothesis that decision makers so allocate the resources under their control that there is no alternative allocation such that any one decision maker could have his expected utility increased without a reduction occurring in the expected utility of at least one other decision-maker.

To make the model yield testable hypothesis, we need to add four assumptions:

> (1) *Most* individual transactors treat the prices of all goods and services that they buy or sell, as independent of the quantities that they transact.
> (2) The prices at which individuals *currently agree* to transact are market clearing prices that are consistent with optimization by all decision makers.
> (3) Information bearing on prices and qualities of all things bought and sold, present and future, is acquired in the quantity that makes its marginal cost equal to its price; information is treated like any other commodity.
> (4) Neither monopoly nor government action (through taxation or otherwise) affects relative prices of quantities sufficiently to prevent either marginal products or compensation of identical resources from being made approximately equal in all uses (p. 11).[15]

We may wonder as well what Chicago made of Herbert Simon's receipt of the Nobel Prize in 1979. Simon is most suspicious of the applications of the hypothesis of the heroic rational economic person maximising under constraints of formidable and daunting odds. He says that his contribution to economics is to change the economic person into a sort of Woody Allen satisficing in an environment characterised by uncertainty, and a great deal of ignorance and anxiety. His Woody Allen is content to find the first sharp needle in a haystack that will do for the job in hand, rather than to continue to search for the sharpest (see Baumol, 1979, p. 76).

30. Perhaps the last word on this issue may be had by Hicks (1984, p. 11), who argues that economics lies between, 'on the edges of', science and history:

> It is on the edge of science, because it can make use of scientific, or quasi-scientific, methods; but it is no more than on the edge, because the experiences that it analyses have so much that is nonrepetitive about them. If a scientific theory is good, it is good now, and it would have been good a thousand years ago, if it had been available; but the aspects of economic life which we need to select in order to make useful theories can be different at different times. Economics is in time, and therefore in history, in a way that science is not.

IV

31. One obvious theme that emerges from reading the Nobel Lectures is how technical the discipline has become, both in economic theory and in econometrics. The person most responsible for the mathematisation of economic theory is Samuelson—I have mentioned already how (apart from *The General Theory*) *Value and Capital* and the *Foundations* are the two books most often mentioned as key influences. The philosophy of the *Foundations* is directed towards establishing operational theorems as well as exploiting the unifying influences of the two great principles of the *Foundations*—maximisation or minimisation under constraints and the correspondence principle, the interconnection between statics and dynamics. In his Nobel Lecture (Samuelson, 1970) Samuelson reaffirms his faith in his youthful enthusiasm for such an approach, his disdain for literary economics, as opposed to his appreciation of the preciseness and rigor of the mathematical approach to theory. He does argue that the *theory* is more important, that mathematics is merely the agent (J. Willard Gibbs' saying, 'Mathematics is a language', is on the title page of the *Foundations*), and as I have argued elsewhere (Harcourt, 1982b), Samuelson is no longer regarded in the trade as a mathematical economist, merely as a theoretical one.

32. In arguing this case, Samuelson seems not to have heeded—much—Boulding's review of the *Foundations* (Boulding, 1948). There, Boulding assesses the limitations as well as the advantages and the achievements of the mathematical method in a social science. One point that he makes (which is echoed in Shackle's assessment of Keynes's mode of theorising by use of language) is that mathematics can be a limited, one-dimensional mode of thought, unsuitable for dealing with complex structures. 'It makes very little sense to say "let *Hamlet* equal *H* and *Macbeth* equal *M*"' (p. 236). He adds that it may be:

> an understatement to say that mathematics is a language, for, while it is probably true that all mathematical expressions can be translated into 'literary' language ... it is not true that all 'literary' expressions can be translated into mathematics ... [Boulding knows] of no mathematical expression for the literary form, 'I love you'. [pp. 236–7]

Shackle (see Harcourt, 1981, p. 144) has referred to Keynes's flair for choosing words which are evocative of the multi-dimensional concepts and sets of ideas that he is analysing—he mentions 'sentiment' as a good example. By insisting that truth comes only in the guise of a mathematical model, we may so desiccate the factors that we are trying to include in our models that they become very poor vehicles for interpreting the processes at work in our economies.[16]

33. Moreover, our ability to communicate, both within the boundaries of the trade and outside, to policy-makers and ordinary citizens, is greatly reduced—a danger which Boulding clearly foresaw in 1948. Having admonished those 'literary' economists who 'from wilful egotism . . . refused to acquire that modicum of mathematical training which yields clearly increasing returns', he speculated that 'the greatest danger [now may be] from the other side. The mathematicians themselves set up standards of generality and elegance in their expositions which are a bar to understanding' (p. 247)—they make a virtue of what is clearly a vice. I have, for example, on my desk at the moment, a collection of the important papers on the theory and econometric practice of the influential rational expectations school, edited by Lucas and Sargent (1981). Even in the Introduction, incomprehension sets in after the first couple of pages because the writers insist on using highly technical language. This contrasts with the ability of a Hahn, say, to communicate the gist of technical economics in an easily understood way, to discuss the conceptual issues involved, as he does in his 'Winter of Our Discontent' paper (Hahn, 1973) and his Fred Hirsch Memorial Lecture (Hahn, 1982). We must add that the very best mathematicians who have become economists do *not* try to mystify. As they are not overawed by mathematics as such, they are happy to take an independent look at economics as a separate discipline and to use the mathematics which they believe to be appropriate for it. Many of them are convinced that it is *not* a discipline which needs highly sophisticated mathematical models; they take almost a Marshallian stance, using simple models and often preferring pictures to squiggles, arithmetic to algebra, orders of magnitude as well as qualitative signs, as the most effective

means of understanding and communicating. I think here of A. K. Dixit and Bob Rowthorn, Peter Warr and Ian Steedman as good examples. But it has to be said that they flow against a tide of not-so-convinced practitioners, those who are still dazzled by mathematics as such and who pick problems as much for their mathematical tractability as for their economic importance.

34. To say this is not to say that so-called realism should be the overriding test for all classes of economic problems. Often important conceptual problems can be discussed and analysed within the bounds of distinctly 'unrealistic', that is, highly abstract models. This has been recognised at least since the time of Ricardo and is reflected in some modern debates—for example, the controversies in capital theory and those about whether the existence of surplus labour in the sphere of production is both necessary and sufficient for positive profits in the sphere of distribution and exchange in joint production models (see King, 1982, for a survey). Perhaps the clearest statement of this strategy in recent years is that by Hicks:

> All models are simplifications of reality; they leave out things which are judged to be unimportant, for the purpose in hand, in order to make it possible to think more clearly about the things that are retained. What is ... left out, and what is ... retained, is ... chosen with reference to the problem in hand ... perfectly proper to use one sort of model for one purpose, and another for another. [Hicks 1982, p. 218]

35. In his Nobel Lecture, Gerard Debreu (1984), who holds a joint chair in economics and mathematics at Berkeley, also makes a lucid and succinct set of arguments for his own distinctive brand of axiomatic analysis in economic theory:

> Contemporary developments in the theory of general economic equilibrium took Walras' work as their point of departure, but some of Walras' ideas had a long lineage that included Adam Smith's ... profound insight. Smith's idea that the many agents of an economy, making independent decisions, do not create chaos but actually contribute to producing a social optimum, raises indeed a scientific question of central importance. Attempts to answer it have stimulated the study of several of the problems that every economic system must solve, such as the efficiency of resource

allocation, the decentralization of decisions, the incentives of decision-makers, the treatment of information.

In the past few decades, that wide range of problems has been the subject of an axiomatic analysis in which primitive concepts are chosen, assumptions concerning them are formulated, and conclusions are derived from those assumptions by means of mathematical reasoning disconnected from any intended interpretation of the primitive concepts. The benefits ... have been numerous. Making the assumptions of a theory entirely explicit permits a sounder judgment about the extent to which it applies to a particular situation. Axiomatization may also give ready answers to new questions when a novel interpretation of primitive concepts is discovered. ... Axiomatization, by insisting on mathematical rigor, has repeatedly led economists to a deeper understanding of the problems they were studying, and to the use of mathematical techniques that fitted those problems better. It has established secure bases from which exploration could start in new directions. It has freed researchers from the necessity of questioning the work of their predecessors in every detail. Rigor undoubtedly fulfills an intellectual need of many contemporary economic theorists, who therefore seek it for its own sake, but it is also an attribute of a theory that is an effective thinking tool. Two other major attributes of an effective theory are simplicity and generality. Again, their aesthetic appeal suffices to make them desirable ends in themselves for the designer of a theory. But their value to the scientific community goes far beyond aesthetics. Simplicity makes a theory usable by a greater number of research workers. Generality makes it applicable to a broad class of problems.

The axiomization of economic theory has helped its practitioners by making available to them the superbly efficient language of mathematics. It has permitted them to communicate with each other, and to think, with a great economy of means. At the same time, the dialogue between economists and mathematicians has become more intense. [Debreu, 1984, pp. 274–5]

I have to confess that I would have been more persuaded by these arguments had I understood more of the survey of the work cited by the Royal Swedish Academy of Sciences which preceded it!

36. However, lest it be thought that I wish to put the clock back, let me say that I completely agree with the following statement by Richard Stone, one of the most clear-minded applied thinkers in the discipline and certainly one least prone to unnecessary controversy:

Except in a few obstinate pockets of resistance, the use of mathematics in the social sciences is now generally accepted. The reason is not to be found in the outcome of any high-flown philosophical battle but in a number of simple facts. In the first place, many branches of the social sciences are obviously, one might almost say aggressively, quantitative; demography and economics are clear examples of this. In the second place, while theories about the complex systems which are the subject matter of the social sciences can be expressed verbally, their analysis and comparison are greatly helped by formulating them mathematically. In the third place, the application of such theories must remain very general unless the terms in their relationships can be quantified. In the fourth place, mathematics provides a means of obtaining insight even into subjects whose concepts are rather vague and where precise information is hard to come by. Finally, in the social sciences we are interested not only in a description of what happens and of how the different parts of the social system are related, but also in the rational processes that lie behind effective as opposed to ineffective decisions; to a large extent these processes too can be formulated and analysed mathematically, so that our decisions may eventually come to rest a little more on knowledge and a little less on guess work than they do at present. [Stone 1966, p. 1]

V

37. When we look at the recipients of the Nobel Prize, we see that three great issues of economics—the problems of development, Keynesianism versus Monetarism, and the rise and rise of econometrics—are well represented. As to the first issue, while the plaudits in our trade rarely go to those who work on development problems—they stand in the pecking order marginally above agricultural economists—it is significant that at least five of the Nobel Prize recipients have made development problems their major interests—and that one started his professional life as an agricultural economist. Lewis, Kuznets, Myrdal, Schultz and Tinbergen are most in the mould of our founder, Adam Smith, in that they are intensely interested in the causes of the wealth of nations. Hicks (1973), too, returned to this grand theme in his Nobel Lecture, 'The Mainspring of Economic Growth'. Lewis and Kuznets are as well—and like Smith—great economic historians. Indeed, Findlay (1980), in writing of Lewis and especially of his recent book, *Growth and Fluctuations 1870–1913* (Lewis, 1978), comments (p. 73) that only Lewis could have written it. 'No one else possesses the combination of qualities ... acute theoretical insights, vast historical knowledge and painstaking labor in the collection and

analysis of statistical data. The result is a combination of theory, history and statistics that only a Schumpeter could match'. Lewis himself details the frustrations associated with his various administrative posts over the years which delayed the preparation of the book, and how during the interim he passed from being a rather lonely pioneer in the area to being a member, surely the chief, of a rapidly growing tribe (see Lewis, 1980a, 256–7).

38. I linked Adam Smith with this group of economists because they also have been concerned with theories which either originated with or were greatly developed by Smith himself. Schultz, for example, because of his intimate knowledge of farming communities in the USA, the USSR and developing countries—he was born in Dakota and saw farming depression at first hand, and he spends his study leaves, not attached to a university, but in 'rural communities [and on] actual farms' (Schultz, 1979, p. 239)—has enormous respect for the viability, independence, and shrewdness of peasant farmers, for their ability to respond to the right incentives and raise both their own standards and those of their successors. He has linked what he see as the desirable effect on progress and welfare of cumulative disequilibria (a concept which is characteristic of the work of the other writers as well) with his pioneering work in 'human capital'. He stresses that when people can see the opportunity to invest in their human potential, there will be good old-fashioned economic incentives to encourage people, by their own efforts, to bring potentially explosive population growth under control. The invisible hand is well at work in his models and observations.

39. Lewis has made some wise remarks in these contexts which also would appeal to our founder. He does not think that rising living standards necessarily bring greater happiness, but they do expand the scope for choice and the opportunities for human freedom 'by giving man greater control over his environment' (Findlay, 1980, p. 63). Lewis adds: 'It is open to men to debate whether economic progress is good for men or not, but for women to debate the desirability of economic growth is to debate whether women should have the chance to cease to be beasts of burden, and to join the

human race' (Findlay, 1980, p. 63). Lewis remains the social democrat of his youth, still committed to planning through the price mechanism—he is very sceptical of centralised planning and especially of dictatorships, one-party states, as the means for economic development. Not that he has an uncritical allegiance to the market or to modern neoclassical theory. His single most important contribution, that which makes him a hedgehog rather than a fox (Findlay, 1980, p. 64), is his celebrated 1954 article, 'Economic Development with Unlimited Supplies of Labour' (Lewis, 1954), which is classical in inspiration. In Lewis (1980a) he tells how he came to write it. From his undergraduate days he had pondered on the factors that determined the relative prices of steel and coffee. He mentions how he discarded marginal utility—it 'made no sense ... [The] Heckscher-Ohlin framework could not be used [because it assumed] that trading partners had the same production functions' (p. 257). He also had noticed from his historical work that real wages in the UK had been relatively constant for the first fifty years or so of its industrial economic development so that profits and saving had risen. Suddenly the two problems came together 'in August 1952, walking down the road in Bangkok ... Throw away the neoclassical assumption that the quantity of labour is fixed. An "unlimited supply of labour" will keep wages down, producing cheap coffee in the first case and high profits in the second case. The result is a dual (national or world) economy, where one part is a reservoir of cheap labour for the other. The unlimited supply of labour derives ultimately from population pressure, so it is a phase in the demographic cycle' (p. 257).

40. Lewis uses his theory to explain development until real wages do start to rise, after which he allows neoclassical theory to come into its own (assuming that Keynesian puzzles of lack of effective demand have been cured). So Lewis probably more than any one else joins the old with the new as far as theory goes, the bridge being his emphasis on historical studies, both of the developed world and of the developing world. Another contribution is his explanation of the movements in the terms of the trade between the developing and the developed world, his well-known North–South

model. The North produces steel and food, the South produces coffee and food. If productivity in steel grows more slowly than that of food in the North and productivity in coffee grows faster than that of food in the South, the price of steel will rise relative to that of coffee 'so that the commodity as well as the double factoral terms of trade turn against the South over time . . . a rigorous and elegant argument for . . . the [Prebisch-Singer] thesis of secular deterioration of the terms of trade' (Findlay, 1980, p. 71). This has led Lewis like Schultz to emphasise the importance of technical developments in agriculture and, in Lewis's case, to an emphasis on protection as well. In his Nobel Lecture (Lewis, 1980b) he adds to these themes by considering the consequences for the developing countries of the slowdown in the growth of the developed countries, and especially of world trade, modifying his earlier models in order to capture the forces at work and their implications. Schultz, too, puts great emphasis on the need for rises in agricultural productivity; productivity increases must not be confined to the industrial enclaves of the developing countries.

41. Myrdal stands apart from the others, not in relation to interest or concern, nor in his acute analytical understanding of the power of cumulative processes to bring good or evil, but rather with his emphasis on the normal dimensions of the problems of development. He stresses in particular the destabilising effects of tying aid to what is considered to be the best interests of the giving country, preconceptions which often turn out to be misguided and incorrect. He contrasts Sweden with the USA. The Swedes have been committed to a 25 per cent increase in aid without strings each year. The USA is the greatest giver of all, but it often includes military aid (suitably disguised in the statistics) and is guided by approval of the economic and political institutions of the recipients rather than by need. Myrdal argues that in democratic countries it is basically the citizens who decide over the long haul on these matters and he does not believe that Swedes are more decent and humane than Americans—'I cannot believe that Americans are basically less charitable than Swedes' (p. 419)—only that their decent and humane instincts consistently have been appealed to while that has

not been the case in the USA. Because of his long-standing interest in the political element in economic theory, Myrdal also reaches back to Smith, but in his case it as much to the author of *The Theory of Moral Sentiments* as it is to the author of *The Wealth of Nations*. He is seen at his best when attacking the triage theory whereby only those countries that can be 'saved' by aid should receive aid. 'India is in this literature commonly counted as belonging to the ... group which should be left unaided ... Not giving them food aid is more 'ethical' ... because those who would be saved will breed, and in the end still more millions will ultimately be starving and dying. In the longer run, aid creates more misery than it alleviates' (p. 426).

42. Though Lewis (1980a, p. 255) regrets his lack of training in mathematics in his Bachelor of Commerce degree at the LSE, it is clear from his work—and from the work of Schultz and Myrdal—that simple models combined with thorough empirical studies are powerful and enlightening, both for explanation and for policy. In fact, Lewis's work is a convincing answer to Kuznets' scepticism about, for example, Kalecki's growth and cycle theory as such, that 'the final conclusions are, at most, interesting suggestions of uncertain validity' (see Lundberg, 1971, p. 445), though I do think that he has more than a point with regard to optimum-growth theory. It is no accident, I believe, that Koopmans' and Kantorovich's works were of much more practical importance when set in a micro context at the level of the firm or industry or related to a specific choice, for example, optimum transport arrangements under fixed constraints in wartime conditions, than when they turned their attention, laudable though their objectives may have been, to optimum planning models. Morever, the issues with which this group of authors have dealt are not only amongst the most vital that concern us all but also have been the interests of other 'giants' in the trade, so far overlooked by the Nobel Prize electors. In particular, Kaldor has developed a model of the world economy which has some similarities to Lewis's (see Thirlwall and Vines, 1983), and Boulding's thoughts in these areas, especially his emphasis on the importance of agriculture and technical advances in it as well as in industry,

owe something to his time at Ames with Schultz, as well as at Edinburgh (see Harcourt, 1983b).

VI

43. As to the second issue, Keynesianism versus Monetarism, a conjecture arises as to whether the electors are reacting to or are trying to influence the course of the debate itself. (In making the 1982 award to Stigler for his work on regulation, the electors may be responding to another current trend, the deficiencies of big government in general, in particular the attempts to do by regulation what the market could do better.) Thus Friedman received the prize in 1976, when monetarism as a theoretical challenge was probably at its strongest.[17] But then in recent years we have had Meade and Ohlin (1977), Klein (1980), who pioneered big econometric Keynesian macro-models, and James Tobin (1981), who, with Samuelson, Solow, the late Arthur Okun (who surely would have got a Nobel Prize, had he lived), Robert Eisner, and George Akerlof, are the outstanding American Keynesians.[18] What is significant is that the recipients have addressed themselves to the policy questions of inflation and unemployment in open economies or, in the case of Tobin, how to model effectively the processes in such economies, in order to have a suitable basis for appropriate policy. Tobin (1981) is concerned to supplement the Keynesian income and expenditure accounts with explicit asset, liability, and flow-of-funds statements, in order to bring out the Keynesian view of the interrelationships between the real and the monetary sectors of the economy.

44. Explicit in all these essays is the view that economies are not self-regulating mechanisms, that they do not tend to settle at optimum positions from the points of view of the individual citizens of the economies concerned, so that there *is* a role for active, discretionary intervention in economic life. Increasingly this is being extended from traditional fiscal and monetary policies to related policies in labour markets, a situation forced on policy-makers and the profession alike by the decline in competition in most markets and the

experience during the Long Boom of higher levels of activity, employment—and growth—than when Keynes wrote. Of course, such intervention is not acceptable to either Friedman or Hayek, both of whom have a commitment to the market and to the use of the price mechanism, on both philosophical and, particularly in the case of Hayek, epistemological grounds. Hayek draws the following conclusion:

> If man is not to do more harm than good in his efforts to improve the social order, he will have to learn that in this, *as in all other fields where essential complexity of an organised kind prevails*, he cannot acquire the full knowledge which would make mastery of the events possible. He will therefore have to use what knowledge he can achieve, not to shape the results as a craftsman shapes his handiwork, but rather to cultivate a growth by providing the appropriate environment, in the manner in which the gardener does this for his plants. [Hayek 1975, p. 442; emphasis added]

Keynes wanted us to be humble folk like dentists—he obviously had good teeth. Hayek now wants us to be gardeners. I prefer Hayek's solution and Keynes's arguments.

45. Let me add two reflections in conclusion—I have not the competence to discuss the econometric contributions. The first is that these policy debates turn on whether we believe that there is or there is not a unique resting place of the economy, what Friedman has called the natural rate of unemployment. The concept itself is related to the arguments of the classical economists who believed that their role was to explain the forces which determine the centres of gravitation of the system, its natural prices, including those of wages, profits and rents, all the outcome of sustained and dominant forces which it was the province of political economy to discover and analyse. If there *were* such centres of gravitation, the forces of competition would tend to drive market prices to equality with the natural prices. To this list Friedman has added, as a further centre of gravitation, the natural rate of unemployment, together with his empirical and theoretical arguments concerning the tendency of the economy to find its way there, and of the harmful effects of using policies to try to run the economy anywhere else.[19] However, if it is believed that there is *not* a unique level, that

the economy *is* subject to cumulative movements which reinforce each other, for example, or that even if there *is* a stable resting place, it is *not* one which is optimal but, rather, one where the persons most adversely affected by it, the wage earners, are unable effectively to signal to the key decision-makers in the private sector that they would prefer to be elsewhere (i.e., working), then the case for intervention which Meade and Ohlin, for example, discuss so eloquently is more likely to be established. I mention the second possibility—a centre of gravitation which is nevertheless not optimal—because Keynes long ago in commenting on this said:

> But we must not conclude that the mean position thus determined by 'natural' tendencies, namely by those tendencies which are likely to persist, failing measures expressly designed to correct them, is, therefore, established by laws of necessity. The unimpeded rule of the above conditions is a fact of observation concerning the world as it is or has been, and not a necessary principle which cannot be changed. [Keynes, 1936, p. 254]

I mention it, secondly, because there is currently emerging a debate as to whether Keynes's theory (in *The General Theory*) was concerned to provide a rationale for such a centre of gravitation or whether, rather, he was providing an analysis of the cyclical, crisis-prone nature of capitalism itself (see Harcourt, 1982d, for a survey of these issues).

46. My final reflection is to note the changes that have occurred over the decades in positions and emphases. Prior to Keynes (of *The General Theory*) and during the early neoclassical era in particular, emphasis was on prices—the overall price level *à la* the quantity theory of money and the relative price system as the mechanism of allocation. With Keynes (and, of course, historical events), quantities and employment, activity and output, took centre stage, and adjustment policies and stability all tended to be discussed in terms of these variables. (Even in *Value and Capital*, though, stability problems were still discussed primarily in terms of changes in prices, not in quantities; and Keynes himself used changes in expected prices as the motivating signals at the level of the firm.)[20] Now, with the emergence of monetarism Wave 1, itself superseded by monetarism Wave 2—the

rational expectations school—we are back to an emphasis on prices, the policy implication of which is the inflation-first strategy of most capitalist economies. Implicit in the natural-rate hypothesis and the deliberations of the rational expectations school is the belief that the market *can* successfully solve the problem that Keynes isolated in *The General Theory*:

An act of individual saving means—so to speak—a decision not to have dinner today. But it does *not* necessitate a decision to have dinner or to buy a pair of boots a week hence or a year hence or to consume any specified thing at any specified date. Thus it depresses the business of preparing today's dinner without stimulating the business of making ready for some future act of consumption. It is not a substitution of future consumption-demand for present consumption-demand—it is a net diminution of such demand ... If saving consisted not merely in abstaining from present consumption but in placing simultaneously a specific order for future consumption, the effect might indeed be different. For in that case the expectation of some future yield from investment would be improved, and the resources released from preparing for present consumption would be turned over to preparing for the future consumption ...

The trouble arises, therefore, because the act of saving implies, not a substitution for present consumption of some specific additional consumption which requires for its preparation just as much immediate economic activity as would have been required by present consumption equal in value to the sum saved, but a desire for 'wealth' as such, that is for a potentiality of consuming an unspecified article at an unspecified time.

Tobin (1981, p. 7) adds:

In short, the financial and capital markets are at their best highly imperfect coordinators of saving and investment, an inadequacy which I suspect cannot be remedied by rational expectations. This failure of coordination is a fundamental source of macro-economic instability and of the opportunity for macro-economic policies of stabilization.

So, it is a sobering thought that, after all these years of reflection and research in our trade, I am tempted to sum it all up as a dilemma as to whether we should mind our P's or our Q's.

NOTES

1. This article is a revised version of a paper presented to the History of Economic Thought Conference which was held at the University of Nottingham, 7–9 September 1982. It is published in *History of Political Economy* (Winter 1984), pp. 489–517. An earlier version was the 1982 G. L. Wood Memorial Lecture which was given on 21 June 1982 in the Copland Lecture Theatre, University of Melbourne, Australia. I am grateful to Bruce McFarlane, to the participants on the Monday Economics Workshop, University of Adelaide, and to an anonymous referee for their comments on a draft of the paper.
2. It makes us speculate how many people may have missed out because of the β– quality of the essays on them.
3. Possibly the one exception to this is the late Harry Johnson's essay on James Meade (Johnson, 1978), which is certainly the most critical of all the essays. This, no doubt, was Johnson's way of showing his respect and admiration for Meade—that Meade would still emerge as a giant despite the critical evaluations of his work. Aubrey Silberston (1977, 1978) did the same thing for Johnson himself.
4. 'The humanitarian idealism which Nobel wanted to reward has no representative in our profession as fine and noble as Jan Tinbergen. As much as he is respected in the privileged world, he is beloved by the underprivileged. Always at their service, always on their side, always working to improve their conditions, Tinbergen would be an equally worthy candidate for the Nobel Peace Prize' (Hansen, 1969, p. 336). 'One could not improve on this as a tribute also to Gunnar Myrdal' (Reynolds, 1974, 492).
5. The person least easily classified under this heading, if we may judge from his writings, is the 1983 recipient, Gerard Debreu, who seems to be rather remote from the human problems that provide the rationale for economics as a discipline. He is delightfully candid about his attitude, expressing wonder at the 'dazzling recognition ... in Stockholm for something [he] enjoyed so much doing, [for the] unsurpassed, addictive intellectual pleasure' of solving scientific problems. He adds, a 'scientist knows that his motivations are often weakly related to the distant consequences of his work. The logical rigor, the generality, and the simplicity of his theories satisfy deep personal intellectual needs, and he frequently seeks them for their own sake. But here, as in Adam Smith's famous sentence, he seems to be 'led by an invisible hand to promote an end which was not part of his intention,' for his personal intellectual fulfillment contributes to promoting the social interest of the scientific community. The logical rigor of his theories provides a secure foundation to build upon; their generality makes them applicable to a broader class of problems; their simplicity makes them usable by a greater number of research workers' (Debreu, 1983).
6. The first English translation from the original Polish of Kalecki's review of *The General Theory* recently appeared in the December 1982

issue of *Australian Economic Papers*, together with a commentary by two young European scholars, Ferdinando Targetti and Bogulslawa Kinda-Hass. Kalecki's work has long been admired in Australia, not only in Melbourne but also in Adelaide through Brian Tew, Ron Hirst, and the late Eric Russell, and in Sydney.

7. For an assessment of Piero Sraffa's role in twentieth-century economics, *see* Harcourt 1982a, 1983a.
8. '(not the "Economics of Keynes" Leijonhufvud would say, but so much the better, say I).'
9. *See* Harcourt, 1982b, Ch. 23; 1982c, for Lorie Tarshis's memories of the same period.
10. Hansen compares Tinbergen's work and approach with the Anglo-Saxon work on welfare economics of the 1940s and 1950s, which he considers to be elegant and refined but 'sterile and difficult to apply to practical policy problems'. One amusing side effect of the Nobel Prize awards is that the Scandinavians seem to be getting their own back on the Brits in particular for the arrogance, the 'unnecessary originality', which the British economists displayed in their heyday.
11. It may lie behind their research strategy of 'wanting policy rules to be kept simple so that quantitative tests of the effects of alternative policies may be properly judged'. That their recommendations in practice are usually in favour of non-discretionary interventions—rules rather than discretion—may well be related to this insight as well. I am indebted to an anonymous referee for these comments.
12. For Keynes's methods in *The General Theory* and after, *see* Kregel 1976.
13. Koopmans was delighted to be coupled with Kantorovich for the award; he felt that economics had come of age when two scientists in very different societies nevertheless dealt with the same problems in a similar way. I am indebted to Ugo Pagano for this observation.
14. *See*: Bharadwaj, 1978; Walsh and Gram, 1980; Harcourt, 1982a, 1983a.
15. In his Nobel Lecture, Stigler (1983, p. 533) states what in his view is the fundamental rationale for such a methodology: 'If the problems of economic life changed frequently and radically and lacked a large measure of continuity in their essential nature, there could not be a science of economics. An essential element of a science is the cumulative growth of knowledge, and that cumulative character could not arise if each generation of economists faced fundamentally new problems calling for entirely new methods of analysis. The change of problems and methods would also undermine the training of economists: if the young studied under the old, the young could be confident that they were learning things that were rapidly becoming obsolete. A science requires for its very existence a set of fundamental and durable problems. In economics the most fundamental of these central problems is the theory of value.'
16. Shackle (1983, p. 116), has a typically kind and perceptive comment on this issue: 'I think there are two kinds of economics. One of them

aims at precision, rigour, tidiness and the formulation of principles which will be permanently valid: an economic science. The other is ... rhetorical ... often used disparagingly [—] a modern unscholarly abuse. The rhetorician employs reason ... appeals to logic, but ... is a user of language at its full compass, where words are fingers touching the keyboard of a learner's mind. I do not believe that human affairs can be exhibited as the infallible and invariable working of a closed and permanent system'.

17. Hayek was coupled with Myrdal in 1974 but his award was not so much, if at all, for his challenge to Keynes as for his broad philosophical and all-round contributions—the nature of economic knowledge, the case for economic freedom, the relationship between society and its institutions, especially its legal ones. Indeed, his essayist, the late Fritz Machlup, thinks that Hayek's *Pure Theory of Capital* (1941) is his finest work (*see* Machlup 1974, p. 509).
18. I leave to one side the American branch of the Post-Keynesian school—Paul Davidson, Donald Harris, Jan Kregel, Hyman Minsky, Edward Nell, the late Sidney Weintraub—not because they are not important but because they are not going to figure prominently in either central mainstream debates nor, alas, in Nobel Prize awards. For a discussion of Post-Keynesianism, *see* Harcourt, 1982d.
19. This does not rule out policies which affect the rate itself—anti-minimum-wage policies, deregulation legislation, institutions which improve knowledge and mobility, and so on.
20. I am indebted to Bob Rowthorn for this point.

REFERENCES

Baumol, W. J. 1979. 'On the Contributions of Herbert A. Simon to Economics.' *Scandinavian Journal of Economics* 81, no. 1: 74–82

Bharadwaj, K. 1978. *Classical Political Economy and Rise to Dominance of Supply and Demand Theories.* R. C. Dutt Lectures on Political Economy 1976, Centre for Studies in Social Sciences, Calcutta

Boulding, Kenneth E. 1948. 'Samuelson's Foundations: The Role of Mathematics in economics'. *Journal of Political Economy* 56, no. 3:187–99

Debreu, Gerard 1983. Speech given after the banquet on December 10, 1983, *Les Prix Nobel 1983* (Stockholm)

——— 1984. Nobel Lectures: 'Economic Theory in the Mathematical Mode.' In *Les Prix Nobel 1983* (Stockholm); and *American Economic Review* 74, no. 3:267–78

Dorfman, R. 1973. 'Wassily Leontief's Contribution to Economics.' *Swedish Journal of Economics* 75, no. 4:430–49

Findlay, Ronald 1980. 'On W. Arthur Lewis' Contributions to Economics.' *Scandinavian Journal of Economics* 82:62–79

Friedman, Milton 1977. Nobel Lecture: 'Inflation and Unemployment.' *Journal of Political Economy* 85, no. 3:451–72

Frisch, Ragnar 1933. 'Propagation Problems and Impulse Problems in Dynamic Economics.' In *Economic Essays in Honor of Gustav Cassel*. London, pp. 171–205

Hahn, F. H. 1973. 'The Winter of Our Discontent.' *Economica*, n.s. 40, no. 159:322–30

—— 1982. *Reflections on the Invisible Hand*. Fred Hirsch Memorial Lecture, University of Warwick, November; printed in *Lloyds Bank Review* 144:1–21.

Hansen, Bent 1969. 'Jan Tinbergen: an appraisal of his contributions to economics.' *Swedish Journal of Economics* 71, no. 4:325–36

Harcourt, G. C. 1972. *Some Cambridge Controversies in the Theory of Capital*. Cambridge

—— 1981. 'Notes on an Economic Querist: G. L. S. Shackle.' *Journal of Post Keynesian Economics* 4, no. 1:136–44

—— 1982a. 'The Sraffian Contribution: An Evaluation.' In Ian Bradley and Michael Howard, eds., *Classical and Marxian Political Economy: Essays in Honour of Ronald L. Meek*. London, pp. 255–75

—— 1982b. *The Social Science Imperialists: Selected Essays of G. C. Harcourt*. Edited by Prue Kerr. London

—— 1982c. 'An Early Post-Keynesian: Lorie Tarshis (or: Tarshis on Tarshis by Harcourt).' *Journal of Post Keynesian Economics* 4, no. 4:609–19

—— 1982d. 'Post Keynesianism: Quite wrong and/or Nothing New?' *Thames Papers in Political Economy*, Summer

—— 1983a. 'On Piero Sraffa's Contributions to Economics.' In Peter Groenewegen and Joseph Halevi, eds., *Altro Polo: Italian Economics—Past and Present*. Sydney, pp. 117–28

—— 1983b. 'A Man for All Systems: Talking with Kenneth Boulding.' *Journal of Post Keynesian Economics* 6, no. 1:143–54

Hayek, F. A. von 1941. *The Pure Theory of Capital*. London

—— 1975. Nobel Lecture: 'The Pretence of Knowledge.' *Swedish Journal of Economics* 77, no. 4:433–42

Hicks, John 1973. Nobel Lecture: 'The Mainspring of Economic Growth.' *Swedish Journal of Economics*; reprinted in John Hicks, *Economic Perspectives: Further Essays on Money and Growth*. Oxford (1977), pp. 1–19

—— 1979. 'The Formation of an Economist.' *Banca Nazionale del Lavoro Quarterly Review* 130:195–204

—— 1982. *Money, Interest and Wages: Collected Essays on Economic Theory*, vol. 2. Oxford

—— 1984. 'Is Economics a Science?' *Interdisciplinary Science Review*, forthcoming

Johansen, Leif 1969. 'Ragnar Frisch's Contributions to Economics.' *Swedish Journal of Economics* 71, no. 4:302–24

Johnson, H. G. 1978. 'James Meade's Contribution to Economics.' *Scandinavian Journal of Economics* 80, no. 1:64–85

Kaldor, N. 1966. 'Marginal Productivity and Macroeconomic Theories of Distribution.' *Review of Economic Studies* 33:309–19; reprinted in G. C. Harcourt and N. F. Laing, eds., *Capital and Growth*. Harmondsworth, 1971

Keynes, J. M. 1936. *The General Theory of Employment, Interest and Money*. London

——— 1973, *The General Theory and After. Part II: Defence and Development*. Vol. 14, *Collected Writings of John Maynard Keynes*, ed. Donald Moggridge. London

King, John A. 1982. 'Value and Exploitation: Some Recent Debates.' In Ian Bradley and Michael Howard, eds., *Classical and Marxian Political Economy: Essays in Honour of Ronald L. Meek*. London, pp. 157–87

Koopmans, T. 1977. 'Examples of Production Relations Based on Microdata.' In G. C. Harcourt, ed., *The Microeconomic Foundations of Macroeconomics*. London

Kregel, J. A. 1976. 'Economic Methodology in the Face of Uncertainty: The Modelling Methods of Keynes and the Post-Keynesians.' *Economic Journal* 86, no. 342:209–25

Leontief, Wassily 1974. Nobel Lecture: 'Structure of the World Economy: Outline of a Simple Input–Output Formulation.' *Swedish Journal of Economics* 76, no. 4:387–401

Lewis, W. A. 1954. 'Economic Development with Unlimited Supplies of Labour.' *Manchester School* 22:139–91

——— 1978. *Growth and Fluctuations 1870–1913*. London

——— 1980a. 'Sir Arthur Lewis.' In *Les Prix Nobel 1979*. Stockholm, pp. 255–58

——— 1980b. Nobel Lecture: 'The Slowing Down of the Engine of Growth.' In *Les Prix Nobel 1979*. Stockholm, pp. 259–69

Lucas, Robert E., and Thomas J. Sargent, eds. 1981. *Rational Expectations and Econometric Practice*. London

Lundberg, Erik 1971. 'Simon Kuznets' Contribution to Economics.' *Swedish Journal of Economics* 73, no. 4:444–61

Machlup, Fritz 1974. 'Friedrich von Hayek's Contribution to Economics.' *Swedish Journal of Economics* 76, no. 4:498–531

Mincer, Jacob 1983. 'George Stigler's Contributions to Economics.' *Scandinavian Journal of Economics* 85, no. 1:65–75

Myrdal, Gunnar 1975. Nobel Lecture: 'The Equality Issue in World Development.' *Swedish Journal of Economics* 77, no. 4:415–32

——— 1977. 'The Nobel Prize in Economic Science.' *Challenge* 20, no. 1:50–52

Reddaway, W. B. 1936. Review article of *The General Theory of Employment, Interest and Money*. *Economic Record* 12, no. 22:28–36

Reder, M. W. 1982. 'Chicago Economics: Permanence and Change.' *Journal of Economic Literature* 20. no. 1:1–38

Reynolds, Lloyd G. 1974. 'Gunnar Myrdal's Contribution to Economics, 1940–1970.' *Swedish Journal of Economics* 76, no. 4:479–97

Robinson, Austin 1977. 'Keynes and his Cambridge Colleagues.' In Don Patinkin and J. Clark Leith, eds., *Keynes, Cambridge and the General Theory*. London, pp. 25–38
Samuelson, Paul A. 1970. Nobel Lecture: 'Maximum Principles in Analytical Economics.' In R. C. Merton, ed. *The Collected Scientific Papers of Paul A. Samuelson*. Cambridge, Mass., 1972
——— 1972. 'Economics in a Golden Age: A Personal Memoir.' In Gerald Holton, ed., *The Twentieth-Century Sciences*. New York, pp. 155–70
Schmalensee, Richard 1983. 'George Stigler's Contributions to Economics.' *Scandinavian Journal of Economics* 85, no. 1:77–86
Schultz, T. W. 1980. 'Theodore W. Schultz.' In *Les Prix Nobel 1979*. Stockholm, pp. 239–41
Schumpeter, J. A., 1946. Review of F. A. Hayek, *The Road to Serfdom* in *Journal of Political Economy* 54:269–70
Shackle, G. L. S. 1983. 'A Student's Pilgrimage.' *Banca Nazionale del Lavoro Quarterly Review* 145:107–16
Silberston, Aubrey 1977. 'Harry Johnson as a Young Man.' *Economic Analysis and Policy* 7, no. 2:39–52
——— 1978. 'Harry Johnson as a Young Man, Errata.' *Economic Analysis and Policy* 8, no. 1:87–88
Sraffa, Piero 1961. Debate at the Corfu Conference on the Theory of Capital, organized by the International Economic Association (4–11 Sept. 1958.). In F. A. Lutz and D. C. Hague, eds., *The Theory of Capital*. London, pp. 305–6
Stigler, George J. 1983. Nobel Lecture: 'The Process and Progress of Economics.' *Journal of Political Economy* 91, no. 4:529–45
Stone, Richard 1966. *Mathematics in the Social Sciences and Other Essays*. London.
Targetti, Ferdinando, and Bogulslawa Kinda-Hass, 1982. 'Kalecki's Review of Keynes' *General Theory*.' *Australian Economic Papers* 21, no. 39:244–60
Thirlwall, A. P., and David Vines 1983. 'A general Model of Growth and Development on Kaldorian lines.' Mimeo. Cambridge
Tinbergen, Jan 1969. 'The Use of Models: Experience and Prospects.' Nobel Memorial Lecture. Stockholm
Tobin, James 1981. 'Money and Finance in the Macro-Economic process.' Nobel Memorial Lecture. Stockholm
——— 1982. 'James Tobin.' Mimeo. Yale University
Walsh, V., and H. Gram 1980. *Classical and Neoclassical Theories of General Equilibrium*. New York

2 A Man for All Systems: Talking with Kenneth Boulding[1]

I

1. Kenneth Boulding has always been one of my heroes, so it was reassuring to find out, when I spent Sunday 25 May talking with him in Melbourne,[2] that he really *is* a hero; it was even more reassuring to find that he has two Achilles' heels. He thinks sports are boring and he does not like Marx or Marxism, neither entirely unprejudiced judgments, he readily admits. Born in 1910 in Liverpool, the only son of a plumber and an only grandson—Elise Boulding says he had three mothers—Boulding was the first in the family for 300 years to go on to secondary and then tertiary education. He had a brilliant undergraduate record at New College, Oxford (1928–32), went to Chicago as a Commonwealth Fellow in 1932, and subsequently taught at Edinburgh (1934–37), Colgate (1937–41), Iowa State (1943–49), Michigan (1949–67) and Colorado (1967–81). Now a vigorous seventy-two, he is Distinguished Professor of Economics Emeritus at Colorado, and is about to do a stint at Swarthmore following an extraordinary itinerary as R. I. Downing Research Fellow at the University of Melbourne. He still packs more illumination into his famous one-liners than most of us get into even a Marshallian-type footnote.

2. Heilbroner says somewhere of Boulding that his real trouble is that he is not interested in power, just in having fun. Certainly there can be as few free spirits as Boulding, a happy man with a remarkable partner in Elise Boulding, their five children and a host of grandchildren. Boulding has a deep religious faith—Elise and Kenneth Boulding are Quakers—and a tolerance and love of people as well as gentle exasperation with their often silly, sometimes wicked ways. Boulding himself is a tall man and, until an Australian barber

played Delilah to his Sampson, his shock of white hair suitably completed the image of twentieth-century prophet, which he is. Beneath the wit and laughter and ready conversation, delivered with a slight stutter, sometimes used to good effect to drive points home, is the serious purpose of a man who has reflected deeply on the processes at work in human society. Boulding refuses to be contained within traditional boundaries. Furthermore, he sees it as much the role of a social scientist to work for world peace as to understand the workings of contemporary capitalism, the socialist countries and the developing Third World countries. Boulding sings the Methodist hymns of his childhood, recites poetry from memory, writes poetry himself, disciplining himself by writing sonnets,[3] sums up conferences in verse and sketches and paints where ever he goes.

II

3. Boulding originally meant to be a chemist. His secondary school, Liverpool Collegiate, specialised in preparing bright boys for Oxford and Cambridge scholarships. Boulding tried for a scholarship at Sidney Sussex College, Cambridge in 1927 but was unsuccessful. (Two years ago Sidney Sussex was host to a conference on the grants economy, at which a principal speaker was the person to whom they refused a grant so long ago.) He won an open major scholarship in Natural Sciences to New College, Oxford, in 1928. He became bored after a year of chemistry—he wanted to know more about the malfunctioning of his own country, and he was also the victim of one aspect of the Oxford system. His tutor had long lost interest in chemistry; their weekly tutorials, Boulding says, were principally about the sociology of the family as the tutor struggled to bring up the child which his estranged wife had left with him. So Boulding changed to Modern Greats—Politics, Philosophy and Economics (PPE)—through the intervention of Lionel Robbins, who was about to leave New College for the LSE.

4. Boulding asked Robbins what he should read in the Long Vacation (Oxbridge students work in the vac., come up and have a good time during term; see *Brideshead Revisited*).

Robbins told him to read Marshall (the *Principles*), Pigou (*The Economics of Welfare)*, Cassell (*Theory of Social Economy*) and Hawtrey (*The Economic Problem*)—Boulding says he has never read as much economics since, though he did read Adam Smith, Ricardo, Marx and Mill for his set books examination. Boulding's first tutor in economics was Henry Phelps Brown, then a historian, who was sent to Michigan after one year to be trained as an economist. While he was there, Maurice Allen from Balliol tutored Boulding. (Allen subsequently became the economist at the Bank of England, presumably because, says Boulding, as he had never published anything they thought he must be discreet.) His most eccentric tutor was the philosopher, H. V. W. Joseph, who took tutorials sitting under a table. Boulding wrote him an essay on evolution (the start of his own abiding interest in evolutionary processes). The voice from under the table: 'All very well to talk about evolution, Mr Boulding. What evolves? What evolves?'

5. Boulding obtained the top First in 1931, failing to get an α only in a history paper. In his last year as an undergraduate he published his first paper, Boulding [1932]—this greatly impressed his tutor. The subject was displacement (now opportunity) cost. Frank Knight, of whom Boulding was very fond and who was to be a great influence on him, responded to the receipt of an offprint of the paper: 'Professor Knight thanks Mr Boulding for his paper, which he thinks is as wrong and as confused as possible'. Characteristically, Boulding was not shattered but instead welcomed criticism—he 'went on to learn more from ... Knight...than from any other teacher ... except perhaps Schumpeter' (Boulding, 1971a, p. viii]).[4] He is always willing to try out his ideas on any audience, even if they are still unformed or even half-baked. Criticism helps him think through his ideas—indeed, he has had so many that it would be quite remarkable if they all were to be as well presented as some of his better-known papers and his admirable *Economic Analysis* (1948). Probably it is no accident that many of the people he admired—Knight and Commons, for example—could inspire their students and contemporaries even though they were often awful expositors in their

classrooms and sometimes in their written work. Certainly, Boulding's seminar style is one of organised chaos.

6. After a year of graduate work at Oxford in which he wrote a thesis on international capital movements for a B. Litt., which he never took out, Boulding received a Commonwealth Fellowship to go to Chicago. He went first class on a Cunard Liner. Fellow passengers were Alastair Cook and Joseph Schumpeter. Boulding became friendly with Schumpeter, who read his thesis during the voyage and discussed it with him. Subsequently, Boulding spent a term at Harvard with Schumpeter (where he wrote a paper on Böhm Bawerk). He was ill for much of the time and spent eight weeks in the Harvard Infirmary, which helped him to form a 'lasting aversion' to Harvard. Boulding never did a Ph.D. either. When Viner told him what he would have to do, he said: 'If I do that, I'll be a broken man'. I think that Boulding's great originality, exuberance, freshness and openness of mind, together with his prodigious output, a continuously flowing spring of ideas, may well be due to his Oxford training and his refusal to lock himself into the grind of the course work of the American Ph.D.[5] Viner also was not impressed with Boulding's response, 'that he'd done all that stuff', to the suggestion that he take 301. Instead, Boulding worked with Henry Schultz, learning statistics, correlation analysis, slogging away on a Marchand calculator, 'getting familiar', as Schultz said, 'with the data'. Nowadays, says Boulding, it is the computer that gets familiar with the data. Boulding thought that Schultz was a most compassionate man; had he not been killed in a car accident in 1937, Boulding feels the Econometrics might now be a more humane subject.

7. Boulding's best friend amongst the Chicago graduate students was A. G. Hart who 'threw off ideas like a Catherine Wheel, talked twice as fast as any one else and always made sense'. Boulding liked but did not feel close to Henry Simons, whom he thought was an unhappy man. All the graduate students liked Aaron Director, who was lively and witty—and very conservative (Samuelson, 1972, p. 159, tells of Director referring to Milton Friedman as his radical brother-in-law). Some of Boulding's early papers, under

Knight's influence, were on capital theory, and Knight put Boulding on the profession's map with his paper, 'Mr Boulding and the Austrians'—'It really had little to do with either Boulding or the Austrians, it was about Frank Knight'. Boulding's paper on Böhm Bawerk for Schumpeter was never published—it may be amongst the '40 boxes of junk' which Boulding unloaded on the University of Michigan when he moved to Boulder in 1967. Boulding had great affection for Schumpeter; so he was 'dismayed' to find when, a few years ago, Boulding used *History of Economic Analysis* as the set book for a History of Economic Thought course, that he felt that it was not only an awful book for students but also that Schumpeter was wrong about 'virtually everything'. He greatly undervalued 'A. Smith', and his admiration for Walras was 'incomprehensible' to Boulding, who regards Walras as a catastrophe for economics!

III

8. Boulding's father died while Boulding was on a summer tour—he heard the news in the Grand Canyon. Boulding returned to Liverpool to find that his father's business (it never employed more than two or three workmen) had been insolvent for twenty years; it was kept going by the banks and his suppliers in the hope that something might turn up. In any event, nothing was to be gained by making him bankrupt. Boulding says that he learnt more economics during the ten days which he spent sorting out the affairs of the business than in the rest of his life! It is tempting to speculate that one of Boulding's most important contributions—the emphasis that he places on the balance sheet and the flow-of-funds statement as well as the profit-and-loss account—may reflect this experience, together with his close association with William Baxter at Edinburgh where, as the two bachelors on the staff, they hiked and holidayed—and talked—together. Boulding and his mother, by putting in their own savings, managed to pay the creditors 12 shillings in the pound. Mrs Boulding then joined Boulding in Harvard (he was ill at the time, so Taussig arranged and paid for her accommodation—an exceptionally kind man, says Boulding of Taussig, even though he was a terrifying teacher whose

Socratic method of seizing on some poor kid in class could reduce him or her to tears!). Mrs Boulding kept house for Boulding in America and then later at Edinburgh (1934–37) and Colgate. At Edinburgh Boulding dropped from his scholarship of $3,000 a year to £250 a year as an Assistant—he reckons it took him forty years to become as well off again as he was as a graduate student in the 1930s in the United States.

9. Boulding loved Edinburgh as a city and found the Scots very kindly—but it would have taken him 500 years to become a Scot, especially when Alexander Gray—a Scot—took over as the professor. Nor does Boulding regret not getting a post at Oxford—a working-class Methodist from Liverpool at Oxford in the 1930s was like a black from Mississippi at Harvard, whereas Methodist culture '*was* the USA', so he felt immediately at home there. (Nevertheless, after the Second World War he still had considerable trouble in becoming a US citizen because of his refusal to bear arms. He became a pacifist as a boy partly because of the traumatic experience of the death of an Australian cousin in the First World War, partly from seeing as a child the impact of the fighting on the Western Front on an uncle, a gentle and fastidious grocer, whose lice ridden clothing his mother washed when he was home on leave. Boulding never forgot the look on his face when he returned from the Western Front. Boulding could not reconcile the Christian/Methodist precept 'to love thine enemy' with modern warfare. (The judge who heard his case was a conservative of considerable integrity who had unshakable respect for the law. Though he had been putting conscientious objectors away for five years without compunction, when he was persuaded that the law said Boulding *could* be a citizen, he assented even though his being was revolted by it.) While Boulding's adopted country has treated him well—he was J. B. Clark Medallist in 1949, President of the AEA in 1968, and recently (1979), President of the AAAS (the only economist to be so since Wesley Mitchell in the 1930s)—the land of his birth has not treated him as well.[6] Oxford has never done anything, Edinburgh remained loyal and gave him an honorary degree and the LSE was where the embryonic *A Reconstruction of Economics* was delivered in 1949—but that is it.

10. So when the three years (limited-term appointment, as we would say now) at Edinburgh was up, Boulding went to Colgate in up-state New York. Mrs Boulding joined him (after a year) in Hamilton and lived there for most of the rest of her life. They lived thirty miles 'from the nearest sin', he was a member of an excellent faculty—the president, 'a blue nosed Baptist from Nova Scotia', 'waited until the depression to get a good faculty cheap'.

IV

11. When Boulding was at Oxford he though of himself as a socialist—'we all did'—and he was by that time a Quaker and a pacifist. He read deeply in the Fabians—Shaw, G. D. H. Cole, Beatrice Webb. Then he read Volumes 1, 2 and 3 of Marx; that ruined him as a Marxist/socialist. He thought Marx was not nearly as good as Adam Smith—a great favourite. He is inclined to agree with Samuelson's judgment (now scrapped by Samuelson) that in matters of theory Marx *is* a minor post-Ricardian! Boulding cheerfully admits he may be wrong and that the many conversations with his new-made friend at Melbourne, Robert Dixon, have made him think again. Nevertheless, I do not think that this will shake his belief that communism itself is a religion of hate, associated with violence and hypocrisy. Perhaps the following quartet best sums up his stance:

> When faced with Rhetoric of Marx,
> My inner mental watch dog barks,
> And even turns into a snarl,
> For Groucho's much more fun than Karl.

At Oxford itself Boulding started with a friend from Liverpool Collegiate a socialist journal called *Plan*. While writing an article for it on how to establish socialism in Britain, Boulding realised that it would have to be either by violence or by deception—people could not be persuaded to do it outright because too many people would be injured to allow a majority for socialism to be obtained. The two means were inconsistent with his Christian beliefs. So he is now a somewhat anarchistic social democrat, rather apolitical in a party sense.[7]

12. Apolitical he may be in a party sense; nevertheless, he *is* political in a profound sense. Indeed, he was part of the first snowball which created the avalanche which ultimately removed President Johnson. In 1966, when Boulding was at Michigan (Ann Arbor), the younger faculty (in the wake of the disillusion of having defeated Goldwater only to have elected him anyway in the guise of Johnson) wanted to strike as a protest against the Vietnam War. The Center for Research on Conflict Resolution, of which Boulding was Research Director, was called in by the Dean: 'Gentlemen, I have a conflict, can you resolve it?' The Professor of Education said, 'Why don't we teach all night instead of all day?' Boulding sold the idea to the Dean and the strike committee—and the first teach-in was born, an institution which was suited to the skills of the university community in a way in which a strike never could be—I mean, who ever would notice if we *did* go on strike?

V

13. During the last twenty-seven years Boulding has been concerned with the General Systems approach. His interest dates from when he was one of the first group of distinguished social scientists who in 1954–55 received a year at the famous Stanford 'Think Tank', the Center for Advanced Study in the Behavioural Sciences. Prior to this break, in effect, with conventional economics, Boulding was moving from being a gifted expositor of, on the whole, orthodox economics[8] to a very thoughful reinterpretation of Keynes's ideas. This came from his absorption of *The Treatise* (partly due to A. G. Hart's influence) and his interest in accounting. When *Economic Analysis* was first published in 1941, Boulding had not properly absorbed *The General Theory*; by the revised edition of 1948, though, it was thoroughly Keynesian—of *The General Theory.*[9] Boulding went to Ames (1943–49) to become a labour economist. He 'did not really succeed . . . but the effort ruined [him] as a pure economist. [He] became convinced that in any applied field one had to

use all the social sciences ... indeed [develop] a general social science. [So began his] gradual transformation from a pure economist into a very impure one' (Boulding, 1971a, p. xi).

14. Boulding thought that *The General Theory* was a badly written book: 'It read like it had been written on brown paper bags on the train between Cambridge and London'. But he also thinks that a combination of *The Treatise* and *The General Theory* can give a profound understanding of the monetary and real interactions that constitute the processes at work in a capitalist economy. He feels that Keynes was acutely intuitively aware of the cybernetic processes which characterise capitalism (well before cybernetic processes themselves had been discovered). Keynes *analytically* never escaped from Marshall—Boulding does not like celestial mechanics or pendulums as models. Cumulative processes—exploding upwards or downwards—rather than a pendulum returning to rest after an external shock seem to Boulding to characterise economic and social systems. Boulding also was initially very much impressed and influenced by *Value and Capital.* He had been struggling with similar ideas but could not get them clear and he wrote to Hicks at the time to thank him for clarifying his mind. Now he is not so sure (neither is Hicks). As with Marshall and Keynes, Boulding likes to stress the importance of built-in stabilisers. Marshall's concept of the 'normal', Keynes's stress on the central importance of a stable 'efficiency' wage, Boulding's stress on the importance of taboos in social relations, all reflect the same insight—an insight that has completely escaped those modern neoclassicals who think that price flexibility is the clue to the efficient functioning of an economic system.[10]

VI

15. As I have mentioned, Boulding is a great fan of Adam Smith. He is especially enamoured of the central idea of the surplus which characterises classical political economy.[11] His studies in economic history led him to emphasise the overriding importance of the surplus in agriculture. (For a Liver-

pool lad who had never seen an English spring until he went to Oxford, there is something of the physiocrat in Kenneth Boulding.) He stresses the vast importance of technical progress in the agricultural sector—fallow fields, clover, for example—which he sees as the real base for the historical Industrial Revolution. The early industrial inventions were not nearly as revolutionary—'the tag end of the Middle Ages'. Indeed, the fall in the death rate and the rise in the birth rate in the nineteenth century was 'due to milk'. Little children were employed in the factories in the industrial towns because this was the first time that there *were* little children—'a sign of development, not of exploitation'.

16. His classical ideas gelled with the main idea that he obtained from *The Treatise*—the widow's cruse theory of profits. (Boulding thought the 'fundamental equations' 'rather silly'.) Along with Kalecki, Hahn, Kaldor and Joan Robinson, Boulding is an independent discoverer of modern macro theories of distribution. He combined this with his emphasis on the importance of stocks as well as flows—hence the role of the balance sheet in his theory. Irving Fisher was an important influence here; Boulding read *The Nature of Capital and Income* at Oxford and was 'tremendously influenced' by it. It knocked over the absurd illusion that household purchases are equivalent to consumption. The most important contributions to welfare are the stocks, not the flows, though flows are important, for eating can be as important as being well fed. We get no satisfaction at all from the effects of moths and rust—that our clothes and houses wear out—these are negatives to which production is the positive offset.

17. Boulding was at Ames as a labour economist, an experience which he says almost made him a neo-institutionalist. He read the Webb's *Industrial Democracy,* the older Perlman's works and, of course, Commons.[12] He also visited eighty-five union head-offices and many local unions in the State of Iowa. He thought that to understand labour economics, you also needed to know political science, sociology, history and psychology, yet he found that mainstream political scientists were uninterested in the politics of labour unions. Boulding himself increasingly has

read wider and wider and his latest books and papers reflect the ponderings of a person who knows no traditional boundaries—he is Renaissance man in the late twentieth century, a Wasp Woody Allen without Allen's self-loathing and despair. Boulding in fact left Ames for Michigan in 1949, not because he was unhappy there but because of the promise of a seminar in the integration of the social sciences. Sadly, he found that 'social scientists did not want to be integrated very much'. Nevertheless, his abiding interest in general systems has left him optimistically hopeful that some fruitful integration is possible. He is very critical of the operational value of the traditional triad of labour, land and capital; he regards them as hopelessly heterogeneous aggregates. Rather, 'know how' which comes from our genes and learning capacity is the essential genetic factor, but its potential may fail to be realised because of the limiting factors of energy, materials, space and time. These limits, however, can be pushed back by quantum jumps in 'know how'. He has a vision of evolutionary interactions under changing parameters: 'The automobile is a species like a horse; it just has a more complicated sex life'. The price mechanism has a prominent place in his system of thought, as does some form of intervention: 'The major case for intervening is to make expensive things which are cheap now but will be expensive later'.

18. Boulding's little book, *The Image* (1956), 'a nine-day wonder written in nine days in August' at the end of his year at the Stanford Think Tank, probably has had more interdisciplinary impact than any of his other books.[13] The notion of images of the future, of images in people's minds, has illuminated not only how we think in economics but also in anthropology, cognitive geography—but, sadly, it has not penetrated psychology, not even social psychology! His writings on the grants economy now—to the author rather sadly—have become almost respectable. In 1971, when he first presented these ideas, 'they nearly created a riot—Hicks turned pale, Harry Johnson stopped whittling and Kuznets jumped up and down'—the profession just could not accept the outrageous idea of a one-way transfer, a redistribution of net worth, because we are so wedded to exchange.

VII

19. In the Introduction to Volume I of his collected papers, Boulding (1971a) refers to them as 'in a sense a record of failure' and to himself 'as a voice crying in the wilderness, to which nobody has paid much attention'. He sees himself as 'not much of a radical ... close to the "main line" ... that goes from Smith to ... Keynes [but] in terms of the reception of [his] ideas [he feels] much closer to ... the American institutionalists ... especially to John R. Commons ... the most influential and most neglected American thinker of the twentieth century' (pp. vii and viii). Boulding shies away from a Guru's role—'can't stand it'. I was tempted to call this essay, 'The Magnificent Failure', but on reflection I thought it too sombre a judgment, for Boulding is too hard on himself. The sanity of Boulding's one-liners may not by themselves secure peace but for generations of students they will continue to provide hope, and his example of tolerant, witty charity to all will continue to inspire long after the latest technical fad has been confined to the W.P.B. 'There is a spirit'. Indeed: it is alive and well and living as Distinguished Professor of Economics Emeritus in Boulder, Colorado.

NOTES

1. This essay is reprinted from the *Journal of Post Keynesian Economics* (Fall, 1983), pp. 143–54. The author is grateful to Bob Dixon, Alastair Fischer, John Hatch and Donald McCloskey for their comments on a draft of the essay.
2. In his flat at Queen's College, University of Melbourne, where he was spending a term as R.I. Downing Research Fellow.
3. The Nayler Sonnets (1945), 'There Is a Spirit'—which are sonnets based on the statement of the seventeenth-century Quaker James Nayler just before he died—were written 'partly as a purely personal act of meditation and devotion, but partly also in the hope that they may call the attention of others to the depths of truth in the passage[s] which fathered them' (Boulding, 1945, p. ix).
4. Boulding told me that he now wonders whether he got a lot of his ideas from Knight; he feels that he must reread him.
5. Boulding—quite rightly—hated the class snobbery at Oxford. He tells with wry amusement how, after he failed to get a Fellowship at an

Oxford college (he had a vigorous debate with Harrod at the interview), with typical Oxford inefficiency they sent to him the confidential references, one of which read: 'a very bright young chap, but not really one of us'. Born a Methodist, going to a grammar school, Boulding did not mix socially even with his fellow Quakers at Oxford as they had been to boarding schools and so belonged to a different class. He felt completely at home in the United States—'a Methodist haven'. Yet the tutorial system whereby students read one or two essays a week to their tutors, which by the standards of the American graduate system is not overwork, left Boulding's creative powers unstunted, his stamina unsapped—and his confidence unsquashed. Of course, it left him also with the Oxbridge style of few footnotes—'easier to think up than look up'. Viner thumbed through Boulding's B.Litt. thesis and said disparagingly, 'Huh, Oxford, no footnotes'—so Boulding referred to Viner in the first footnote of *Economic Analysis* (p. 3).

6. Boulding's only mild gripe about the United States—he is not one to complain—is that the *J. Econ. Lit.* never reviewed the five volumes of his collected papers (Boulding, 1971a, 1971b, 1973, 1974, 1975).
7. Just the same, he recently resigned from the Republican Party and joined the Democrats as a protest against President Reagan's 'irresponsible radical ideology'.
8. Few people have used orthodox analysis—for example, supply and demand analysis—in as illuminating a manner as Boulding. A minor classic (of which Bruce McFarlane reminded me) is his 1947 paper on the theory of the black market (*see* Boulding, 1971a, pp. 215–18), while Part I of *Economic Analysis* takes demand and supply analysis about as far it can go.
9. Samuelson is five years younger than Boulding. It was *The General Theory* that turned him on at the age of twenty-one (eventually!), while it was *The Treatise* that turned on Boulding. Both quoted Wordsworth's lines on the French Revolution:

    Bliss it was in that dawn to be alive
    But to be young was very heaven!

    Samuelson looked them up and got them right; Boulding quoted from memory and got them wrong (sic.)! Or so he told me; in fact, in his 1967 Ely Lecture he got them right (*see* Boulding, 1971b, pp. 378–9).
10. Boulding is fond of saying that habit is important for keeping the system going. Otherwise, no one but a fool or an altruist would have kept on investing when expected rates of profit were negative and real rates of profit were positive, as in the 1930s depression. And now?
11. He 'half believes' in the wage fund. At Edinburgh after six weeks of term they have a Meal Monday Holiday. In the old day the stores of oatmeal which the students brought from their farms were finished by then and they had to return to the farms to replenish their stocks. The wages fund doctrine reflects the truth that when the landlord and

farmer have taken their share (of oatmeal), the remainder must be used for wages because otherwise it would decay if stored too long. This insight is closely related to the truth that Marx, Kalecki, Arthur Lewis and Joan Robinson, for example, have stressed, that the real wages of the investment goods workers have to be found from the surplus created by the consumption goods workers.

12. Commons' students dominated the early days of the New Deal—'another terrible teacher who yet inspired a generation to go out and change the world'.
13. 'Space-ship earth' is another household phrase.

REFERENCES

Boulding, Kenneth E. (1932). 'The Place of the "Displacement Cost" Concept in Economic Theory.' *Economic Journal* 42: 137–41, reprinted in Kenneth E. Boulding (1971a) *Collected Papers,* Vol. I, (edited by Fred R. Glahe), Boulder, Colorado Associated University Press, pp. 3–7

Boulding, Kenneth E. (1945). *There Is a Spirit* (The Nayler Sonnets), New York, Fellowship Press

Boulding, Kenneth E. (1948). *Economic Analysis* (rev. ed). New York, Harper

Boulding, Kenneth E. (1971a, 1971b, 1973, 1974, 1975). *Collected Papers,* Vols. I–V, edited by Fred R. Glahe (I and II), Larry Singell (III to V). Boulder, Colorado Associated University Press

Samuelson, Paul A. (1972). 'Economics in a Golden Age: A Personal Memoir', in Gerald Holton (ed.), *The Twentieth-Century Sciences.* New York, W. W. Norton, pp. 155–70

3 A Twentieth-Century Eclectic: Richard Goodwin[1]

I

Richard Goodwin is a remarkable person. He has had three professional careers: first, at Harvard (which included a spell as a lecturer in physics during the Second World War); second, at Cambridge, England, where he taught for thirty years and was a Fellow (and wine steward) of Peterhouse, Girdlers' Lecturer and ultimately a Reader of the University; and now a splendid metamorphosis (he is 71) at Siena as Professor of Economics Emeritus (for the first four years of his retirement from Cambridge he was Professor of Economics at Siena, the first non-Italian to hold such a post). He lives in Siena during the Italian academical year; for the rest of the year he lives with his wife Jacquie in a thatched cottage in that part of the countryside where Cambridgeshire starts to have hills. There, he works on economic theory. His mind is as fertile now as in any part of his working life and the strands of thought that he has developed over the years have come together in a grand synthesis, his own vision of the nature of the development of the capitalist economy. This has been included in his lectures in Siena, which are given jointly with Lionello Punzo. These lectures both complement and significantly add to his ideas in his two volumes of collected essays (Goodwin, 1982; 1983). His vision continues to inspire the work of his research students and younger colleagues at Siena and elsewhere.[2]

Goodwin also paints, another of his loves, though not as much as he would like. His aunt was a painter but his family vetoed his own youthful ambition to be one also, by saying that she could not support herself. This was a cardinal sin against the ethos of the good folk of Newcastle, Indiana, where Goodwin was born in 1913. Nevertheless, over the years Goodwin has always found time for painting. He refused to do those things necessary to secure an entrée to the art world, so, while his abstract canvases are properly in demand,[3] he has never been a full-time painter.

As with the best social scientists, Goodwin is also politically aware. He was appalled by the Great Depression (he had first-hand experience of its impact on his own family, mainly farming stock, who experienced either bankruptcy or near bankruptcy during the Depression), and by the rise of fascism. The young Goodwin became a Marxist and a member of the British Communist Party (while a Rhodes Scholar at Oxford) and, then, of its American counterpart when he returned to the United States in the late 1930s. He admired the communists for their actions and regarded them as the only effective bulwark against fascism—other groups were either ineffective or half in agreement. The latter were correct to endorse their countries fighting in the Second World War but as often as not they did so for reasons associated with power and greed. Goodwin left the Communist Party following the Hitler–Stalin pact in 1939, but he retained a humane, progressive commitment to planning a more just and equitable society than unfettered capitalism could provide. In this, his evolving understanding of how economic systems work and what economic theory can (and cannot) contribute to our understanding of these processes has been a major passion. His thought moves in quantum jumps, with major insights every five years or so, following a seemingly fallow but really deeply sown gestation period. He is an eclectic and draws on the contributions of Marx, Wicksell (perhaps his favourite economist),[4] Keynes, Schumpeter, Kalecki, Harrod, Leontief, Joan Robinson, Sraffa and Kahn in order to form his own distinctive models. As we shall see, his spell as a physicist, his friendship with Philippe Le Corbeiller, the influence of 'Norbert Wiener's generalisation of the engineering concept of negative feedback control' (Goodwin, 1982, p. viii), his introduction of 'the Frobenius theorem into economics'[5] in the sequel to his classic paper, 'The Multiplier as Matrix' (see Essays 2 and 3 in Goodwin, 1983) and, more recently, the influence of Rene Thom's concepts have allowed him to take a unique approach, culminating in the Siena lectures. Important staging posts on the way were his early papers on non-linear theories of the cycle and his seminal paper in the Dobb *Festschrift* (Feinstein, 1967), 'A Growth Cycle', in which he brought to maturity his desire as expressed in the 1953 *Yorkshire Bulletin* paper to construct a model which would 'fuse indissolubly the cycle and the trend' (Goodwin, 1982, p. 117).

II

His maternal grandfather was a lawyer and Goodwin consulted him on what he should be—he was told to go to Harvard and become a lawyer. Harvard had an entrance examination whereby it took the brightest regardless of wealth. Goodwin, who regarded Harvard merely as a means to the end of getting on—the uncomplicated American dream—got a scholarship, only to find out that law was a postgraduate degree; he asked a lawyer friend of his family what he should do and politics was suggested as at least being relevant for law. Goodwin loved his four years (1930–34) as an undergraduate; he completely changed his attitudes as he read in politics, philosophy and economics—and in maths, which he nearly failed because of his 'awful schooling' at Newcastle. He obtained the equivalent of a First—A. B. Summa Cum Laude—and the Rhodes Scholarship to Oxford to read PPE in the mid-1930s. At Harvard he wrote a thesis on Marx, *A Critique of Marxism* (1934).[6] He also met Joseph Schumpeter at a seminar—Schumpeter was to become one of Goodwin's heroes and, towards the end of Schumpeter's life, a close friend. Schumpeter, who had been in Böhm-Bawerk's seminar in Vienna, knew Marx's work thoroughly, provided a learned and intelligent critique which caused the young Goodwin to take a great dislike to Schumpeter because he could not bear to have Marx, his newfound hero, criticized!

Goodwin used his Oxford years not so much for work—his Harvard result ensured a job for him when he returned—but for gathering information to back up his emerging social and political awareness and for improving his knowledge of art history and his technical skills as an artist—he went to Ruskin for life classes. He immersed himself in early Hitlerian Germany in order to try to find out why a great nation could fall for such a monster; and he spent a lot of time in Italy, not so much to study fascism as to absorb the great works of art there—and to start a life-long love affair with the country itself. He got little out of his tutor at St John's in the first year, but the tutor was perceptive enough to send Goodwin to Harrod at Christ Church in his second year. With Harrod he read *The General Theory* from the proofs which Keynes had sent to Harrod for comment. *The General Theory* had a major impact on Goodwin, though he thought it neglected the cycle. He was to return to Harvard in the late 1930s 'most enthusiastic', only to confront a wall of hostility and incomprehension.[7]

At the same time, Goodwin read Harrod's *Trade Cycle* (1936)[8] and, because he read German, Tinbergen's review of it. Tinbergen, who was originally a physicist, said Harrod's theory implied not a cycle but growth (or decay) because it was not possible endogenously to obtain sustained oscillations from the first-order linear differential equation implied by the accelerator plus multiplier. Goodwin told Harrod this. Harrod only said, 'I'll look into it', and never referred to it again—but published his dynamics essay two years later in 1939.[9] Goodwin, however, felt that 'Harrod and not Tinbergen had the sounder view of capitalist dynamics' and he 'continued to mull over the issue' until illumination came during his 'spell of teaching physics at Harvard during the war' (Goodwin, 1982, p. viii).

III

Goodwin did PPE in two years. He stayed on at Oxford for another year in order to do a B.Litt. thesis which was supervised by Henry Phelps Brown. As Goodwin wanted to try an empirical subject with econometric backing, he worked on the control of the money supply in the United Kingdom from 1919 to 1937—in the process constructing the first series of M and V for the UK. Goodwin thought that Keynes's (liquidity preference) theory was correct but was non-operational because it depended on expectations, a non-measurable variable. He concluded that the central bank could not control activity because *M* and *V* tended to follow movements in *N* and *Q*.[10] Phelps Brown was extremely helpful, telling Goodwin about the pitfalls of empirical research and data collection and referring him to the appropriate series. The one thing which he forgot to tell him was that he was constructing the same series himself! Goodwin returned to Harvard, took his Generals in one year, and wrote up his UK material as his Ph.D. dissertation. Phelps Brown published the series he had constructed in a descriptive article in *Oxford Economic Papers* (Phelps Brown and Shackle, 1939). This had a traumatic effect on Goodwin as it prevented him from publishing his own findings as a book.[11] It put him off money for life (he became a real rather than a money man)—and reinforced his already acquired conviction 'that the "real" behaviour of the economy ... would be wave-like, quite without any help from the banks' (Goodwin, 1982, p. vii).[12] This conviction was acquired in his last year at Oxford when he went to Jacob Marschak's 'superb seminar', where they went through Tinbergen's survey of business cycle theory.

At Harvard, Goodwin took part in the debate about Keynes. He was assistant to John Williams and taught Keynesian economics as part of a money and banking course. (Goodwin used a four-quadrant, rather than the Hicks–Hansen two-quadrant, diagram which he never published, though one of this students—he forgets who—did.)[13] Goodwin also became a close friend and pupil of Schumpeter, turning a full 180 degrees from his attitude to him in the days when he heard him criticise Marx. Schumpeter held a workshop/surgery twice a week at which interested pupils were encouraged to talk about books or issues which interested them. Schumpeter let them go on as long as they were serious; if they were not (on *his* definition), he was ruthless in getting rid of them. Goodwin thought that Schumpeter was not that good a lecturer, principally because he tried to get too much in, to be encyclopaedic, and so he always ran out of time. It was Schumpeter who told Goodwin that if you want to do fundamental work you must not get bogged down in administration, a maxim to which Goodwin has adhered. Indeed, when he was first appointed to Harvard he asked whether he could do half the work for half the pay so as to leave enough time for thinking, painting and, in those days, his intense political activities. Of course, such a request was unheard of and was not granted; it was un-American and helped earn for Goodwin a false reputation of not 'being serious'.[14]

A great influence on Goodwin at Harvard was Philippe Le Corbeiller, whose work on the theory of oscillations was crucial for anyone thinking fundamentally about the cyclical processes at work in capitalist economies. The other stroke of luck was when Goodwin became a lecturer in physics during the Second World War—getting himself up on the theoretical structures of physics gave Goodwin a new armoury of techniques. (It also alerted him to how much more complex economic and social structures are than physical or astronomical ones so that ever afterward he has been sceptical of the ability of economists completely to master our subject matter—it is just too difficult, too complex.)[15] He was invited to a mathematical colloquium where he learned some of the mathematical techniques which were to allow him to illustrate his intuitive understanding and conjectures about the interrelationship between trend and cycle. In particular, he was absorbed with the problem of the lower turning point and he sought out mathematical systems which would give them endogenously. This led to an original contribution which Le Corbeiller called 'the Goodwin Characteristic' (see Goodwin, 1982, p. 196).[16] Goodwin was ahead of Hicks in his understanding of the cycle, 'that the right way to visualise the process was of an elastic system bumping repeatedly against a rising "ceiling" [so that he] was critical of the use of a "floor" along with a "ceiling"'. All investment has to be endogenous, with the 'rising trend. . . not a datum but a part of the system. The basic, single, given, short-run nonlinearity is full employment, whether of capacity or labour' (Goodwin, 1982, p. ix). Goodwin now had the answer as to why Harrod's intuition had been correct, that Harrod *did* have a cycle in his 1930s book. Tinbergen had been wrong.

IV

Through his association with Leontief and Schumpeter, Goodwin also was developing his own analysis of the productive interrelationships which input–output analysis represents, on the one hand, and of the nature of the impact of technical progress through the innovating entrepreneur, whereby underlying structures are crucially altered, on the other. He was invited to the first input–output conference (*not* through Leontief, who, though a close friend, did not perceive Goodwin's essential seriousness). There he met Richard Stone, who suggested that he come to the United Kingdom. Goodwin welcomed this both for old times' sake and because he knew he was not going to get tenure at Harvard.[17] He went to Cambridge on a Fulbright Fellowship in 1951 and during that year was elected to a lectureship in the Cambridge Faculty. Joan Robinson and Richard Kahn were among his backers and Harry Johnson was the 'messenger boy' who was sent to tell him to apply. So began thirty happy years at Cambridge.

What Goodwin especially liked about working at Cambridge was that he could lecture on whatever he wished to and that there was complete democracy in the transmission and criticism of ideas among junior and senior faculty. Of course, people had to be tough to take, say, Joan Robinson's criticisms (both their style *and* content), but they knew that she was after truth, not the person, and that the person concerned might receive what equally well could have applied to Kahn, or other senior members, or to herself. Moreover, he recalls that when Jan Graaf was leaving Cambridge after the publication of his book on welfare economics, the results of which left him thoroughly disillusioned with economics, he read a paper to the 'secret' seminar through which he told them so and why. He was given much credit for this performance, an index of what Goodwin liked about the intellectual atmosphere in the first place. Goodwin in fact became a member of the 'secret' seminar in its most creative period when both Cambridge growth theory and the critique of neoclassical orthodoxy through capital theory were being thought through.

In the mid-1950s Goodwin was elected a Fellow of Peterhouse. Previously pupils reading for the Economics Tripos at Peterhouse had been taught by Joan Robinson, who, because she was a woman, had never been allowed to dine there. When the rule against women dining was relaxed, Goodwin had great pleasure in taking Joan Robinson as his first woman guest—and she, wryly, had great pleasure in going. Goodwin likes teaching, especially one-to-one as in the Cambridge supervision system. Because he feels that 'economics is too difficult for most students and [really] only suitable for very able students with a serious interest in the subject', he kept down the numbers admitted to read for the Economics Tripos at Peterhouse. This had a happy by-product—it preserved space and time for his thoughts to mature; it allowed him to paint and, for many years as wine steward, to improve his enjoyment and knowledge of wine.

For some years Goodwin gave the vital second-year Principles lectures. They were the origin of his book *Elementary Economics from the Higher Standpoint* (Goodwin, 1970). He wanted to be the Marshall of the twentieth century by teaching linear models entirely in geometry (he still prefers geometry and geometric proofs to algebra). When he started giving the lectures the undergraduates asked what books they could read to back up the lectures. There were none. The Faculty Office refused to produce the huge amounts of paper needed to get out his notes three times a week to a class of well over a hundred, so Goodwin decided to write the book instead. Alas, because the finished diagrams are so complicated (built up step-by-step as in a lecture they are clarity itself) and because the book was badly proofread, it never really took off. By contrast, the volumes of his collected essays have sold out very quickly—clearly his time has now come.

Of the thirty years at Cambridge, Goodwin recalls a stretch when he gave more time to painting than to economics as he felt that he was a little stale and also he was not able to follow his usual plan of lecturing on new things so as to communicate a sense of excitement in his lectures. For example, he gave the research students in 1954 a splendid set of lectures on Tustin's engineering systems as applied to economics; in

1956 as a result of a year in India there was another splendid set in which he discussed his views on planning. (The gist of these lectures is in Goodwin, 1983, Essay 6—'how to determine an economic plan for a growing economy in the medium run', p. 121.) Goodwin also demonstrated Phillips' National Income Machine to undergraduate classes for many years, graphically showing pupils the nature of the cycles which result from feedback processes in the Keynesian system as modelled by Phillips.

During the Cambridge period Goodwin's own ideas on the trend and cycle whereby they should be regarded as 'fused indissolubly' (see Goodwin, 1982, p. 117) evolved considerably. A seminal paper, 'The Problem of Trend and Cycle', was published in the *Yorkshire Bulletin* in 1953 (it is reprinted as Essay 9 in Goodwin, 1982). In addition to arguing out this central point, he made good use, in filling in the details of the phases of the cycle, 'of Marshall's famous principle that the short period is very much shorter for expansions than for contractions' (Goodwin, 1982, p. 117), the insight through which the young Kahn was to influence Keynes as he moved from *The Treatise* to *The General Theory* (see Kahn, 1984, p. 174). Goodwin took part in the discussions of growth theory in the 1950s and 1960s but he always saw the need to have the trend and cycle intertwined. His ideas came to fruition in his 1967 paper (in the Dobb *Festschrift*), which, significantly, is entitled 'A Growth Cycle'. There, he took the Volterra prey–predator model whereby the analogy of 'the symbiosis of two populations—partly complementary, partly hostile—is helpful in ... understanding ... the dynamical contradictions of capitalism, especially when stated in a ... Marxian form' (Goodwin, 1982, p. 167). Thus he analysed the fight over wages and profit and the feedback on real variables—and spawned a literature which is still expanding.

Nevertheless Goodwin was not satisfied. He needed effectively to integrate effective demand into the model—Joan Robinson said (characteristically), 'You've made the same mistake as Marx, you have not escaped from Say's Law'. The development of catastrophe theory and the concept of 'bifurcation' have rekindled Goodwin's intuitive understanding of Schumpeter's contributions: he now concentrates on the nature of evolutionary structures which experience from time to time large jumps and breaks, regarding these as the key to the explanation of cyclical development of economies characterised by production interdependencies. There has also been an interlude in which he has pondered the capital theoretic aspects of Piero Sraffa's contributions. He has attempted to use a generalised version of the Standard commodity to clarify Marxian economics and overcome the 'obstinately aggregative' characteristics of cycle models. In retrospect he is inclined to think that these particular strands have ended in a *cul de sac.*

V

When Goodwin retired from Cambridge in 1979 he was appointed to a Chair in the economics department at Siena. There he became extremely productive in a congenial atmosphere; stimulated and admired by his colleagues, his life-long ideas came together in a splendid synthesis. Previously, his thoughts had evolved along two separate lines—on the one hand, the nature of cyclical processes in aggregative models, on the other, the nature of production interdependence in multi-sector models. Now the two have been integrated into an impressive whole. Unlike Martin Luther King, Jr., Goodwin has lived to see his dream come about, to see the fruits of those sensibly acquired and guarded periods for thought. He says ruefully that he never reads now but draws on the inspiration of his past reading of the greats and the modes of analysis which he absorbed during his years as a physicist.

Indeed, Italy is the appropriate place for him, for he calls to mind those Renaissance master painters who planned the broad canvases, setting out the structures and left the details for their followers and pupils to fill in and subsequently to develop. Richard Goodwin is a happy, fulfilled person who enjoys civilised living. He is wonderful company as he sits, relaxed, in his garden in Cambridgeshire, reminiscing over past events, never with rancor but with detached amusement and with infectious enthusiasm when he discusses technical problems. At the same time, his work is getting better known as a new generation of students as well as his old friends read his collected essays, a process which will greatly accelerate when his Siena lectures (with Lionello Punzo) come to be published.[18]

NOTES

1. Reprinted from the *Journal of Post Keynesian Economics* 7 (Spring, 1985)3:410–21. The essay is based in part on notes taken while talking to Richard Goodwin in the garden of his Cambridgeshire home in August 1984. The author is grateful to Sukhamoy Chakravarty, Mohammed Dore, Jayati Ghosh, Graeme Snooks, and David Vines for their comments on a draft.
2. They join an honour roll of outstanding people who have been his pupils; for example, Robert Solow, Luigi Pasinetti, Hollis Chenery, Kumaraswamy Velupillai (*see* Velupillai, 1982, pp. 73–4), and in learning mathematics, Schumpeter and Haberler. (When Goodwin was teaching economics at Harvard he became a friend of Schumpeter. Schumpeter, who had no mathematics, said that if Goodwin would give a maths course he would attend; so Goodwin gave a course on maths and cycle theory to which Schumpeter, Haberler and three or four others came. Goodwin is thus unique in being both a 'student and a teacher of Schumpeter'!)
3. A number of them hang on the walls of the Faculty Building in Sidgwick Avenue.
4. 'As a student I found Wicksell more inspiring, more illuminating, more sympathetic to my own way of seeing things than any other economist' (Goodwin, 1983, p. 153).
5. The first economist to do so.
6. The chapter headings are typically Goodwinian—Introduction; By Way of Beginning; Marxism: An attempt at Understanding; Marxism: A Further Attempt at Understanding; By Way of Ending.
7. Years later when Kuhn published his book on the nature of scientific revolutions, Goodwin says he recognised in the tale of paradigm clashes exactly what he and others who had been at Cambridge or Oxford when *The General Theory* came out experienced: either you see it, in which case it is the great illumination, or you do not, in which case it is gobbledygook, quite wrong and/or nothing new.
8. He 'was, and still [is], much impressed by that largely forgotten book, but [he] felt that its intuition far outran its analytic expertise' (Goodwin, 1982, p. vii).
9. Many years afterwards R. C. O. Matthews asked Harrod if he remembered the conversation; he said he had no recollection of it. Goodwin adds that to Harrod he was 'a not very bright student' (he did little work and got a Second) and that Harrod, while very

stimulating, was not an approachable person. Indeed, Goodwin thought him 'standoffish'.

10. 'Especially in the short run the supply of money cannot be separated from the spending of it' (Goodwin, 1982, p. 24).
11. They were published in an article in *Oxford Economic Papers* in 1941 (*see* Essay 1 in Goodwin, 1982).
12. Goodwin recently gave a paper on inflation. A young listener said at the end that it was the first time he had ever heard a paper on inflation in which the quantity of money was not mentioned.
13. Kumaraswamy Velupillai has traced the forgotten student—he is Ira O. Scott, Jr. In n. 3, p. 13 of his 1951–52 paper in the *Review of Economic Studies,* 'An exposition of the Keynesian System', Scott writes: 'After preparing a draft of this paper, the author benefited greatly from reading an unpublished manuscript in which Professor Goodwin presents a slightly different version of the Keynesian system in diagrammatic form'.
14. That it was false is witnessed to, for example, by Karl Brunner's remarks that when he came to Harvard in the late 1940s there were only two of the faculty with whom he could talk: 'Haberler and a young man by the name of Richard Goodwin. He later left for England, I believe' (*see* Klamer, 1984, p. 180).
15. He says in the preface to Goodwin, 1983 (p. vi) 'In my view economies are so impossibly complex as to defy any completely satisifactory analysis ... the best that can be hoped for is a number of different approaches, each of which yields valuable but incomplete insights.'
16. 'The first example of a two-stroke oscillation appeared in the work of an economist, Dr Richard M. Goodwin, who communicated it to the writer in December 1950' (Le Corbeiller, 1960, reprinted in Goodwin, 1982, p. 186).
17. In fact Schumpeter and Haberler were the only ones to 'support' his continuing appointment. Goodwin charitably attributes the decision as a mistaken one made purely on academic grounds but I, less charitably, suggest that McCarthyite funk also was a factor influencing some of the decision-makers. For though he had worked on 'technical' problems, his Marxist and Communist past were likely to return to haunt them.
18. To be called *The Dynamics of a Capitalist Economy*.

REFERENCES

Feinstein, Charles H. (ed.) *Socialism, Capitalism and Economic Growth: Essays Presented to Maurice Dobb.* Cambridge, Cambridge University Press, 1967

Goodwin, Richard M. *A Critique of Marxism.* Harvard, Mass., 1934

——— *Elementary Economics from the Higher Standpoint.* Cambridge, Cambridge University Press, 1970

—— *Essays in Economic Dynamics*. London, Macmillan, 1982
—— *Essays in Linear Economic Structures*, London, Macmillan, 1983
Harrod, Roy F. *The Trade Cycle: An Essay*. Oxford, Oxford University Press, 1936
Kahn, Richard F. *The Making of Keynes' General Theory*. Cambridge, Cambridge University Press, 1984
Klamer, Arjo. *The New Classical Macroeconomics: Conversations with the New Classical Economists and Their Opponents*. Brighton, Wheatsheaf Books, 1984
Le Corbeiller, Philippe. 'Two-Stroke Oscillators'. Institute of Radio Engineers Transaction of the Professional Group on Circuit Theory, 1960, reprinted as the Appendix to Goodwin, 1982, pp. 181–213
Phelps Brown, E. H., and Shackle, G. L. S. 'British Economic Fluctuations 1924–38'. *Oxford Economic Papers*. (May 1939), no. 2:98–134
Scott, Ira O. Jr., 'An Exposition of the Keynesian System.' *Review of Economic Studies XIX* (1951–52), 12–18
Velupillai, Kumaraswamy. 'Linear and Nonlinear Dynamics: The Contributions of Richard Goodwin'. *Economic Notes* (1982), no. 3: 73–91

PART II
Piero Sraffa and Joan Robinson

4 On Piero Sraffa's Contributions to Economics[1]

I

Piero Sraffa has always found writing difficult—indeed, the introductions to the great edition of Ricardo's works and correspondence were finally written only because Maurice Dobb collaborated with Sraffa. They discussed each paragraph, Dobb wrote it, Sraffa corrected the draft until it was to his liking, and then they went on to talk about the next paragraph (see Eatwell, 1979, pp. 143–4). The core of *Production of Commodities by Means of Commodities* (1960) was written in the late 1920s, 'particular points ... were worked out in the thirties and forties', and it was only when Sraffa put the 'old notes' together in the second half of the 1950s that he filled in the 'gaps which had become apparent in the process', Sraffa (1960, p. vi). I recently asked him whether the conjecture of Peter Sallans (see Harcourt, 1982, pp. 271–2, n.7) was correct, to wit, that it was Hume's *Abstract*, which Keynes and Sraffa edited together in the 1930s (see Hume, 1938) that led him to write *Production of Commodities* in such a sparse, stark manner. He answered that it was because he disliked writing so much that he wrote *Production of Commodities* in as few words as possible. Of course, his reply was partly a joke, a tease. As Krishna Bharadwaj reminds me (letter of 1 Jan. 1982), Sraffa 'could compose prose quite easily [and] could draft letters in no time'. It was with the final product, which had to meet the extraordinarily high standards which he set himself, his 'insistence on perfection', that the 'difficulty' partly lay. In all his published works, including the introductions to the Ricardo volumes, 'the style, the choice of words, the economy of phrases, the compactness of content, the tightness of the logic' are entirely due to Sraffa. Anyway, we have from his pen relatively little for a lifetime (he is now well into his eighties), but what we have has had a revolutionary impact on economic theory. In particular, his 1925 and 1926 articles, his edition with Maurice Dobb of Ricardo's works and correspondence (1951-55) and *Production of Commodities* itself, will survive long after the ephemeral scribbling which passes for so much of economic analysis these days has been forgotten.

What has Sraffa been trying to *do* in his writings? I think, as I have argued elsewhere (see Harcourt, 1982), that he has been trying to teach the orthodox, without them necessarily knowing it, important lessons from Marx. More generally, he has been trying to re-establish the approach to economic analysis which originally was to be found in the classical political economists and in Marx, the core of which is the concept of the surplus of commodities over the necessaries required for their production. This approach had been lost—'submerged and forgotten'—or at least emasculated, with the emergence of the marginal school and the 'marginal' method and the accompanying dominance of the subjective theory of value, itself brought to its most refined form in the neoclassical version of general-equilibrium theory. Krishna Bharadwaj (1978) calls this process the 'rise to dominance of the supply and demand theories'. Sraffa himself in 1926 referred to the near end product of the process, 'the almost unanimous agreement at which economists have arrived regarding the theory of competitive value', as a 'striking feature of the present position of economic science'. He contrasted this 'state of things . . . with the controversies on the theory of value by which political economy was characterised during the past century' (1926, p. 535). As is now well known, Sraffa, as an adolescent, became a pacifist socialist (see 'Introduction—the Unknown Sraffa', *NLR*, 1978, p. 62). Many of his student friends were Marxists, but his teachers would not allow Marx or Marxist issues to be discussed explicitly in class. However, while a student, Sraffa read Ricardo's *Principles* and discovered that much of what Ricardo had to say bore a close resemblance to what he had been reading in Marx's works. As Ricardo was eminently respectable and so acceptable to their teachers, Sraffa and his fellow students took to discussing Marxist issues under the guise of a study of Ricardo. This ploy, evidently so successful then, he used again in his 1960 classic, teasing us now just as he teased his teachers long ago.[2]

In order to prepare the ground for the acceptance of his project Sraffa needed to attack on two fronts: the first was to overthrow neoclassical economics, especially the marginal theory of value and distribution, including the theory of value as it was presented to the English-speaking world in Marshall's work in particular, using supply and demand analysis. The 1925 and 1926 articles were specifically directed against Marshall's schema, as Sraffa makes plain in his reply to D. H. Robertson in the 1930 *Economic Journal* Symposium on 'Increasing Returns and the Representative Firm':

> We seem to be agreed that [Marshall's] theory cannot be interpreted in a way which makes it logically self-consistent, and at the same time, reconciles it with the facts it sets out to explain. Mr Robertson's remedy is to discard mathematics, and he suggests that [Sraffa's] remedy is to discard the facts; perhaps I ought to have explained that . . . I think it is Marshall's theory that should be discarded. [1930, p. 93]

The introductions to the Ricardo volumes and *Production of Commodities* were directed against the neoclassical theory of value and distribution, which itself invoked supply and demand, in the sense that the fundamental idea was that the relative prices of 'capital' and 'labour', and their relative shares, were what they were because of relative scarcities—the rate of profits, for example, was high or low depending upon whether or not the economy in question had a 'little' or a 'lot' or 'capital' in relation to its supplies of 'labour'. This notion, allied with 'the dynamical principle of "substitution" . . . seen ever at work' (Marshall, 1890, p. xv), were the principal clues to the levels of normal profits and wages in a competitive economy.

Sraffa has exacting standards concerning measurement, theory and the criteria which they should meet. He succinctly stated his views at the Corfu Conference on capital theory in the late 1950s:

> [O]ne should emphasize the distinction between two types of measurement. First, there was the one in which the statisticians were mainly

interested. Second, there was measurement in theory. The statisticians' measures were only approximate and provided a suitable field for work in solving index number problems. The theoretical measures required absolute precision. Any imperfections in these theoretical measures were not merely upsetting, but knocked down the whole theoretical basis. One could measure capital in pounds or dollars and introduce this into a production function. The definition in this case must be absolutely water-tight, for with a given quantity of capital one had a certain rate of interest so that the quantity of capital was an essential part of the mechanism. One therefore had to keep the definition of capital separate from the needs of statistical measurement, which were quite different. The work of J. B. Clark, Böhm-Bawerk and others was intended to produce pure definitions of capital, as required by their theories, not as a guide to actual measurement. If we found contradictions, then these pointed to defects in the theory, and an inability to define measures of capital accurately. It was on this—the chief failing of capital theory—that we should concentrate, rather than on problems of measurement.[3]

It was by these standards that he found orthodox theory wanting. He himself merely stated the results in *Production of Commodities*—reswitching in Part III, the famous passage in parenthesis in the Reduction to Dated Labour chapter (p. 38), the 'remarkable effect' on page 70 of the chapter on fixed capital. It has been left to his younger colleagues, especially Krishna Bharadwaj, John Eatwell, Pierangelo Garegnani, Luigi Pasinetti, Ian Steedman, to spell them out and for Alessandro Roncaglia [1978] to document the story insofar as it applies to Piero Sraffa himself. These now are all old stories, but it should not hurt if I go over some of the same ground in what follows.

What I want to do in this paper is, first, to discuss the 1925 and 1926 articles; second, to relate Sraffa's work to the approach of the classical economists in which the key concept was the origin, extraction and allocation of the surplus; and, third, to point out how Sraffa's Standard commodity and Standard system represent the end of a line which starts with Quesnay and goes through Ricardo and Marx, in a theory of the origin of profits. Overall—and this is the second front, from which he advanced his positive contribution—Sraffa's work forms an integral part in the account of modern classical analysis which Walsh and Gram give in their outstanding book, *Classical and Neoclassical Theories of General Equilibrium* (1980). Simultaneous determination *is* an aspect of classical thought, but so, too, are sequences, for classical political economy was principally concerned with a dynamic analysis of the creation, extraction and allocation of the surplus and the *analytical* role which the various classes of capitalist society played in this process.

II

Sraffa's 1925 and 1926 articles are attacks on the logical foundations of Marshall's theory of competitive value. The theory itself depends upon 'the fundamental symmetry existing between the forces of supply and demand', using the method of partial equilibrium—Sraffa calls it 'particular equilibrium' (1926, p. 539)—so that 'the essential causes determining the price of particular commodities may be ... grouped together so as to be represented by a pair of intersecting curves of collective demand and supply' (1926, p. 535). Sraffa's conclusion is that the only case which is *logically* consistent with the approach is one of constant costs—'In normal cases the cost of production of commodities produced competitively ... must be regarded as constant in respect of small variations in the quantity produced' (1926), pp. 540–1). Moreover, as Sraffa adds in a footnote (n. 1, p. 541), the constancy arises from the 'absence of causes which tend to cause the cost either to increase or diminish' and not from an improbable 'accidental balancing of two opposite tendencies' as Sidgwick (as quoted by Sraffa) and Marshall would have it. In which case, we are back with the discredited classical theory of value which the demand and supply theories, together with the subjective theory of value and the marginal method, were meant to supercede.

We have stressed that Sraffa's work led him in 1925 and 1926 to argue that partial-equilibrium *analysis* only applied to constant costs; that is, to do otherwise was to be inconsistent with the method used (though not necessarily with the 'real world' facts which he also discusses). His criticism is a logical and methodological one; that is to say, a search for the set of conditions which allows the method logically to be applied. Sraffa starts by showing that the 'laws' of returns historically belonged in different parts of the discipline, diminishing returns in the theory of distribution (rent) rather than in the discussion of *relative* values, increasing returns in the discussion of 'general economic progress' rather than in a discussion of 'increase[s] in the scale of production' (1926, p. 537). Therefore, to combine them together in one theoretical whole is both contradictory and restrictive. Especially was this true of increasing returns, *for to be consistent with competitive theory*, the division of labour had to be limited to the case of 'independent subsidiary factories coming into existence as the production of an industry [increased]' (1926, p. 537). Internal economies associated with the growth in the size of an individual firm had to be 'entirely abandoned [because they were] incompatible with competitive conditions' (1926, pp. 537–8). 'External economies' were therefore more and more emphasised.

The fixed-factor aspect of diminishing returns meant that the more broadly we defined an industry, the more likely it was that diminishing returns (arising from using one factor) arose. By contrast, the more homogeneous we made the commodity which the industry was to produce (for example, we move from agriculture to fruit), 'the greater will be the probability that the forces which make for increasing returns will predominate' (1926, p. 538). Sraffa likens these effects to the effects of time; in particular, the time allowed for adjustments to occur and the consequent impact of this on returns.

However, it is the independence assumption (of demand and supply schedules in relation to small variations) which is most at risk. For, as Sraffa says, 'it is primarily in [the] ... category that ... when a variation in the quantity produced by [an] industry ... sets up a force which acts directly, not merely upon its own costs, but also on the costs of other industries [, so that] the conditions of the 'particular equilibrium' which it was intended to isolate are upset ... that the applications of the laws of returns fall, in the great majority of cases' (1926, p. 539).[4] As far as diminishing returns are concerned, we are left with 'the study of that minute class of commodities in the production of which the whole of a factor of production is employed' (1926, p. 539). While for increasing returns, we may consider only those economies which are external to the firm but internal to the industry, 'precisely the class which is most seldom to be met with [in practice] (1926, p. 540).

So we have Sraffa's conclusion, the logic of which is as impeccable as the neglect of its implications by the orthodox has been staggering, that 'the supply schedule with variable costs cannot claim to be a general conception applicable to normal markets ... In normal cases the cost of production of commodities produced competitively—as we are not entitled to take into consideration the causes which may make it rise or fall—must be regarded as constant in respect of small variations in the quantity produced' (1926, pp. 540–1). Hence the discarded cost of production theory of value returns 'as a simple way of approaching the problem of competitive value ... [It] is as important as it is useful: it emphasises the fundamental factor ... the predominant influence of cost of production' (1926, p. 541). It also makes it possible to bring in other factors in more detailed analyses of the exchange values of particular commodities because 'it does not conceal from us the fact that we cannot find the elements required for this purpose *within the limits of its assumptions*' (1926, p. 541, emphasis added).

In the 1926 article, Sraffa turned his back on general equilibrium, the conditions of simultaneous equilibrium in a number of industries, 'while keeping to the path of free competition', because he felt it did not offer an accessible way out for *theory*. Instead, he spawned the imperfect competition, monopolistic competition 'revolutions' when he sketched a logically watertight theory which served to illuminate the 'real world' facts of the time—competitive structures with which were associated differentiated products and unutilised opportunities for lower costs with higher rates of output. While this approach was enthusiastically taken up, at least for a time, by the profession, Chicago always excepted, Sraffa himself by 1930 had already turned in another direction: to the models of the centres of gravitation or prices of production of what eventually was to become *Production of Commodities by Means of Commodities*. In order to explain the patterns of relative prices in the competitive capitalist mode of production, Sraffa isolated as persistent and dominant factors, *not* variations in costs with respect to output, nor variations in quantity demanded with respect to price, which was characteristic of neoclassical economics, but, rather, the technical conditions of production at a given moment of time—Roncaglia's snapshot, Roncaglia (1978, p. 21)—together with a given value of one of the distributive variables, either the wage or the rate of profits. (The distributive variables are assumed to have a tendency to equality in all uses, allowance being made for differences in skills in the case of labour and differences in risk and other factors in the case of capitals.) The corresponding factors which determine levels of output and sales were abstracted from—taken as given—for this *particular* task of theory in order to analyse the factors which were thought to be most responsible for the patterns of relative prices, the centres of gravitation of the system; that is to say, to elucidate 'such properties of an economic system as do not depend on changes in the scale of production or in the proportions of "factors"' (Sraffa, 1960, p. v).[5]

III

The late Ronald Meek was the first of the reviewers of *Production of Commodities* to discern in the book a rehabilitation of classical economics (including in this description, Marx's contributions). In his perceptive review article 'Mr Sraffa's Rehabilitation of Classical Economics', (Meek, 1961; reprinted in Meek, 1967), especially in the last section, he showed that the structure of Sraffa's system was such as to provide a rigorous framework for the theory of the origin of profits in the capitalist mode of production. That is to say, Sraffa provided a rigorous formal content for Marx's insight that the origin of profits was the surplus labour extracted in the sphere of production from the wage-earning class by the capitalist class. This showed itself as surplus value—here the form which Marx gave to the labour theory of value is relevant—which was reflected in the sphere of distribution and exchange as the component of average profits in the prices of production. The prices of production themselves, and their divergence from the Marxian labour values of the sphere of production, could be predicted from the knowledge of these labour values and two other embodied labour amounts, those associated with the net product and the means of production of Sraffa's Standard system, which, when expressed as a ratio, constituted the maximum rate of profits of the economic system (R). According to Meek, Marx himself has used his own construction of an average industry—one which showed the characteristics of the economy as a whole in its organic composition of capital—in order to make the same point as Sraffa in his (Marx's) solution of the transformation problem (see Meek, 1967, pp. 175–8].[6]

The argument here then is that Sraffa's approach to Marx's puzzle was through his concepts of the Standard system and the Standard commodity. Some commentators (e.g. Blaug, 1968), have interpreted these concepts and the analysis in which they are used as Sraffa's solution to Ricardo's unsolved problem, the search for an invariable standard of value. As I have argued elsewhere (see Harcourt, 1982, pp. 257–61), this is a mistake or, at least, too limited an interpretation. Insofar as Sraffa's contribution bears on Ricardo's problem—it will be remembered that Ricardo wanted to find such a unit because he wanted to be able to say rigorous things about the distribution of the surplus of heterogeneous commodities between classes when both distribution changed and technical advances occurred—Sraffa shows conclusively that Ricardo was searching for a Will 'o the Wisp. While it is true, at least in a circulating commodity model without joint production, that there is always awaiting to be found, at a particular point of time, a Standard commodity which is invariant to changes in distribution, any changes in the level of any of the basic industries (unless they exhibit constant returns to scale), or any technical advance in the basic industries which alters the amounts of the means of production and/or labour needed to produce any basic commodity, immediately implies that there is another, completely different Standard commodity involved. It follows that while the Standard commodity (under the assumptions stated) will serve to solve one aspect of Ricardo's problem—the impact of changes in distribution on the measurement of the surplus (the exact form of this relationship must be interpreted very carefully)—it does not solve the other aspect associated with changes in activity, and with technical advances. Even with the first aspect, we must note that what is revealed, having previously been hidden, is an inverse relationship between the *rate* of profits and the wage (which in terms of the Standard commodity is a simple linear relationship), not necessarily an inverse relationship between the *shares* of profits and wages. Sraffa is *very* careful to state this: 'Reverting to our example, if in the actual system ... (...with R = 20%) the wage is fixed in terms of the Standard net product, to w = 3/4 there will correspond r = 5%. But while the share of wages will be equal in value to 3/4 of the Standard national income, it does not follow that the share of profits will be equivalent to the remaining 1/4 of the Standard income' (1960, p. 23). Some commentators have not been so careful and have claimed more than its author did for the construction.[7]

However, as we have seen, the principal purpose of the Standard commodity and the Standard system, together with the associated relationship, $r = R(1 - w)$ (where r = rate of profits, R = maximum rate of profits, and w = the wage measured in terms of the Standard commodity and as a share of Standard national income), is rigorously to reveal what Ricardo and then Marx were striving for in their theory of the origin of profits.[8] As Meek and Christopher Gregory have shown, the line which runs from Ricardo to Marx to Sraffa may be shown schematically as follows:[9]

$$\text{(1)}\quad r = \frac{\text{Corn as output} - \text{corn as capital, i.e. advances of necessaries to labour}}{\text{Corn as capital, i.e. advances of necesaries to labour}} \quad \text{(Ricardo of the \textit{Essay})}$$

$$\text{(2)}\quad 1 + r = \frac{\text{Total labour}}{\text{Labour in necessaries}} \quad \text{(Ricardo of the \textit{Principles})}$$

In Marx's terms this becomes:

$$\text{(3)}\quad 1 + r = \frac{s + v}{v}$$

And for Marx himself:

$$\text{(4)}\quad r = \frac{(s + v) - v}{v + c} = \frac{s + v}{c} \cdot \frac{c}{c + v} \cdot \frac{s}{s + v} = R.k\left(1 - \frac{v}{s + v}\right)$$

where:

$\frac{s+v}{c}$ is the maximum rate of profits, R,

$\frac{c}{c+v}$ is the organic composition of capital, k,

s = surplus value,
v = variable capital,
c = constant capital,
all measured in terms of labour time.

Because the wage is paid out of the surplus in Sraffa's formulation, we have:

$$(5)\quad r = \frac{s}{c} = \frac{s+v}{c}\left(1 - \frac{v}{s+v}\right)$$

(Note that there is now no longer a place for the organic composition of capital in this formulation.)

Finally, in Sraffa's analysis, (5) becomes:

$$(6)\quad r = R(1 - W)$$

rigorously measured in terms of the Standard commodity, as Meek showed long ago.

Nor does the story stop here. Garegnani has pointed out the essential similarity between the Standard system, Standard commodity approach of Sraffa's book and his own approach through the concept of the integrated consumption or wage goods industry. He first introduced this concept in his 1959 Ph.D. dissertation, Garegnani (1959), and used it to good effect in his 1970 *Review of Economic Studies* paper, (Garegnani, 1970), and his 1984 *Oxford Economic Papers* paper (Garegnani, 1984). In the last paper he shows that if *w* is given—for the purposes of analysis, that is, at the place and point in time where we cut into the system, as it were, in order to start the analysis—then *r* for the whole economy is determined by the labour commanded by the wage goods themselves and the labour commanded by the direct and indirect amounts of labour needed to produce them, using the techniques of production at the time, and taking account of the 'time' processes of production. Both approaches serve to 'give transparency to a system and render visible what was hidden' (Sraffa, 1960, p. 23). They do, of course, contradict Marx's (sometime) view that the rate of profits depends upon *all* industries, and not just the wage goods industries (see Howard and King, 1975, p. 155 and p. 177, n. 41).

IV

In concluding, therefore, I want to stress again that Sraffa's contributions constitute an alternative approach, a return to the tradition of classical political economy, and not refinements within a unified, evolutionary body of thought called economics. Walsh and Gram (1980), for example, have shown very clearly that while classical and neoclassical general equilibrium theory often share the same formal structure, the contexts of the models are entirely different. The former is concerned principally with the dynamic creation, extraction and allocation of the surplus between further accumulation and luxury consumption as a result of the decisions of the accumulating class (i.e. the capitalists). The latter, even when it is set ostensibly in a neoclassical growth model, is concerned with the allocation of an arbitrarily given set of initial endowments between alternative ends by individuals whose class is irrelevant for the formal analysis itself. Since Sraffa is in the former tradition, and is attempting to rehabilitate it, he is right to take the view that his model is concerned with production of commodities by means of commodities; that is, with the circular interdependence of production and consumption, as opposed to the 'one-way avenue that leads from "Factors of production" to "Consumption goods"' (1960, p. 93) which is characteristic of the neoclassical tradition.

Finally, there sometimes arises a confusion concerning the nature of the (classical–Marxian) rate of profits and (neoclassical) rates of return (or interest rates), to which both Sraffa's critique of orthodoxy and his positive contributions are addressed. These concepts, though they share the same dimension, nevertheless belong to completely different contexts. As Walsh and Gram (1980) argue, 'the interest rates ... derived in a [neoclassical] model of the allocation of resources over time, are not ... linked to the concept of surplus, since surplus is not defined in the quantity relations of the model [whereas] the [rate of profits] of classical theory ... arises *only* when a surplus is defined'. It is perhaps ironical that they invoke Hahn's plea to avoid 'the source of much controversy and muddle' when they add 'that we shall insist on a *conceptual* distinction between the commodity interest-rate of neoclassical theory (in which inputs and outputs are differentiated according to delivery dates) and the [rate of profits] of classical theory (which is associated with capitalist relations of production in the allocation of surplus output)' (p. 236).

Surplus is the concern therefore both of the classical economists and Marx, and of Sraffa's system. His criticisms of the neoclassical approach—the impossibility of finding a unit in which to measure 'capital' which is independent of distribution and prices, the reswitching results—*are* a critical part of the critique of the neoclassical theory of distribution. Milgate (1979) especially has shown how the transformation of the questions asked and concepts used has occurred because of 'a growing realisation ....that if the demand and supply approach to the theory of capital and interest was to be retained, something would have to be done to free it from the bounds imposed by its need to work in terms of a "quantity of capital"' (p. 1). In *that* growing realisation, the works of Piero Sraffa play the pivotal role.

NOTES

1. Reprinted from P. D. Groenewegen and J. Halevi (eds.), *Altro Polo: Italian Economics Past and Present*, Frederick May Foundation of Italian Studies, University of Sydney, Sydney 1983, Ch. 4. I am grateful to Krishna Bharadwaj, Bob Dixon, Peter Groenewegen and Mike White for comments on a draft of this essay.
2. T. W. Hutchison wrote two perceptive reviews of Sraffa's edition of Ricardo's works and correspondence (*see* Hutchison, 1952, 1953). It is clear that he sensed what Sraffa's main purpose was; it is also clear that Hutchison was (and is) antagonistic to it. He therefore wrote the reviews in such a way as to play down Sraffa's purpose and, indeed, indirectly to mock his principal thesis by writing off Marxian economics and, by implication, Ricardo's contributions to it, as both unsound and unimportant for modern economics.

3. Keynes put forward similar views in *The General Theory* in Ch. 4 on 'The Choice of Units' (*see* Keynes, 1936, pp. 39–40). His discussion ends:

   To say that net output today is greater, but the price-level lower, than ten years ago or one year ago, is a proposition of a similar character to the statement that Queen Victoria was a better queen but not a happier woman than Queen Elizabeth—a proposition not without meaning and not without interest, but unsuitable as material for the differential calculus.

4. The parallels of this criticism with the criticism of the Cambridge, England, School of IS/LM analysis may be noted; *see* Moggridge (1976, Appendix, pp. 173–5).
5. The section on the choice of techniques of production in Part III is an exception to this general principle. Sraffa himself acknowledges this: "No changes in output and (at any rate in Parts I and II) no changes in the proportions in which the different means of production are used by an industry are considered, . . ." (1960, p. v).
6. Meek further developed these arguments in the introduction to the second edition of *Studies in the Labour Theory of Value*, Meek (1973). *See also* Krishna Bharadwaj (1980).
7. For further elaboration of this point, *see* Harcourt (1982, p. 260).
8. The next pages draw heavily on Sections 3 and 4 of Harcourt (1982).
9. Christopher Gregory has a fine paper which shows that the initial link in this chain is Quesnay. Sraffa himself provides convincing evidence of this viewpoint in Appendix D of Sraffa (1960), "References to the literature", see, especially, pp. 93–94.

REFERENCES

Bharadwaj, Krishna. 1978. *Classical Political Economy and Rise to Dominance of Supply and Demand Theories.* 1976 R. C. Dutt Lectures on Political Economy, Calcutta, Orient Longman

—— 1980. 'On Certain Theoretical Issues in Classical Political Economy: A Review Article' *Australian Economic Papers* 19:349–63

Blaug, M. 1968. *Economic Theory in Retrospect.* 2nd edn, London, Heinemann

Eatwell, J. L. 1979. 'Dobb, Maurice', in David L. Sills (ed.), *International Encylopaedia of the Social Sciences. Biographical Supplement*, Vol. 18, New York, Free Press, pp. 142–4

Garegnani, Pierangelo. 1959. *A Problem in the Theory of Distribution from Ricardo to Wicksell.* Unpublished Ph.D. dissertation, Cambridge

—— 1970. 'Heterogeneous Capital, the Production Function and the Theory of Distribution.' *Review of Economic Studies*, XXXVII, 3: 407–36

—— 1984. 'Value and Distribution in the Classical Economists and Marx', *Oxford Economic Papers*, 36, 291–325.
Harcourt, G. C. 1982. 'The Sraffian Contribution: An Evaluation', in Ian Bradley and Michael Howard (eds.), *Classical and Marxian Political Economy: Essays in Honour of Ronald L. Meek*. London, Macmillan, pp. 255–75
Howard, M. C. and J. E. King. 1975. *The Political Economy of Marx*, Harlow, Longman
Hume, David. 1938. *An Abstract of a Treatise of Human Nature* (1740). Ed. with an introduction by John Maynard Keynes and Piero Sraffa, Cambridge, Cambridge University Press
Hutchison, T. W. 1952. 'Some Questions about Ricardo.' *Economica* 19: 415–32
—— 1953. 'Ricardo's Correspondence.' *Economica* 20:263–73
Keynes, John Maynard. 1936. *The General Theory of Employment, Interest and Money*. London, Macmillan
Marshall, Alfred. 1890. *Principles of Economics: An Introductory Volume*. Vol. I, 9th ed, (Variorum), London, Macmillan, 1961
Meek, R. L. 1961. 'Mr Sraffa's Rehabilitation of Classical Economics', in R. L. Meek, *Economics and Ideology and other Essays: Studies in the Development of Economic Thought*. London, Chapman and Hall, 1967
—— 1973. *Studies in the Labour Theory of Value*. 2nd ed, London, Lawrence and Wishart
Milgate, M. 1979. 'On the Origin of the Notion of "Intertemporal Equilibrium".' *Economica* 46: 1–10
Moggridge, D. E. 1979. *Keynes*. London, Macmillan
Roncaglia, Alessandro. (1979). *Sraffa and the Theory of Prices*. Chichester, John Wiley and Sons
Sraffa, Piero. 1925. 'Sulle Relazioni fra Costo e Quantità Prodotta.' *Annali di Economica* 11. 277–328
—— 1926. 'The Laws of Returns under Competitive Conditions.' *Economic Journal* XXXVI, 535–50
—— 1930. 'A Criticism' and 'Rejoinder'. *Economic Journal*, XL, 89–93
Sraffa, Piero with the collaboration of Maurice Dobb, eds. 1951–55. *Works and Correspondence of David Ricardo*. Cambridge, Cambridge University Press
Sraffa, Piero. 1960. *Production of Commodities by Means of Commodities. Prelude to a Critique of Economic Theory*. Cambridge, Cambridge University Press
—— 1961. Interventions in the debate at the Corfu Conference on the 'Theory of Capital' organised by the International Economic Association (4–11 September, 1958), in F. A. Lutz and D. C. Hague (eds.), *The Theory of Capital*. London, Macmillan
Walsh, Vivian and Harvey, Gram. 1980. *Classical and Neoclassical Theories of General Equilibrium. Historical Origins and Mathematical Structure*. New York, Oxford University Press

5 On the contributions of Joan Robinson and Piero Sraffa to economic theory[1]

I

Joan Robinson and Piero Sraffa died within a month of each other in 1983. Sraffa, who was born in August 1898, was five years older than Joan Robinson; they had known one another for over fifty years. Joan Robinson had been to Sraffa's lectures in Cambridge in the late 1920s, and they were colleagues in the Faculty of Economics and Politics from 1931 on when Joan Robinson was appointed to an Assistant Lectureship. Sraffa himself had been appointed to a teaching post in 1927 but, as Austin Robinson (1977, p. 29) recalls, in 1930 he begged to be taken off teaching. He retained the post of Marshall librarian and soon after resigning his lectureship, the post of mentor to the research students was created for him. This allowed him to work on the Ricardo volumes, and it relieved him of the anxieties which teaching, especially the critical destruction of the arguments of people whose work he admired (Marshall, for example) caused him. Joan Robinson's first major work, *The Economics of Imperfect Competition* (1933a), was inspired by the 'pregnant suggestion' in Sraffa's 1926 *Economic Journal* article concerning the generality of monopoly rather than competition as the way forward in the theory of value. They were both part of the small group of exceptional young people who constituted the 'circus' which in the early 1930s argued out the *Treatise* and discussed with Keynes (through the Messenger Angel from the Gods, Richard Kahn; see *JMK* XIII, 339) the emerging questions to be tackled and the arguments of *The General Theory*. Joan Robinson remained an ardent Keynesian, though increasingly she was to adopt the structures by which Kalecki independently discovered the principal propositions of *The General Theory*. If we may judge from the written record (but let us not do a Patinkin),[2] Sraffa was more and more to distance himself from Keynes of *The General Theory*. Partly this may have been because he conceived of his own project of the revival of classical political economy, especially of the concept of the surplus as the core of the theory of value and distribution, as both at a higher level of abstraction and as dealing with more fundamental or, at least, more basic issues. To someone who was deeply influenced by the whole corpus of the work of Ricardo and Marx (and of Marshall), whose interest was more in the class struggle and the notion of internal contradictions, Keynes's solution of the realisation problem inevitably must have seemed to have been of relatively narrow scope even if of profound practical importance in the aftermath of a deep depression. (Certainly, it is possible to get a suggestion of a similar attitude to Keynes from Maurice Dobb, who was later to be Sraffa's collaborator on the Ricardo volumes.) Partly also, Sraffa may have been unhappy with the use which Keynes made of Sraffa's construct of own rates of interest in Chapter 17 of *The General Theory*. Sraffa (1932) employed the construct in order to criticise internally the argument of Hayek's *Prices and Production* rather than to provide an integral part of a positive theory of the operation of capitalist markets.

Joan Robinson's *magnum opus, The Accumulation of Capital* (1956), was also much influenced by Sraffa's contributions, this time his remarkable introduction to Volume I of the Ricardo volumes (Sraffa with Dobb, 1951). Here he set out the first major step of his attempt to revive the surplus approach of the classical economists which had 'been submerged and forgotten since the advent of the "marginal" method' (Sraffa, 1960, p. v). And, of course, when Sraffa's own *magnum opus,* albeit a slim volume of less than a hundred pages, was published in 1960, Joan Robinson wrote one of the most perceptive reviews of it (1961; Vol. III, 1965) and joined forces with Sraffa in a combined attack on the orthodox theory of value and distribution. For a while they were as one, detecting in the capital-reversing and reswitching results the Achilles' heel of orthodoxy and arguing that the theory of profits in capitalist economies was to be found in the surplus approach. But towards the end of their lives they were to part in their views on what was most damaging to their shared opponents, as Joan Robinson shifted the emphasis of her attack to one on methods rather than particular results, while Sraffa, or at least the Sraffians, concentrated on the results obtained within a particular methodology. The latter it was argued had been common to economic theory from the classical political economists to Hicks's *Value and Capital,* or at least until Hayek's work in the late 1920s. Hayek sensed the inconsistencies associated with the concept of capital within the supply and demand framework which were made explicit in the 1960s, and responded by changing both the questions asked and the concept of equilibrium used (see Milgate, 1979; Garegnani, 1976; 1983).

As well as being a great intellectual influence on Joan Robinson, it is clear from those parts of their correspondence which have survived,[3] that they were extremely close friends who had great affection for each other and also cared very much about the other's well-being. Much of the contents consists of the intimate discussion of close friends who share a common language and who enjoy gossip, but it also includes some fascinating debates, in which invariably Sraffa emerges as the winner. In a battle of champions even Joan Robinson's renowned logic and insights had to give way to Sraffa's quite remarkable powers of criticism and illumination. He could take what seemed to be a neat and powerful definition or contrast and shown that it was empty of meaning. This was done without rancour and with affection and wry humour. Even as one's head came off the sensation was as much one of amusement as of amazement, certainly there was no immediate pain. Moreover, his own self mockery and sense of irony were much in evidence, especially in the letters in which he discusses whether he should accept a Fellowship at Trinity which had become available because D. H. Robertson had left Cambridge for a Chair in London.

Joan Robinson continued to work into the last year of her life. She gave the prestigious Tanner Lectures at Utah in 1981 and two of her last papers were substantial contributions: 'Spring Cleaning' (1980), where amongst other things she summed up where she stood with regard to Sraffa's contributions in particular and economic theory in general; and (with Frank Wilkinson) on 'Ideology and Logic' (1983; 1985), a preoccupation which was to the forefront of her interests all through her life. 'Spring Cleaning' and its aftermath left her near despair, feeling that she had been discussing economic theory for over fifty years and that it had come to pieces in her hands, an almost nihilistic conclusion, typically harsh and honest but too hard on herself and her achievements. Gram and Walsh (1983) give a more hopeful account of them and the promise which they hold for workers in the future.

Sraffa was in ill health for much of the last ten years of his life. While he was still able to discuss issues which excited his attention, he did not write anything after the publication of *Production of Commodities* and the few postscripts to it—the reply to Harrod, for example, (Sraffa, 1962)—though he gave considerable help to the many serious and devoted scholars who came to see him. It should be stressed that Sraffa was much more a loner than Joan Robinson, at ease with his own company and in thinking issues through, though he did, of course, take part in discussions and welcomed the company of congenial minds. Joan Robinson by contrast liked to discuss and to exchange written comments. For many years she went on long weekend walks with Richard Kahn and others, including Sraffa, in order to thrash out problems in economic theory, and she used regularly to circulate drafts of her papers, and to correspond with people on issues. While generally Joan Robinson was a fearless person, handing it out without fear or favour, she held Sraffa in awe and was wary of arousing his wrath. (No one can blame her for *that*; see Austin Robinson, 1977, p. 29, and Harcourt, 1984a, p. 468).

II

The first major point to make about Joan Robinson is that for good or ill she was much influenced by Marshall and by his methods, his principal preoccupations and by his acute insights. (She is on record as saying that 'the more I learn about economics the more I admire Marshall's intellect and the less I like his character'—Joan Robinson, 1953, p. 14;

Vol. IV, 1973, p. 259). That she understood profoundly and very early on his system of thought in the *Principles* is evident from the delightful essay, 'Beauty and the Beast', which was written jointly with her great friend Dorothea Morison, afterwards Mrs R. B. Braithwaite, while she was still an undergraduate. It concludes: 'With this happy union of producer's and consumer's surplus they then lived happily ever after, constantly keeping in mind their higher ideals and maximizing their satisfaction by equalizing the marginal utility of each object of expenditure' (Vol. I, 1951, 1978, p. 233). Of the essay she says, '[It] owes nothing to Keynes, but everything to Marshall' (p. ix).

Much of her early technical work was explicitly Marshallian static in method. This is obvious in *The Economics of Imperfect Competition* and is the fundamental reason why eventually she was to repudiate much of the analysis. It depended upon the 'shameless fudge' that implicitly assumed that equilibrium points could remain stable while economic agents (as we would say now) actively searched for them. The same method lies behind her classic paper on 'The Foreign Exchanges' (1937b, 1947), which reads as though the author, having drawn up the arguments in terms of supply and demand curves and their movements, translated the findings into English. (Joan Robinson denied though that this was how it was written.) The lasting impact that Marshall had on her thinking was not only through the forces of supply and demand as presented in the statical method but also through his discussion of the meaning of equilibrium and the basic inconsistency in his own system between his vision of an accumulating economy moving forwards through time, on the one hand, and the static-equilibrium method, on the other. Joan Robinson for many years thought that Marshall admitted this himself but hid it away in Appendix H. There, the irreversibility of the long-run supply curve is revealed even though in the text, in his central discussion of long-period normal prices (what Kahn, 1929, p. 1, has described as 'the real business of the *Principles*'), long-period supply and demand curves are integral parts of the analysis.

In writing *The Economics of Imperfect Competition*, Joan Robinson developed her ideas from Sraffa's 'pregnant suggestion' that each firm was its own little monopolist in a nevertheless competitive environment, but she virtually ignored the message of his argument that it was, except for some minor, empirically unimportant exceptions, inadmissible in competitive theory to assume that supply and demand curves were independent of each other. As Sraffa said in the 1930 symposium on 'Increasing Returns and the Representative Firm', '[Marshall's] theory cannot be interpreted in a way which makes it logically self-consistent and, at the same time, reconciles it with the facts it sets out to explain [so that] Marshall's theory . . . should be discarded' (Sraffa, 1930, p. 93). The significance of this general criticism, that it may be inadmissable in general to draw a schedule because any actual movement along it may alter its position (and those of other schedules), was to have its full impact on Joan Robinson after the Second World War, when it became the basis of the central criticism she was to make of what she considered to be the method of orthodox economic theory. In retrospect she was to argue that Marshall, too, had known this all along, that he had confined his formal statement to equilibrium points, and had considered only notional changes around them. He also had stressed the importance of equilibrium positions being stable ones—otherwise they would not be of interest in explanations through the medium of supply and demand curves of the outcome of sustained and dominant, or persistent, forces. Joan Robinson herself was to make a unique contribution here, when finally she departed radically from both the Marshallian and the neoclassical general-equilibrium tradition whereby a problem was always framed so as to discuss first existence and uniqueness and then local and global stability. She was to say, in effect, that these were distinctions or dichotomies without content. If a market or an economy were in equilibrium, no question of stability arose—it was as if expectations were always realised. If either were not in equilibrium, then the question of existence did not arise, because the market or the economy evolved under the influence of past and present happenings, and expectations of the future, reacting to any inconsistencies now present but with no presupposition that they would seek out positions where, once again, they were absent. Hence we have her statements: 'The short period is here and now, with concrete stocks of the means of production in existence. Incompatibilities in the situation . . . will determine what happens next. Long-period equilibrium is not at some date in the future; it is an imaginary state of affairs in which there are no incompatibilities in the existing situation, here and now' (1962, p. 690; Vol. III, 1965, p. 101).[4]

Accompanying this change in views was another 180-degree change over her lifetime with respect to another aspect of methodology.[5] Very early on, she set out her youthful views on method in an essay published in 1932, 'Economics Is a Serious Subject' (1932). There she argued that 'the subject matter of economics is neither more nor less than its own technique' (p. 4). Joan Robinson then went on to distinguish between manageable sets of assumptions and realistic sets, adding that 'generally speaking, the optimistic, English, economist will choose the manageable set and the pessimistic, methodological, Continental, economist will choose the realistic set' (pp. 6–7), and firmly allied herself with the optimists. By the end of her life, though, she was to adopt the Continental economist's approach (and also, alas, his pessimism) and to scrap any faith that she may ever have had in 'complete theories'. (It has sometimes been said that Joan Robinson did not have the influence she should have had because she did not provide an alternative 'complete theory' to replace that of the neoclassicals. She herself considered that 'any other "complete theory" would be only another box of tricks', adding that 'we need . . . a different habit of mind—to eschew fudging, to respect facts and to admit ignorance of what we do not know', (Vol. V, 1979, p. 119).

As we have argued, Sraffa's aim in his 1925 and 1926 papers was to show the logical incoherence of Marshall's method and its applications; that is, that when it was legitimate to apply it, because the supply and demand curves could be taken as independent of one another, the application itself was to a very small part indeed of the real world. For example, if there were increasing returns, the economies responsible had to be external to the firm but internal to the industry; when there were decreasing returns, the fixed factor had to be used entirely in one industry. It was these arguments which constituted the main thrust of the two papers, but in the 1926 paper, following his masterly succinct summary of the argument of the 1925 paper, he added the section about monopoly which spawned the imperfect competition revolution. He himself did not follow this up but went in another direction (which was also mentioned in the 1926 paper (see Sraffa, 1926, p. 541), that of examining the interrelatedness of production and the relationship of this to the theory of value and distribution, the revival of the surplus approach which reached its fullest statement in *Production of Commodities*. (Evidently, he had the basic structure clearly in his mind in the 1920s.) Theorising at this level of abstraction may not have been of much interest to Keynes, while Joan Robinson probably was not aware of the early drafts (which Sraffa had shown to Keynes in 1928; see Sraffa, 1960, p. vi) when she was writing her first big book in the late 1920s and early 1930s. In addition to Sraffa's influence, Joan Robinson mentions the overriding importance of Shove's work, principally in his lectures, and, of course, of Kahn's guiding hand on virtually every page. Indeed, Keynes was to say in his report on the book to Harold Macmillan in 1932 that he had 'a great deal of confidence that it [was] resonably free from minor slips and errors and fallacies because it had been very elaborately and carefully criticised by R. F. Kahn. [He] is the most careful and accurate of all the younger economists, and mistakes do not easily get past him ... Knowing the part that he has played ... [Keynes had] much greater confidence in its being free from the blunders which so very easily creep into a treatment of this kind' (*JMK* XII, 867). Keynes himself thought that 'the book will be for a little while to come an essential one for any serious student of the modern theory of value' (p. 867). When writing this, Keynes did not know of Chamberlin's (1933) parallel work, which probably was to prove more fruitful than Joan Robinson's work and which was not influenced, at least to the same degree, by Sraffa's work.[6]

In any event, Joan Robinson had already become excited about the critique of the *Treatise* and the emerging propositions of *The General Theory*. She took an active part not only in writing papers which were progress reports on the way—for example, 'The Theory of Money and the Analysis of Output' (1933b; Vol I, 1951, 1978)—but also in commenting on drafts of *The General Theory* as Keynes prepared them and in drafting even before its publication her own 'told to the childen' version, what was to become *Introduction to the Theory of Employment* (1937a). Already in 1933 Joan Robinson had a very clear perception that the theory of money, the theory of the demand and supply of output (as a whole) and the theory of prices should be intertwined. (She was not alone, of course. Others had been there before; for example, D. H. Robertson and R. G. Hawtrey.) She gives a very clear description of how a decline in output (in the *Treatise* framework) will bring about the equality of saving with a (given) level of investment, commenting that Keynes had missed the profound significance of this result, '[throwing] it out in the most casual way without pausing to remark that he [had] proved that output may be in equilibrium at any number of different levels ... that while there is a natural tendency towards equilibrium between savings and investment ... there is no natural tendency towards full employment of the factors of production ... [Keynes had] failed to notice [when he wrote the *Treatise*] that he had incidentally evolved a new theory of the long-period analysis of output' (Joan Robinsion, 1933b, p. 25; Vol. I, 1951, 1960, 1978, p. 56). As Keynes moved towards the publication of *The General Theory*, Joan Robinson was extending his analysis in two directions, her first try at a long-period theory of effective demand (1936a; 1937b, 1947) and her work on the international aspects of Keynes's theory (e.g. Part III of Joan Robinson, 1937b, 1947). Her work on the long-period theory of employment was still Marshallian in method and neoclassical in regard to the treatment of the distribution of income, though, of course, it took into account Keynes's theory of output as a whole and of the monetary nature of the rate of interest. Thus, she took as given the level of the rate of interest and asked the analytical question, if, when the stock of capital goods has adjusted optimally to this rate of interest, so that we have a stationary state (a Marshallian long-period position) in which net investment is zero, would we find associated with that stock a fully employed labour force? The concept of the elasticity of substitution plays a key role in the determination of the overall distribution of income both in the long-period position and in the discussion of the transition to it.[7] Keynes's insight concerned whether the long-period level of income which allowed net saving to be zero also implied long-period unemployment. The paper contains, as well, an extension to the long period of the proposition established in the short-run analysis of *The General Theory* that a rise in the desire to save may in fact decrease output and employment.

As we mentioned earlier, Sraffa was increasingly distancing himself from these particular discussions, though it is clear from his correspondence with Joan Robinson over the 1930s that he was trying to persuade her and others close to Keynes of the 'emptiness' of the marginal productivity theory of value and distribution. Indeed, he argued that there was quite a theological flavour to the concepts and arguments of the subjective theory of value. For example, there is a letter in October 1936 in which he explicitly refers to the incoherence of the concept of a quantity of capital (measured in a unit which is independent of distribution and prices) relative to the concepts of land and labour. He suggests that if Joan Robinson should ask her gardener what a quantity of capital is, he would think her dotty, though he would have no trouble in understanding what quantities of land and labour are. It seems reasonable to suppose that the force of these arguments impressed itself upon her when she began to think about the problems of growth and accumulation in the post-war period.

As I have argued elsewhere (see Harcourt, 1979, 1982, 1984b), the quantum jump in Joan Robinson's thinking came when she started seriously to study Marx and Marxism. It is interesting to compare her early views, as expressed in her review, 'Some Reflections on Marxist Economics' (1936b; 1937b, 1947), of John Strachey's *The Nature of Capitalist Crisis* (1935), where she appears to argue that Marx was a classical economist because he accepted Say's Law, with her later much more incisive and sympathetic views (except in regard to the labour theory of value) in, for example, her 1942 *Essay on Marxian Economics*[8] and her 1951 introduction to the English edition of Rosa Luxemburg's *Accumulation of Capital* (which is reprinted in Joan Robinson, Vol. II,

1960, 1975). Sraffa, of course, had always 'known' his Marx from his early student days and saw in Marx's work the fulfilment of the surplus approach, the origins of which were to be found in the physiocrats and Adam Smith and Ricardo. Reading Marx's work, writing her book on him, together with her friendship with Kalecki which dates from the mid-1930s radically changed Joan Robinson's perspective. In particular, the reproduction schemes from which Kalecki started his discussion of the theory of effective demand, the nature of the trade cycle and the theory of distribution were increasingly to become Joan Robinson's mode of thought, so that when she started to write on capital and growth theory, it was the natural framework to use. It is also significant that in her introduction to Rosa Luxemburg's book, she poses as the key question, 'Where does the demand come from which keeps the accumulation going?' (Joan Robinson, Vol. II, 1960, 1975, p. 65).[9]

Harrod's work on dynamics was also another major influence, though she was able to show him that he exemplified that attractive English vice of unnecessary originality, that essentially his theory was to be found in Volume II of *Capital* (see Joan Robinson, 1953, p. 17; Vol. IV, 1973, p. 263). Harrod himself thought he was doing something much more fundamental for economic theory than Keynes had, because he was providing the foundations of dynamic analysis; that is, rediscovering Volume II in which it is shown that once a capitalist economy 'slips off [an equilibrium line of development] it will never get back between now and doomsday' (see Joan Robinson, 1953, p. 17; Vol. IV, 1973, p. 263).

III

The Accumulation of Capital (1956) is Joan Robinson's *magnum opus*. She published it when she was the same age as Keynes had been when he published *The General Theory*, and she meant it to do for the long-period problems of growth and distribution what he had done for the short-period problems of the theory of effective demand. As it was to do with the long period, she felt that she needed a theory of the rate of profits and that Sraffa (in his introduction to the Ricardo volumes—Sraffa with Dobb, 1951) had provided a coherent theory to replace what she discerned as incoherent in Marshall, from whom she originally learnt her theory of value and distribution. There is in her papers a draft of a preface to a later edition of *The Accumulation of Capital* which explains very clearly the four main sorts of issues and questions with which she was concerned. This lists also shows why it was a difficult book to grasp in its entirety. As far as I have been able to discover, the preface has never been published, at least in English; it appears from internal evidence to have been written either in or after 1959.

Joan Robinson considers a model of an unregulated free enterprise economy in which firms 'within the limits set by their command of finance' determine the rate of capital accumulation, while the members of the public, constrained 'by their command of purchasing power, are free to make the rate of expenditure what they please . . . [a] model . . . not . . . unrealistic in essential respects'.

The model may be used 'to analyse the chances and changes of the development of an economy as time goes by' by considering 'four distinct groups of questions':

1. We make comparisons of situations, each with its own past, developing into its own future, which are different in some respect (for instance the rate of accumulation going on in each) in order to see what the postulated difference entails.
2. We trace the path which a single economy follows when the technical conditions (including their rate of change) and the propensities to consume and to invest are constant through time.
3. We trace the consequences of a change in any of these conditions for the future development of the economy.
4. We examine the short period reaction of the economy to unexpected events.

The first group of questions is more naturally handled in terms of comparisons of steady states (including stationary states). The conditions for steady states to be achieved are set out, but there is no implication that the unregulated behaviour of the decision-makers will in fact ever bring them about. When discussing the choice of techniques, the relationship between the value of capital and physical capital in the economy as a whole becomes relevant and 'takes up several chapters (Book II, Section II) and is difficult out of all proportion to its importance'.

The second set of questions concerns what happens when one of the conditions for steady growth (other than technical conditions and the consumption propensities) are not satisfied. The third set relates to the path which the economy will follow when, having been in a steady state, a basic change, for example, 'an increase in monopoly which causes profit margins to increase', occurs. The fourth set concerns the reactions of the inducement to invest to current events in an uncertain world and relates to the possibility of oscillation in the transition from one state of affairs to another, or even to the generation of a trade cycle by 'mere uncertainty' without any change in basic conditions. In principle, says Joan Robinson, 'this type of analysis enables us to deal with all the possible vicissitudes of a developing economy, and prepares the way for discussions of public policy'.

We mentioned on page 101 why the list showed that *The Accumulation of Capital* was a difficult book to grasp in its entirety. Tom Asimakopulos (letter of 14 Jan. 1985) has suggested to me that the list also provides a clue as to 'why it "failed" despite the many excellent things in it', that Joan Robinson 'never discussed the various strands of her analysis, their interrelationships and their compatability, or lack of it, with her "Keynes" view of the world. Her later critical essays provide some insight into how she would handle these questions, but she never published anything directly on them'.

Parallel with Joan Robinson's developments and discussion of these issues was her attack on the neoclassical theory of value and distribution, as expressed principally in the aggregate production function version of, for example, J. B. Clark and Hicks's *Theory of Wages*. This was extended into her critique of neoclassical growth models when Solow, Swan, Samuelson and Meade responded to the questions opened up by Harrod (and Domar) by trying purposefully[10] to provide neoclassical answers. While Joan Robinson's critique started within the context of the overall choice of technique within a growth model, it soon developed into both a methodological critique and a discussion of the *meaning* of capital within the supply and demand frameworks (of Marshall, Walras and Fisher), and within a model of a capitalist economy generally. Perhaps the most comprehensive statement of her ultimate position (except in regard to Sraffa's model, for which we must go to 'Spring Cleaning' (1980)), is her paper in the *Revue d'économie politique* symposium of 1977. (The English translation is Essay 5 of Joan Robinson, Vol. V, 1979.) In the early days of the debate, it was the former issues which dominated and this emphasis was reinforced by the publication of *Production of Commodities* in 1960. The chapters on reduction to dated labour, and fixed capital, and Part III—Sraffa's discussion of capital-reversing and reswitching—reinforced and put into focus the results that had come out of Joan Robinson's work and comments upon it, especially the remarkable comment in 1953–54 by David Champernowne. For some little time these arguments were thought to be conclusive, especially when Samuelson accepted them in his 'summing up' paper in the 1966 *Quarterly Journal of Economics* symposium, following the failure through his pupil Levhari to refute them in 1965. But while Joan Robinson initally welcomed these results, she had decided by the late 1960s that they were a side issue and that her methodological critique relating to changes versus differences was the central issue. (I know because the major complaint that she made about the first draft of my 1972 book which I sent to her in about May 1970 was that I had not emphasised sufficiently the methodological critique.) This emphasis was to separate her for the rest of her life from her former allies, probably Piero Sraffa himself and, more actively, John Eatwell, Murray Milgate and Pierangelo Garegnani. Indeed, it is necessary to separate her attitude to Sraffa from her attitude to the other three scholars, partly because her discussions with them concerned Keynesian questions—whether Keynes himself had provided a short-period or long-period analysis and, if he had not, or had not done it adequately, what form would the long-period theory of effective demand take? In 'Spring Cleaning' she got Sraffa's contributions into focus, insofar as they bore on her particular interests, making a distinction between the nature of the model which underlay the first two parts of the book, on the one hand, and that which underlay the third part, on the other. In the first two, we enter the world just as it is at the moment with the stocks of means of production already established because of past decisions in the light of past expectations. We are given the value of one distributive variable (Joan Robinson makes it the share of wages in value added) and then find the corresponding values of the prices of production and the other distributive variable, here, the rate of profits. Because we assume a uniform rate of profits, we have prices of production. This is not a description of 'reality', or a theory of market prices, but an analytical construction. In Sraffa's system, certainly as used by the Sraffians, though not in anything Sraffa himself wrote, the prices of production are centres of gravitation. Presumably, therefore, they have some explanatory power for the patterns of actual market prices—but this is not so in Joan Robinson's interpretation. She has, though, abandoned her earlier interpretation whereby the means of production were such that, in effect, a stationary state with all things in their correct proportions was established. Now, she says, this may or may not be, we take the world as we find it and do our thought experiments.

When we get to Part III, we change our perspective, as Sraffa hints in his preface—'No changes in output and (at any rate in Parts I and II) no changes in the proportions in which different means of production are used by an industry are considered' (p. v). We now look at a producer who is to make a choice between two (or more) possible ways of producing a commodity. Sraffa takes great pains to allow such a comparison to be logically made. Joan Robinson says that it cannot be done:

> [We] can imagine a variety of techniques for producing a single flow output set up in a 'book of blueprints' but we cannot imagine switching from one to another at an instant of time. A switch would require availability of the appropriate stocks of inputs already in existence. Moreover, differences in techniques are introduced successively through time as research and development goes on responding to historical changes not merely to shifts in the rate of profit... To put the point in methodological terms, it is not correct to draw two or more wage-profit curves in the same axes, for the *y* axis represents the flow of net output in only one particular technique. [1980, p. 10]

Moreover, there is a further problem of measurement, even in terms of Sraffa's own construction of a Standard commodity. Each system has its own, and therefore it is not possible to find a consistent measure with which to make comparisons between the systems. Ricardo's search for an invariant standard of value was really a search for a will 'o the wisp. Thus, Joan Robinson argues that Sraffa's procedure is an illegitimate comparison in that it cannot illuminate processes actually going on in historical time. Such a procedure *is* allowed a role in doctrinal debates whereby the marginal productivity theory of distribution is attacked and the concepts of the marginal product of capital and the demand curve for capital are argued to be vacuous. At this point, she says, we leave Sraffa and take up again with Keynes—and Kalecki (see Bhaduri and Robinson, 1980).

Finally, in her debates with Garegnani, and with Eatwell and Milgate, Joan Robinson used her views on the inadmissibility of long-period comparisons for describing processes, which she developed in her critique of neoclassical theory,[11] to criticise the central stress by these authors on the notion of centres of gravitation or long-period positions. Here, her final departure from Marshall's definition of the long period which we noted above (see pp. 93–6) is relevant, for it was this that made her reject in a theory of accumulation and distribution, a process in historical time, any use of the notion of a centre of gravitation. In effect, she was moving close to rejecting the usefulness of the issues discussed under the first three headings in the unpublished preface to *The Accumulation of Capital* above, and to concentrating entirely on the fourth issue, as it was developed, for example, in Kalecki's theories of cyclical growth.[12] It was in *that* form, she argued, that we were to find the essential messages of Keynes—and of Marx. This was a brave if depressing and nearly nihilistic conclusion to which to come. As ever, as we said before, she may have been too hard on herself.

Sraffa, I believe, saw his positive contribution as having sorted out some unfinished or incoherent problems within the whole corpus of Marx's theory of the laws of motion of capitalism, by reviving the surplus approach in a rigorous manner. As far as his prelude to a critique was concerned, it does seem fair to say that he helped to undermine the central thrust of the supply and demand theories by showing some of their principal messages to be incoherent or illogical. The debates themselves still continue, now placed more securely within the context of general-equilibrium analysis (see, for example, Hahn's 1982 paper on 'The Neo-Ricardians'. But, whatever the outcome of this particular strand, the following passage from Gramsci on 'The Intellectuals', which was read at the memorial service for Piero Sraffa in November 1983, will stand as a valid account of the ideals and objectives of these two great twentieth-century political economists.

> In a political and military struggle it can be correct tactics to break through at the points of least resistance in order to be able to assault the strongest point with maximum forces that have been precisely made available by the elimination of the weaker auxiliaries... On the ideological front, however, the defeat of the auxiliaries and the minor hangers-on is of all but negligible importance. Here it is necessary to engage battle with the most eminent of one's adversaries. Otherwise, one confuses newspapers with books, and petty polemic with scientific work. The lesser figures must be abandoned to the infinite casebook of newspaper polemic.
>
> A new science proves its efficacy and vitality when it demonstrates that it is capable of confronting the great champions of the tendencies opposed to it and when it either resolves by its own means the vital questions which they have posed or demonstrates, in peremptory fashion, that these questions are false problems.
>
> It is true that an historical epoch and a given society are characterised rather by the average run of intellectuals, and therefore by the more mediocre. But widespread, mass ideology must be distinguished from the scientific works and the great philosophical syntheses which are its real cornerstones. It is the latter which must be overcome, either negatively, by demonstrating that they are without foundation, or positively, by opposing to them philosophical syntheses of greater importance and significance.
>
> Quaderni del carcere—ANTONIO GRAMSCI

NOTES

1. This essay is a longer version of an article entitled 'On the Influence of Piero Sraffa on the Contributions of Joan Robinson to Economic Theory', which is published in the *Economic Journal* (Supplement), March 1986. I thank, but in no way implicate, Tom Asimakopulos, Andrea Boitani, Lilia Constabile, Sukhamoy Chakravarty, Phyllis

Deane, Meghnad Desai, Keith Frearson, John Hatch, Jan Kregel, Peter Kreisler, Michael Lawson, Terry O'Shaughnessy, Ian Steedman and Michael White for their comments on a draft of this essay.

2. 'Don Patinkin disputes the importance commonly attributed to [the 'circus'] in assisting Keynes to write *The General Theory. Insofar as he relies on documents*, he is fully entitled to make his case' (Kahn, 1984, p. 105; emphasis added).
3. So far, we know of eighteen letters from Sraffa to Joan Robinson, spanning from 1931 to 1951, in Joan Robinson's papers in the King's Library. Whether Joan Robinsons's corresponding letters are in Sraffa's papers is not yet known. In a few cases, Sraffa returned Joan Robinson's letters in order that she could follow his detailed comments on her arguments.
4. See, also, Gram and Walsh (1983, p. 531) where they conclude that 'standard stability arguments find no place in Robinson's canon'.
5. This is not criticism but praise. Her favourite story about Keynes is that when someone remonstrated with him for being inconsistent, he responded: 'when someone persuades me that I am wrong, I change my mind. What do you do?'
6. Chamberlin himself says (p. 5, n. 4) that while 'there are striking parallels [in Sraffa's 1926 article] with some of the ideas presented in [Chamberlin, 1933, yet] at the time when Professor Sraffa's article appeared, the present study, submitted as a doctor's thesis at Harvard University, April, 1927 was virtually completed'.
7. While Joan Robinson herself was never to return to this issue in this particular form, there has recently been renewed interest in the paper itself; *see* Eatwell (1983), Kregel (1983) and O'Shaughnessy (1984).
8. Here is Keynes's reaction (20 August 1942) to her 1942 *Essay*. He found it 'most fascinating—as well written as anything you have done. This is in spite of the fact that there is something intrinsically boring in an attempt to make sense of what is in fact not sense'. Keynes was 'left with the feeling ... that [Marx] had a penetrating and original flair but was a very poor thinker indeed—and his failure to publish the later volumes probably meant that he was not unaware of this himself'. I am indebted to Robert Skidelsky for bringing this letter to my attention.
9. Shove pointed out in his review article (1944, pp. 47–8) of her 1942 book that she had misunderstood Marx's analysis with regard to Say's Law and its refutation, that 'it is doubtful whether Marx anticipated modern ideas about the nature and significance of 'effective demand' to the extent which her account of his theory of crises would suggest'.
10. It is perhaps too often forgotten, not least by his critics, that Solow (1956; 1970, p. 189), wrote:

    Everything above is the neoclassical side of the coin...it is full employment economics—in the dual aspect of equilibrium condition and frictionless, competitive, causal system. All the difficulties and rigidities which go into modern Keynesian income analysis have been shunted aside . . . not [Solow's] contention that these problems don't exist, nor that they are of no significance in the long run. [Solow's] purpose was to examine . . . the tight-rope view of economic growth and to see whether more flexible assumptions about production would lead to a simple model.

Even if, as Kregel (1980) has definitively shown, Harrod did *not* assume rigidity of coefficients, Solow's way of putting the issues may be looked at as an interesting problem in its own right.

11. Or possibly even earlier. Jan Kregel (letter of 14 Jan. 1985) refers to 'traces of discussions [of this] with Kalecki dating from the mid-1930s'.
12. Already in 1973 she had written: 'In reality, all the interesting and important questions lie in the gap between pure short-period and pure long-period analysis' (1973; Vol. V, 1979, p. 261).

REFERENCES

Bhaduri, Amit and Joan Robinson. 1980. 'Accumulation and Exploitation: An Analysis in the Tradition of Marx, Sraffa and Keynes.' *Cambridge Journal of Economics* 4 (June), 103–15

Chamberlin, Edward H. 1933. *The Theory of Monopolistic Competition. A Re-orientation of the Theory of Value.* Cambridge, Mass. Harvard University Press

Champernowne, D. G. (1953–54). 'The production Function and the Theory of Capital: A Comment.' *Review of Economic Studies* XXI, 2: 112–35

Eatwell, J. L. 1983. 'The Long-Period Theory of Employment.' *Cambridge Journal of Economics* 7 (Sept./Dec.), 269–85

Garegnani, Pierangelo. 1976, 1983. 'On a Change in the Notion of Equilibrium in Recent Work on Value and Distribution', in M. Brown, K. Sato and P. Zarembka (eds.), *Essays in Modern Capital Theory.* North Holland Publishing Company, 1976. Reprinted in John Eatwell and Murray Milgate (eds), *Keynes's Economics and the Theory of Value and Distribution.* London, Duckworth, 1983, pp. 129–45

Gram, Harvey and Vivian Walsh. 1983. 'Joan Robinson's Economics in Retrospect.' *Journal of Economic Literature* XXI, (June), 518–50

Hahn, F. H. 1982. 'The Neo-Ricardians.' *Cambridge Journal of Economics* 6 (Dec.), 353–74

Harcourt, G. C. 1979. 'Robinson, Joan', in David L. Sills (ed.) *International Encyclopedia of the Social Sciences, Biographical Supplement,* Vol. 18. New York, The Free Press, pp. 663–71

—— 1982. *The Social Science Imperialists, Selected Essays,* edited by Prue Kerr. London, Routledge and Kegan Paul

—— 1984a. 'The End of an Era: Joan Robinson (1903–83) and Piero Sraffa (1898–1983).' *Journal of Post Keynesian Economics* VI (Spring), 466–9

——— 1984b. 'Harcourt on Robinson', in Henry W. Spiegel and Warren J. Samuels (eds.), *Contemporary Economists in Perspective*, Greenwich, Conn., JAI Press, pp. 639–54

Kahn, R. F. 1929, 'The Economics of the Short Period', unpublished Fellowship dissertation, King's College, Cambridge

——— 1984. *The Making of Keynes' General Theory*, Cambridge, Cambridge University Press

Keynes, J. M. 1930, 1971. *A Treatise on Money*, 2 Vols. London, Macmillan for the Royal Economic Society

——— 1983, 1973. *The Collected Writings of John Maynard Keynes*, Vols. XII, XIII. London, Macmillan for the Royal Economic Society

Kregel, J. A. 1980. 'Economic Dynamics and the Theory of Steady Growth: An Historical Essay on Harrod's "knife-edge".' *History of Political Economy* 12 (Spring), 97–123

——— 1983. 'The Microfoundations of the "Generalisation of the *General Theory*" and "Bastard Keynesianism": Keynes's Theory of Employment in the Long and the Short Period.' *Cambridge Journal of Economics* 7 (Sept./Dec.), 343–61

Levhari, D. 1965. 'A Nonsubstitution Theorem and Switching of Techniques.' *Quarterly Journal of Economics* LXXIX, (Feb.), 98–105

Luxemburg, Rosa. 1951, English ed. *The Accumulation of Capital*. London, Routledge and Kegan Paul

Milgate, Murray. 1979. 'On the Origin of the Notion of "Intertemporal Equilibrium".' *Economica* 46 (Feb.), 1–10

O'Shaughnessy, T. J. 1984, 'Long-Period and Short Period Interpretations of the Principle of Effective Demand in a Monetary Economy: Keynes and Joan Robinson', mimeo, Cambridge

Robinson, Austin. 1977. 'Keynes and His Cambridge Colleagues' in Don Patinkin and J. Clark Leith (eds.), *Keynes, Cambridge and The General Theory*. London, Macmillan, pp. 25–38

Robinson, Joan. 1932. *Economics Is a Serious Subject. The Apologia of an Economist to the Mathematician, the Scientist and the Plain Man*. Cambridge, W. Heffer

——— 1933a. *The Economics of Imperfect Competition*. London, Macmillan

——— 1933b. 'The Theory of Money and the Analysis of Output', *Review of Economic Studies* 1, (Oct.), 23–26; reprinted in Joan Robinson (Vol. I, 1951, 1978, pp. 52–58).

——— 1936a. 'The Long-Period Theory of Employment'. *Zeitschrift für Nationalökonomie* VII (Mar.) Heft 1, 74–93; reprinted in Joan Robinson (1937a, 1947), except for section 5, pp. 75–100

——— 1936b. 'Review of John Stratchey, *The Nature of Capitalist Crisis* (1935)', Economic Journal XLVI (June), 298–302

——— 1937a. *Introduction to the Theory of Employment*. London, Macmillan

——— 1937b, 1947. *Essays in the Theory of Employment*. Oxford, Basil Blackwell

——— 1942. *An Essay on Marxian Economics*. London, Macmillan

——— 1951–79. *Collected Economic Papers*, 5 Vols. Oxford, Basil Blackwell

——— 1953. *On Re-reading Marx*. Cambridge, Students' Bookshops; reprinted in Joan Robinson (Vol. IV, 1973, pp. 247–268)

——— 1956. *The Accumulation of Capital*. London, Macmillan

——— 1961. 'Prelude to a Critique of Economic Theory.' *Oxford Economic Papers*, 13, (Feb.), 53–8; reprinted in Joan Robinson (Vol. III, 1965, pp. 7–14)

——— 1962. 'Review of H. G. Johnson, *Money, Trade and Economic Growth* (1962).' *Economic Journal* LXXII (Sept.), 690–92; reprinted in Joan Robinson (Vol. III, 1965, 1974, pp. 100–2)

——— 1973. 'Ideology and Analysis' in *Sozialismus, Geschichte und Wirtschaft. Festschrift für Eduard März*, Europaverlags A. G. Wein, pp. 53–60; reprinted in Joan Robinson (Vol. V. 1979, pp. 254–61)

——— 1980. 'Spring Cleaning', mimeo, Cambridge

——— and Frank Wilkinson (1983, 1985). 'Ideologia e logica', in Fausto Vicarelli (ed.), *Attualita di Keynes*, Editori Laterza, pp. 109–44. English version: 'Ideology and Logic', in Fausto Vicarelli (ed.), *Keynes's Relevance Today*, London, Macmillan, pp. 73–98

Samuelson, Paul A. 1966, 'A Summing Up,' *Quarterly Journal of Economics* LXXX (Nov.), 568–83

Shove, G. F. 1944. 'Mrs Robinson on Marxian Economics,' *Economic Journal* LIV (Apr.), 47–61

Solow, R. M. 1956. 'A Contribution to the Theory of Economic Growth.' *Quarterly Journal of Economics* LXX (Feb.), 65–95; reprinted in A. K. Sen (ed.), *Growth Economics: Selected Readings*, Harmondsworth: Penguin Books, 1970, pp. 161–92

Sraffa, Piero. 1925. 'Sulle Relazione fra Costo e Quantità Prodotta,' *Annali i Economica* III, 1: 277–328

——— 1926. 'The Laws of Returns under Competitive Conditions,' *Economic Journal* XXXVI (Dec.), 535–50

——— 1930. 'A Criticism' and 'A Rejoinder'. *Economic Journal* XL (Mar.), 89–92 and 93

——— 1932. 'Dr Hayek on Money and Capital,' *Economic Journal* XLII (Mar.), 42–53

——— 1960. *Production of Commodities by Means of Commodities. Prelude to a Critique of Economic Theory*. Cambridge, Cambridge University Press

——— 1962. 'Production of Commodities: A Comment,' *Economic Journal* LXXII (June), 477–79

——— with the collaboration of Maurice Dobb, eds. (1951). *Works and Correspondence of David Ricardo*, Vol. 1. Cambridge, Cambridge University Press

Stratchey, John. 1935. *The Nature of Capitalist Crisis*. London, Victor Gollanz

PART III
The Capital Theory Debate

6 Investment-Decision Criteria, Capital-Intensity and The Choice of Techniques[1]

INTRODUCTION

Some aspects of the current theory and practice of investment decisions at the enterprise level in both the United Kingdom and the European socialist countries are discussed in this paper. In recent years in the United Kingdom, government departments, academic and business economists and businessmen themselves have been advocating the use of Discounted Cash Flow (DCF) procedures as aids to investment decisions.[2] At the same time, empirical research and official inquiries have increased the knowledge of actual business practice in the United Kingdom.[3]

While DCF procedures, especially the *internal rate of return* and *present value* of investment projects, are becoming more familiar, they are still used in only a small minority of cases. The most popular measure of the profitablity of invesment projects is some variant of the *accounting rate of profit*, often *before* tax, on the original investment. And replacement decisions, as well as the choice of investment projects, or of different methods of producing the same level of output, are still more likely to be decided by the application of a rough rule of thumb such as the *pay-off period criterion*, or by a comparison of accounting rates of profit, than by the use of DCF procedures. The latter, especially the internal rate of return, are, of course, not without their critics.[4]

This paper is confined to one aspect of the theoretical and practical issues which have been thrown up by the advocates of these various criteria. Suppose that there are a number of known ways of producing a given stream of output per year, and that certain expectations are held concerning the rates of increase of the price of the product, the prices of its raw material inputs, and money wages. What is the *relative* capital-intensity of the techniques which would be chosen by following some of the criteria either in use or recommended in the United Kingdom? Four criteria are considered: (1) the *present value criterion*, (2) the *internal rate of return criterion*, (3) the *pay-off period criterion* and (4) the *accounting rate of profit criterion*. In addition, the capital-intensity of the techniques which would be chosen, given the same basic technology and expectations, by the application of (5) the *recoupment-period criterion*, the criterion that is commonly applied by investment decision-makers in the European socialist countries, is compared with the capital-intensities which result from the use of the four 'capitalist' criteria.[5] The paper is not concerned as such with the 'rightness' or 'wrongness' of particular criteria but with some of the economic implications of putting them into effect.

The paper is in four sections. In section 1 the description of the profitability of investment projects in terms of the internal rate of return and present value is discussed, together with some general comments on the current state of the theory of the firm in capitalist economies and its relevance for investment-decision rules. In section 2, the two rules most used in practice in the United Kingdom for investment decisions—the pay-off period and the accounting rate of profit—are briefly discussed, together with an outline of two possible variants of the recoupment period. The main part of the paper is in section 3, where the capital-intensities resulting from the application of the various rules are compared. The main conclusions of the paper are gathered together in section 4.

1. DESCRIPTIONS OF THE PROFITABILITY OF INVESTMENT PROJECTS

The profitability of an investment project can be described in a number of ways, two of which are discussed here—the *internal rate of return* of a project and the *present value* of a project. These are two examples of what have come to be known as Discounted Cash Flow (or DCF) methods.

Internal rate of return. Suppose that the *initial outlay* on an investment project is £I, and that the project is expected to add to the *net receipts* of the business over the next n years (the expected lifetime of the project) the stream: £q_1, $q_2, \ldots q_n$. The q_i's are the *expected* increases in annual sales receipts *less* the accompanying expected increases in wages, raw material and maintenance costs. The project is expected to have a scrap value, £K, at the end of the *nth* year. Then, the internal rate of return (or *expected rate of profit*) of the project, ρ, is defined as that rate of discount which makes the present value of the expected net receipts, including any scrap value, equal to the initial outlay on the machine. That is, ρ is the rate of discount which satisfies the following equation:

$$I = \left\{ \sum_{i=1}^{n} \frac{q_i}{(1+\rho)^i} \right\} + \frac{K}{(1+\rho)^n} \qquad (1.1)$$

Another interpretation of ρ, perhaps more illuminating, is: if the expected rate of profit of an investment project with an initial outlay of £I and a series of net receipts (including any scrap value) of £q_1, q_2, ... q_n is ρ, it will be possible to provide a series of annual payments at a rate of ρ per year on the initial outlay *and* to accumulate a sum of money which at the end of the life of the project will be equal to the initial outlay; always provided that the *cash surplus* resulting from the difference between the annual net receipts and the annual payments [£$(q_i - \rho I)$] can be reinvested at a rate of return of ρ per year.

Present value of an investment project

The present value of an investment project is calculated by discounting the expected net receipts (including any scrap value) of a project by the *marginal cost of finance* to the business considering the investment[6] and subtractng from this the initial outlay.

Let V' = present value of a project with an expected life of n years;
q_i = expected net receipts of year $i (i = 1, \ldots, n)$;
K = expected scrap value at end of year n;
I = initial outlay;
R = marginal cost of finance to the firm.

Then,

$$V' = \left\{ \sum_{i=1}^{n} \frac{q_i}{(1+R)^i} \right\} + \frac{K}{(1+R)^n} - I \qquad (1.2)$$

If $V' = 0$, then $R = \rho$ (see [1.1] above), that is to say, the project's expected rate of profit, or internal rate of return, equals the marginal cost of finance.

It will be noticed that, in the descriptions of the profitability of investment projects, while I and (in the second description) R may be known, the expected net receipts are estimates derived from expectations about the future courses of revenues and costs.[7] Perhaps the most simple, plausible expectation is that the physical productivity of the plant or equipment involved in the project will be maintained, that the price of the product will rise (for simplicity, at a constant rate) and that costs will rise at a faster rate than price. Thus the expected sales receipts will change at the expected rate of change of the price of the product. Costs will rise at a faster rate than the price of the product, partly because maintenance costs may be expected to rise as the equipment gets older, but mainly because money wages, on average, can be expected to increase at a rate which reflects both the rise in the general level of prices *and* the rise in national productivity. These considerations give the profile of expected net receipts shown in Figure 1*b*, and the rest of this paper proceeds on the assumption that such a profile is typical. If it is assumed that a machine will be scrapped when the net receipts associated with it first become zero, n_1 years is the expected *economic* life of the project shown in Figure 1.

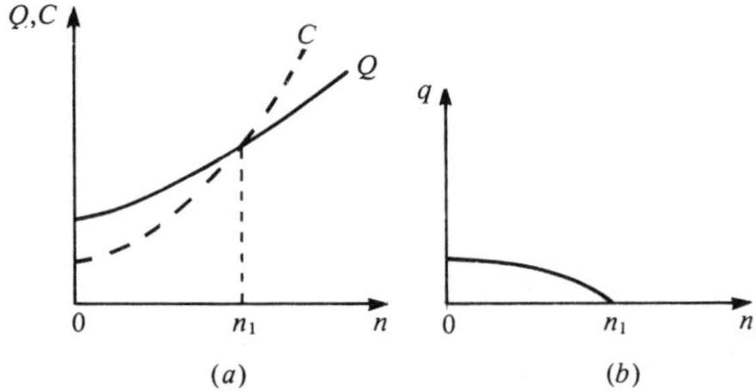

Figure 1: *Profile of expected net receipts*

In principle, three main decisions with regard to investment expenditure may be distinguished: the *amount* of investment to be done per period, including any replacement expenditure; the *sort* of investment to be done—that is, the choice between alternative ways of producing the same product and, sometimes, level of output—and the method and cost of finance. Though in principle these are three separate aspects of the investment decision, it is clear that the criteria which have to be satisfied for each have to be met *simultaneously*. Attention in this paper will, however, be concentrated on the second aspect (the choice of technique).[8]

In deciding the criteria to be used and met, the aims of the decision-makers of the business concerned need to be specified. In the theoretical literature, the most common aim is taken to be the maximisation of the value of the firm to its shareholders, which is one variant of the traditional view that those in charge of firms wish to maximise profits. This basic assumption, however, has been challenged by another school of thought, which argues that managers aim to maximise the rate of growth of the firm, or, sometimes, the rate of growth of its sales, subject to the constraint that the rate of profit does not fall below a minimum or 'satisfactory' level.[9] These conflicting aims obviously *may* imply different levels of investment expenditure per unit of time and, perhaps, different financial structures. It is not clear, however, that they affect the choice of techniques. A cost-minimisation principle, at least with regard to production, seems to be consistent with all three views. In discussions of the choice of technique, the cost-minimisation principle has been said to be satisfied by choosing either the technique with the *highest* internal rate of return, or that with the *highest* present value, though the two criteria do not necessarily result in the same technique being chosen (see sec. 3). This appears to be the implication of the arguments of the authors of *Investment Appraisal*. Meek makes cost-minimisation the correct social criteria for the choice of technique and shows that maximising the present value achieves it. Additional provisos are, in the case of the internal rate of return criterion, that it exceed a required minimum rate, and, in the case of the present value criterion, that it at least be positive.[10]

2. PAY-OFF PERIOD, ACCOUNTING RATE OF PROFIT, AND RECOUPMENT PERIOD

There are two variants of the *pay-off* or *pay-back* criterion, one of which is relevant to the choice of technique, and the other to replacement decisions. The first variant argues that an investment project should be undertaken if it can be expected to 'pay for itself' within an arbitrary period of time, usually between two to five years. By 'pay for itself' is meant that the sum of the expected net receipts should at least equal the initial outlay on the project by the end of the pay-off period. In the context of choosing between investing in different methods of producing the same stream of output per year, the pay-off period criterion requires the choice of the technique which maximises the sum of the expected net receipts over the pay-off period, subject to the constraint that the sum of the expected net receipts at least equal the investment outlay. This is discussed in further detail in section 3.

The variant of the pay-off period which is applied to replacement decisions is that the total savings in operating costs consequent upon replacing an existing machine by a new one should at least equal the initial outlay on the new machine by the end of the pay-off period. Neild found, in his study of a sample of firms in the engineering industry, that three, five and ten years were the most common values of the replacement pay-off period.[11]

There are many versions of the accounting rate of profit. Perhaps the simplest is average annual net profit as a proportion of the initial outlay, where average annual net profit is the average annual expected net receipts for the lifetime of the project *less* an arbitrarily determined, annual allowance for depreciation. It may also be defined as the first year's net profit as a proportion of the initial outlay; or net profit may be related to the average amount of capital employed, itself arbitrarily determined as, say, one half. Whichever variant is used—the first variant is used below—the choice of technique is decided by the instruction to choose the technique with the highest rate of profit, subject to it exceeding some required minimum rate of return.

It should be mentioned in passing that the United Kingdom

company tax system contains very complicated methods of capital allowances, cash investment grants (these have recently replaced investment and initial allowances) and 'wear and tear' allowances, which are sometimes (though not universally)[12] taken into account in the calculations of these various measures. Their *pre-tax* and *post-tax* versions should be distinguished in practice; however, they will be ignored for the remainder of this paper, as will the question of the cost and availability of finance and their relevance to investment decisions.[13]

Essentially, the criterion for the recoupment period requires that the total reduction in operating costs consequent upon choosing a more capital-intensive rather than a less capital-intensive technique should *at least* equal, by the end of the period, the increase in investment expenditure entailed. While the criterion has features in common with the replacement version of the pay-off period criterion, they are *not* the same criteria. It is understood that in Hungary and Poland, a unique recoupment period is used for the economy as a whole; in Czechoslovakia and the Soviet Union, the length of the period varies from sector to sector.[14] The actual periods are said to be five years in Hungary, six years in Poland and between three years (for light industry) and ten years (for heavy industry) in the other two countries; the values most commonly fall between three and six years.

There are two variants of the recoupment period, one which includes only the cost of labour and raw materials in the operating costs (Hungary and Poland), the other which includes an allowance for depreciation (on a straight-line basis) as well (Czechoslovakia and the Soviet Union).

3. THE FIVE RULES

In this section, the choice of techniques at the enterprise level is analysed, presuming the existence of a number of ways of producing a given stream of output per year. The five common rules mentioned in the preceding sections are considered. The decision-makers in the enterprises have to decide which technique to invest in, and they are assumed to take into account the expected rise in the price of the product and in money and wages. For the moment, raw material costs are ignored.

'Capitalist' rules

(1) Choose the technique with the *highest* present value; (the *present value criterion*). (2) Choose the technique with the *highest* internal rate of return (the *internal rate of return criterion*). (3) Choose the technique with the *highest* expected net receipts over the pay-off period, subject to the constraint that these net receipts at least equal the initial investment outlay (the *pay-off period criterion*). (4) Choose the technique with the *highest* average accounting rate of profit (the *rate of profit criterion*).

It is assumed that there is at least one technique (not necessarily the same one in each case) which has a positive present value, or an internal rate of return, or a rate of profit above the required minimum rates.

'Socialist' rule

(5) Choose the technique for which the *sum* of average operating costs per year *and* investment outlay averaged over the standard recoupment period (and, in the second variant, per year as well) is *least* (the *recoupment period criterion*).

Suppose that there are a number of ways of producing a given stream of output per year, characterised by decreasing labour requirements per year as current investment expenditures (initial outlays) increase. The saving in labour requirements is, however, subject to diminishing returns; that is, as the techniques become more capital-intensive, the saving in labour becomes less. The labour requirements per year of each technique are assumed to remain the same for the entire *engineering* life of the equipment associated with each technique. Maintenance costs are ignored; engineering lives are assumed to be *considerably* greater than economic lives (on this, see sec. 4). If investment expenditure (I) is plotted on the horizontal axis and labour requirements per year (l) on the vertical axis, the following curve, ll, is obtained. I_1, I_2 and I_3 are the investment expenditures associated with three of a number of different ways of producing a given level of output (x), and l_1, l_2 and l_3 are their respective annual labour requirements (Fig. 2).

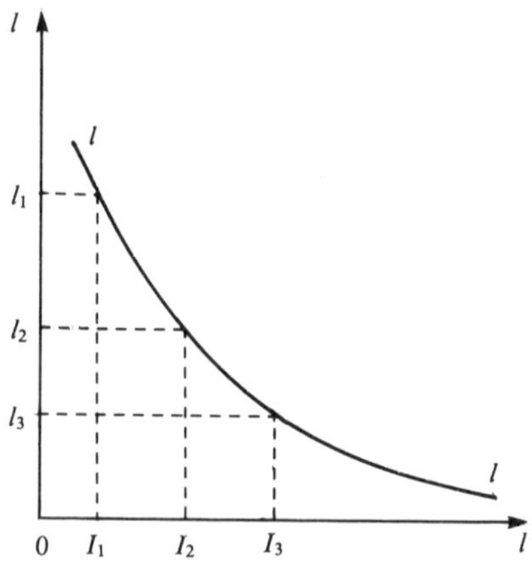

Figure 2: *Annual labour requirements and investment expenditures of the different techniques*

The price per unit of the product is expected to rise at a constant rate (g) per year; this rate of increase is expected to be less than the expected rate of increase (G) of money wages. These expectations have been discussed in section 1 where it is argued that they are likely to be very widely held. The expected economic life of the equipment associated with a given technique is assumed to be given by the point where the expected net receipts first become zero. The expected annual receipts and the labour costs of the three techniques marked on Figure 2, are shown in Figure 3a, together with their expected *economic* lives, n_1, n_2 and n_3 (all of which are assumed to be considerably shorter than their engineering lives). It can be seen that, with the present assumptions, capital-intensity and *economic* durability are positively associated. Length of life in years (n) is measured on the horizontal axis, annual sales receipts (Q) and labour costs (C) on the vertical axis. The curve QQ shows annual sales receipts, the curves C_1C_1, C_2C_2 and C_3C_3 show the annual costs of techniques 1, 2 and 3, respectively. Sales receipts at the end of year $i (i = 1, \ldots, n)$ are $Q_i = p_0 x \, (1 + g)^i$, where p_0 = price at the beginning of year 1, and x = output per year. Labour costs of technique $j (j = 1, \ldots, m)$ at the end of year i are: $C_i^j = w_0 l_j \, (1 + G)^i$, where w_0 = wage at the beginning of year 1, and l_j = annual labour requirement of technique j. The totals of the expected net receipts (q) are the

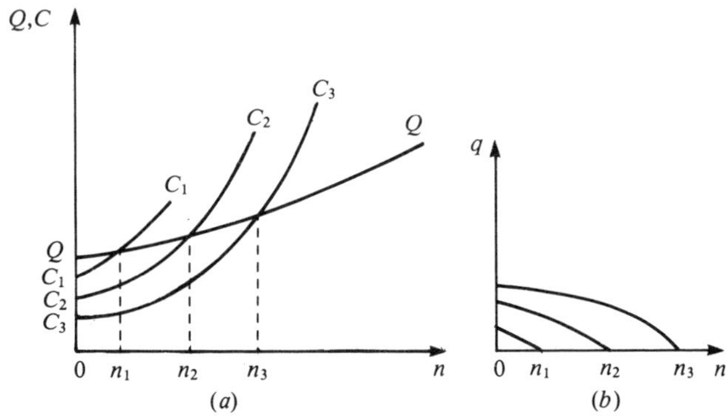

Figure 3: *Expected net receipts of three techniques*

areas between QQ and the respective CC curves; they are shown separately in Figure 3*b*.[15]

(1) Investment-decision rule 1 states:
Choose I_j such that

$$\sum_{i=1}^{n} \frac{(Q_i - C_i^j)}{(1+R)^i} - I_j = max,$$

where R is the marginal cost of finance to the firm.

(2) Investment-decision rule 2 states:
Choose I_j such that ρ in the expression,

$$\sum_{i=1}^{n} \frac{(Q_i - C_i^j)}{(1+\rho)^i} - I_j = 0,$$

is a *maximum*, where ρ is the internal rate of return.

(3) Investment-decision rule 3 states:
Choose I_j such that

$$\sum_{i=1}^{b} (Q_i - C_i^j) = max,$$

subject to

$$\sum_{i=1}^{b} (Q_i - C_i^j) \geqq I_j,$$

where b is the pay-off period, measured in years.

(4) Investment-decision rule 4 states:

Choose I_j such that

$$\frac{\sum_{i=1}^{n} (Q_i - C_i^{\,j}) - I_j}{nI_j} = max$$

(5) Investment-decision rule 5 states:
There are two versions of the recoupment period, one excluding depreciation, the other including it on a straight-line basis.

Variant 1 is to choose I_j such that

$$\frac{I_j}{z} + \frac{\sum_{i=1}^{n} C_i^{\,j}}{n} = min$$

where z is the standard recoupment period, measured in years.[16]

Variant 2 is to choose I_j such that

$$\left(\frac{1}{z} + \frac{1}{n}\right) I_j + \frac{\sum_{i=1}^{n} C_i^{\,j}}{n} = min$$

Now suppose that a decision-maker at the enterprise level decides, on the basis of *one* of these rules, the technique in which to invest. The question with which this section is concerned is: can the resulting six techniques be ordered according to their *relative* capital-intensities?

Consider, first, investment-decision rules 1 and 2. In Figure 4 the present value of the expected net receipts (PV), discounted at the marginal cost of finance, and the investment expenditure on each project are shown on the vertical axis; investment expenditure is also shown on the horizontal axis. II, the investment expenditure line, is clearly a 45 degree line. V_1V_1, the PV curve, is shown as increasing at a *decreasing* rate. Undiscounted expected net receipts increase as I increases, because labour requirements fall, and the lives of the projects lengthen. But, because the saving in labour requirements gets smaller and smaller, and because money wages grow faster than the product price, the *discounted* value of the expected net receipts increases at a decreasing rate.

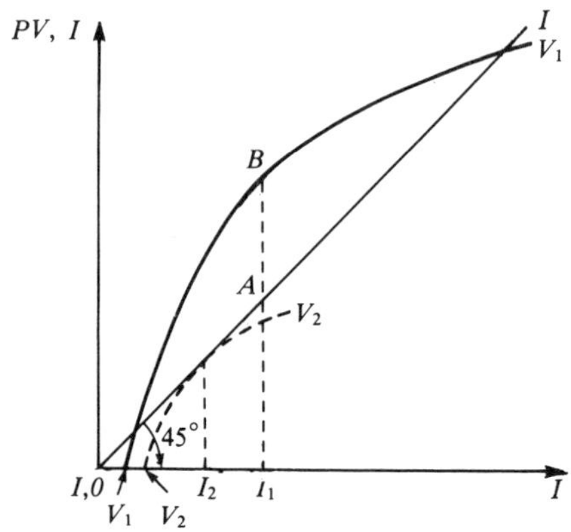

Figure 4: *Choice of technique by rule 1*

If the PV curve is V_1V_1, the technique associated with an investment expenditure of I_1 will be chosen, because at this point V_1V_1 is parallel to II and AB, its present value, is a maximum.[17] (If V_2V_2 were the PV curve, there would be a tangency solution and the technique associated with an expenditure of I_2 would be chosen.)

If now the present values of the projects ($V' = PV - I$) are plotted against their lengths of life, the curve $V'V'$ in Figure 5 is obtained (it will be remembered that there is a positive association between I and n): n_1 is the length of life of the technique associated with an expenditure of I_1 in Figure 4. Any techniques with positive present values must have internal rates of return which are greater than R. ($V' > I$ implies $\rho > R$.) However, because the lives of the projects also vary, it is clear that the rate of interest which would reduce the present value of the technique with a life of n_1 to zero is *not*

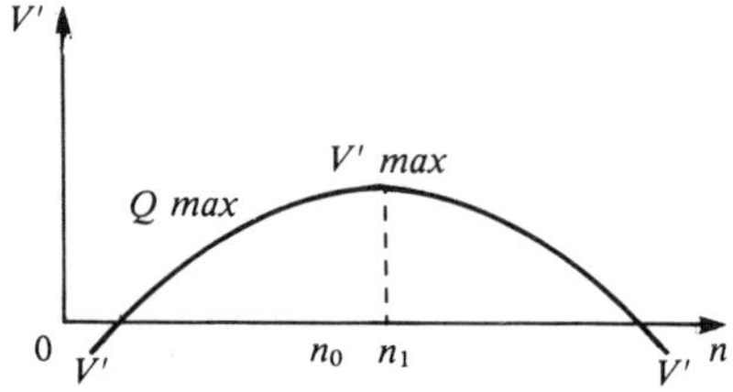

Figure 5: *Choice of technique by rules 1 and 2*

the greatest rate of interest required to reduce the respective present values to zero. The present value at n_1 exceeds those of its neighbours to the immediate left, not only because its undiscounted annual net receipts are greater than theirs, *but* also because it has a longer economic life. A given increase in the length of life has a less than proportional effect on the discounted value of a stream of payments. Somewhere to the left of n_1, therefore, a greater rate of interest will be needed to reduce the present value to zero, say, at n_0. The maximum internal rate of return equals this rate of interest. It follows that investment-decision rule 2 will, with the present technology and price and cost expectations, result in the choice of a *less* capital-intensive technique than investment-decision rule 1. (There is one exception to this statement; if there is a tangency solution [see Fig. 4], the same technique will be chosen by the two rules. A tangency solution implies, of course, that $V' = 0$ and that $\rho = R$.)[18] Because maximising the present value of a project also implies cost-minimisation, it is clear that maximising the internal rate of return does not.

None of the three remaining rules uses a rate of discount or a rate of interest; it is obvious, therefore, that they will lead to different techniques being chosen than those chosen by rules 1 and 2. Consider, first, the pay-off period criterion (rule 3). In Figure 6:

$$\pi_j \left(= \frac{\sum_{i=1}^{b} (Q_j - C_i^j)}{bI_j} \right)$$

is plotted on the vertical axis and I on the horizontal axis. The values of π_j on the vertical axis are the values of the expected average gross rates of profit for the pay-off period of each technique and are the *inverses* of the number of years

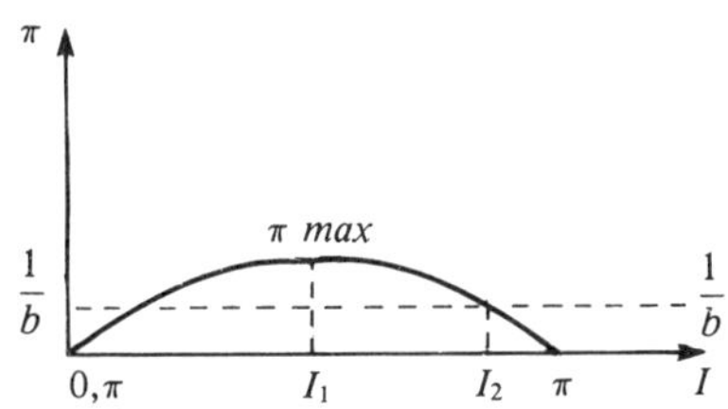

Figure 6: *First choice of technique by rule 3*

that it takes to 'repay' the respective investment outlays. Because the undiscounted net receipts of the techniques are bounded by the pay-off period and because labour requirements decline at a decreasing rate as I increases, π will rise to a maximum and then decline as I increases, giving the curve $\pi\pi$ shown in Figure 6.

If the decision rule were an instruction to choose the technique with the *lowest* pay-off period, the technique associated with an expenditure of I_1 would be chosen and π would be maximised. However, it would be possible both to increase expected net receipts *and* to satisfy the pay-off period criterion by choosing the technique associated with an expenditure of I_2; at which value, $\pi = \frac{1}{b}$, the inverse of the pay-off period.[19] With this technique,

$$\sum_{i=1}^{b} (Q_i - C_i^j) = I_j,$$

and is also maximised.

It is not clear whether this technique is more or less capital-intensive than those chosen under rules 1 and 2. The ordering depends upon the length of the pay-off period, the rate of decline in labour requirements, the rates of increase of the product price and money wages, the lengths of life of each technique, and the value of R. If, however, the expected net receipts for the years outside the pay-off period are ignored, it is clear that the pay-off period criterion results in the choice of a technique which is *more* capital-intensive than that chosen by the present value criterion. Therefore, the greater is b and, thus, the closer is it to the values of n, the economic lengths of life of the techniques chosen under rules 1 and 2, the more likely is it that the pay-off period criterion will result in the choice of a more capital-intensive technique than either rule 1 or 2.

In order to facilitate the remaining comparisons, and to establish rigorously the results of the preceding paragraph, it is necessary to obtain expressions for the rates of substitution of annual labour input for investment expenditure of the techniques which are chosen by rules 1 and 3. (The rate of substitution is $\frac{\partial l}{\partial I}$, the slope of the curve, ll, in Figure 2.)

Rule 1 (the present value criterion) may be written as:

$$V_j' = p_0 x B - w_0 l_j A - I_j = max \tag{3.1}$$

where

$$A = \frac{(1+G)\left\{\left(\frac{1+G}{1+R}\right)^n - 1\right\}}{G-R},$$

$$B = \frac{(1+g)\left\{\left(\frac{1+g}{1+R}\right)^n - 1\right\}}{g-R} \text{ and } R > G > g,$$

by assumption. (For moderate rates of increase of prices and money wages, this seems a reasonable assumption.)

To find the first-order condition for (3.1) to be a maximum, partially differentiate (3.1) with respect to I and put the resulting expression equal to zero.

$$-\frac{\partial l}{\partial I} = \frac{1}{w_0 A - \frac{\partial n}{\partial l}\left(p_0 x \frac{\partial B}{\partial n} - w_0 l \frac{\partial A}{\partial n}\right)} \tag{3.2}$$

is obtained.[20]

Rule 3 (the pay-off period criterion) requires that:

$$p_0 x B' - w_0 l_j A' = max, \text{ subject to } p_0 x B' - w_0 l_j A' \geqq I_j,$$

where

$$A' = \frac{(1+G)\{(1+G)^b - 1\}}{G} \text{ and } B' = \frac{(1+g)\{(1+g)^b - 1\}}{g}$$

Write:

$$l = \frac{p_0 x B'}{w_0 A'} - \frac{I}{w_0 A'} \tag{3.3}$$

(3.3) is a straight line (*LL* in Fig. 7) with a slope of $\left(-\frac{1}{w_0 A'}\right)$ and an intercept on the vertical axis of $\frac{p_0 x B'}{w_0 A'}$.

The curve, *ll*, of Fig. 2—the annual labour requirement, investment expenditure relationship—is also shown in Figure 7. Provided some labour and investment are needed to produce a given level of output, it is clear that *LL* will either

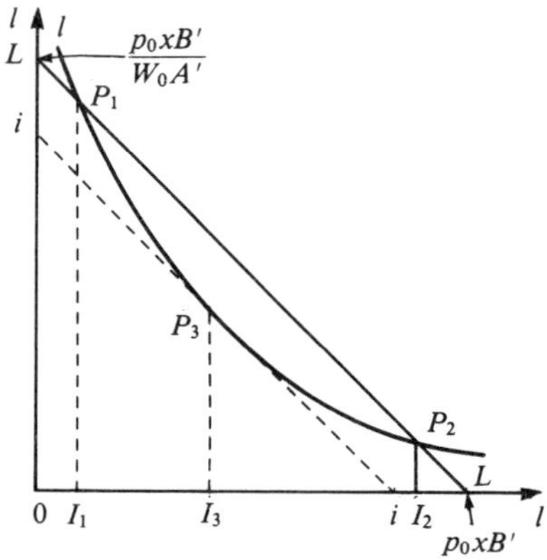

Figure 7: *Second choice of technique by rule 3*

intersect ll at points such as P_1 and P_2, or will be tangential to ll at a point such as P_3 (or not cut ll at all, in which case no technique will satisfy the criterion). At P_2, the pay-off period criterion is satisfied and the technique associated with an investment expenditure of I_2 is chosen (see Fig. 6). At P_2,

$-\frac{\partial l}{\partial I} < \frac{1}{w_0A'}$, because ll cuts LL from below. (The other

possibility is the tangency solution at P_3, and, there,

$$-\frac{\partial l}{\partial I} = \frac{1}{w_0A'}.\text{) Therefore, } -\frac{\partial l}{\partial I} \leqq \frac{1}{w_0A'}.\text{[21]} \qquad (3.4)$$

Now compare (3.2) with (3.4) and suppose, initially, that $n = b$ for all techniques. (3.2) therefore becomes:

$$-\frac{\partial l}{\partial I} = \frac{1}{w_0A''} \qquad (3.5)$$

where

$$A'' = \frac{(1+G)\left\{\left(\frac{1+G}{1+R}\right)^b - 1\right\}}{G-R}$$

Because $A'' < A'$, it is obvious that (3.5) > (3.4).

In (3.2), $\left(p_0x\frac{\partial B}{\partial n} - w_0l\frac{\partial A}{\partial n}\right)$ may be $\gtreqless$ 0. If it $\leqq 0$,

(3.2) > (3.4), for a wide range of values of n;[22] that is to say, the present value criterion results in a *less* capital-intensive technique being chosen. If $\left(p_0 x \frac{\partial B}{\partial n} - w_0 l \frac{\partial A}{\partial n}\right) > 0$, it does not necessarily follow that (3.2) < (3.4) especially as $w_0 A < w_0 A'$, for given n, and $\frac{1}{w_0 A'}$ is the upper value of the inequality, $-\frac{\partial l}{\partial I} \leqq \frac{1}{w_0 A'}$. Thus, it seems reasonable to conclude that, given the present assumptions, in many circumstances, the pay-off period criterion results in the choice of a *more* capital-intensive technique than does the present value criterion (and, *a fortiori*, the internal rate of return criterion).

Another investment decision rule which is often used in practice in the United Kingdom is the accounting rate of profit criterion (rule 4). This may be written as:

$$P_j = \frac{1}{nI_j}\{p_0 x B''' - w_0 l_j A''' - I_j\} = max \qquad (3.6)$$

where

$$A''' = \frac{(1+G)\{(1+G)^n - 1\}}{G}$$

and

$$B''' = \frac{(1+g)\{(1+g)^n - 1\}}{g}.$$

A rough idea of the relative capital-intensity which results from this rule, as compared, first, with the pay-off period criterion, can be obtained as follows. Suppose that annual *net* profits are averaged for a period equal to the pay-off period, and that depreciation is reckoned on the straight-line basis as $\frac{I}{b}$ per year, so that $\frac{I}{b}$ increases as I increases. Then, it is clear that if P_j is plotted against I as the curve PP (Fig. 8) and compared with π_j (see Fig. 6), it will reach a maximum at the *same* investment expenditure (I_1) as π (Fig. 8). Therefore, with these assumptions, rule 4 results in a *less*

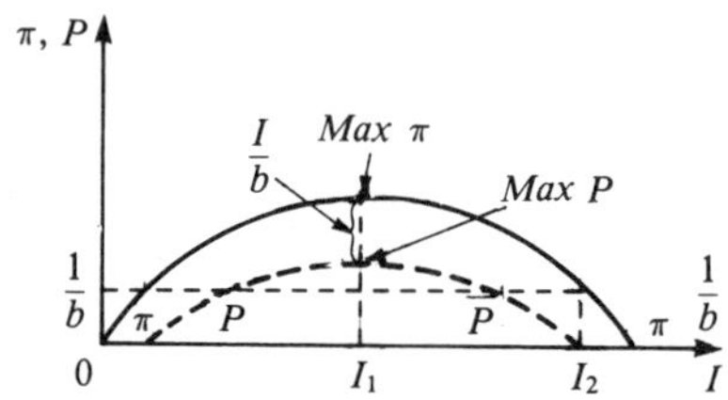

Figure 8: *Choice of technique by rules 3 and 4*

capital-intensive technique being chosen than that resulting from rule 3.[23]

If, now, the assumption that $n = b$ is dropped, the maximum of the accounting rate of profit curve may well occur at a value of I which is closer to I_2; but it does seem that there will be a considerable number of cases where this rule results in *less* capital-intensive techniques being chosen.

What can be said of the ordering of rule 4 (accounting rate of profit) in relation to rule 1 (present value)? To answer this, consider the first-order condition for a maximum P. It is:

$$-\frac{\partial l}{\partial I} = \left\{\frac{p_0 x B''' - w_0 l A'''}{I}\right\}$$

$$\left\{\frac{1}{w_0 A''' - \frac{I}{n}\frac{\partial n}{\partial l} - \frac{\partial n}{\partial l}\left\{p_0 x\left(\frac{\partial B'''}{\partial n} - \frac{B'''}{n}\right) - w_0 l\left(\frac{\partial A'''}{\partial n} - \frac{A'''}{n}\right)\right\}}\right\} \tag{3.7}$$

Comparing (3.7) with (3.2)

$$\left(-\frac{\partial l}{\partial I} = \frac{1}{w_0 A - \frac{\partial n}{\partial l}\left(p_0 x\frac{\partial B}{\partial n} - w_0 l\frac{\partial A}{\partial n}\right)}\right),$$

and ignoring the last two terms of the denominator of (3.7), and the last term of the denominator of (3.2), the ordering is seen to turn on whether the effect of $\frac{p_0 x B''' - w_0 l A'''}{I} > 1$, which tends to make (3.7) > (3.2), outweighs, or is outweighed by the effect of $w_0 A''' > w_0 A_1$, which tends to make (3.7) < (3.2). It appears, therefore, that while both rule 1 and rule 4 result in less capital-intensive techniques being chosen than does rule 3, it is not possible to order the techniques corresponding to rules 1 and 4 themselves.

Comparison of the recoupment period criterion (rule 5) with the pay-off period criterion (rule 3)

As the pay-off period criterion (rule 3) often results in the choice of the most capital-intensive technique of the four 'capitalist' rules, it seems sensible to make it the first 'capitalist' rule to be compared with the recoupment period criterion (rule 5). As defined above, the recoupment period criterion requires that the savings in costs which result from choosing a more capital-intensive technique cover the increase in investment expenditure within the period of time defined as the recoupment period. This can be shown to be equivalent to minimising one of the expressions given in the fifth paragraph of section 3, depending upon which variant of the criterion is used. In order to simplify the comparison with the pay-off period criterion, variant 1 with a recoupment period equal to the pay-off period and with all techniques given the same arbitrarily determined life, $\bar{n}$, is examined (a special case is: $\bar{n} = b = z$). The assumption concerning n is dropped later (see below). The values of the recoupment periods for different industries are mostly within the two- to five-year range associated with the pay-off period.

The recoupment period criterion (variant 1) then is:

$$\frac{I}{z} + \frac{1}{\bar{n}} w_0 l_j A'''' = min \tag{3.8}$$

where

$$A'''' = \frac{(1+G)\{(1+G)^{\bar{n}} - 1\}}{G}$$

and $z = b(= \bar{n})$.

The first-order condition for this to be a minimum is:

$$-\frac{\partial l}{\partial I} = \frac{1}{z}\left(\frac{\bar{n}}{w_0 A''''}\right) \tag{3.9}$$

For

$$\bar{n} = z(= b),\ \frac{1}{z}\left(\frac{\bar{n}}{w_0 A''''}\right) = \frac{1}{w_0 A'},$$

the upper value of the pay-off period criterion. However, except in the special case of a tangency solution, $-\frac{\partial l}{\partial I} < \frac{1}{w_0 A'}$ for rule 3, so that for $\bar{n} = z = b$, the recoupment period criterion results in the choice of a *less* capital-intensive technique.

As $\bar{n}$ increases, $\frac{1}{z}\left(\frac{\bar{n}}{w_0 A''''}\right)$ will fall because, though the numerator increases arithmetically, the denominator increases geometrically. There is, therefore, a value of $\bar{n}$ at which the same technique will be chosen by the two rules. But it seems clear that there may be a considerable range over which the recoupment period criterion results in a *less* capital-intensive technique being chosen.

If the second variant of the recoupment period is considered, that is, depreciation is taken into account, the relevant condition for the recoupment period criterion is that:

$$-\frac{\partial l}{\partial I} = \left(\frac{1}{z} + \frac{1}{\bar{n}}\right)\left(\frac{\bar{n}}{w_0 A''''}\right) \tag{3.10}$$

This results in the choice of a less capital-intensive technique than the first variant, that is,

$$\left(\frac{1}{z} + \frac{1}{\bar{n}}\right)\left(\frac{\bar{n}}{w_0 A''''}\right) > \left(\frac{1}{z}\right)\left(\frac{\bar{n}}{w_0 A''''}\right),$$

which, of course, is to be expected. The range within which the recoupment period criterion results in a *less* capital-intensive technique being chosen is widened.

The comparisons are now repeated, supposing n to be determined by the criterion that the expected net receipts be either positive or zero (see Fig. 3). With variant 1, the condition for the recoupment period criterion becomes:

$$-\frac{\partial l}{\partial I} = \left(\frac{1}{z}\right)\left\{\frac{n}{w_0\left[A''' + l\,\frac{\partial n}{\partial l}\left(\frac{\partial A'''}{\partial n} - \frac{A'''}{n}\right)\right]}\right\} \tag{3.11}$$

This expression is very similar to (3.9), but now has an additional product in the denominator which is negative.[24] If, therefore, $n \leqq \bar{n}$, a less capital-intensive technique will be chosen if this version is used; and there is a range of values of $n > \bar{n}$, where this still holds. It seems possible, therefore, to accept the previous findings, provided n is relatively close to $\bar{n}$.

With the second variant of rule 5, the first-order condition for the recoupment period criterion becomes:

$$-\frac{\partial l}{\partial I} = \left(\frac{1}{z} + \frac{1}{n}\right) \left\{ \frac{n}{w_0 \left\{ A''' + l \frac{\partial n}{\partial l} \left(\frac{\partial A'''}{\partial n} - \frac{A'''}{n} \right) \right\} - \frac{I}{n} \frac{\partial n}{\partial l}} \right\} \tag{3.12}$$

If it is assumed that the last two terms approximately cancel one another

$\left[-\frac{I}{n} \frac{\partial n}{\partial l} > 0 \right]$, for $n = \bar{n}$, the criterion is the same as before. It may be concluded, then, that the assumption of a variable n is unlikely to alter the results significantly.

Comparisons of rule 5 with rules 1 and 4

If variant 1 of rule 5 is considered, and if $\bar{n} = z = b$, then the present value criterion condition is:

$$-\frac{\partial l}{\partial I} = \frac{1}{w_0 A''} \tag{3.5}$$

the accounting rate of profit condition is:

$$-\frac{\partial l}{\partial I} = \left(\frac{p_0 x B' - w_0 l A'}{I} \right) \left(\frac{1}{w_0 A'} \right) \tag{3.7a}$$

and the rule 5, variant 1, condition is:

$$-\frac{\partial l}{\partial I} = \frac{1}{w_0 A'} \tag{3.13}$$

Both (3.5) and (3.7a) > (3.13), that is to say, the recoupment period criterion, variant 1, results in the choice of a *more* capital-intensive technique than either rule 1 or 4.

However, if rule 5, variant 2 is considered, even under the present restricted assumptions, this ordering no longer holds.[25] And when a variable n is considered, nothing definite can be said about the ordering of rule 5, variant 1 in relation to either rule 1 or 4, though the results above suggest that rule 5, variant 1 will result in *more* capital-intensive techniques being chosen in a number of cases, as, perhaps, is to be expected.

Raw material inputs

For completeness, something should be added about the influence of raw material costs on the choice of technique resulting from the five rules. It is assumed that the raw material input per year (k) is the *same* for *all* techniques, and that the rate of increase of the price of the raw material input is the same as that of the product price (g). With these assumptions it can be shown, first, that the present value criterion results in a *less* capital-intensive technique being chosen than when labour alone is considered.[26]

Second, by reasoning similar to that used in the eighth paragraph of this section, it is clear that the internal rate of return criterion will still result in a *less* capital-intensive technique being chosen, relative to rule 1, and that it will be *less* capital-intensive than with labour alone. Third, the choice of technique resulting from the pay-off period criterion is now *less* capital-intensive than that associated with labour alone.[27]

Fourth, if the accounting rate of profit criterion is considered, then, within the bounds of a given period, say b, a *more* capital-intensive technique than previously will be chosen, though it still will be *less* capital-intensive than that chosen by the pay-off period criterion.[28] However, if n is variable, the technique chosen may be either more or less capital-intensive than before.[29]

Both versions of the recoupment period criteria result in the choice of a *less* capital-intensive technique than before,[30] except, of course in the special case of $n = \bar{n}$ (see above), when the choice is not affected. These results therefore confirm the ordering of rules 1, 2, 4 and 5 in relation to rule 3, leave unchanged the ordering of rules 1 and 2, and still leave indeterminate the relative capital-intensities resulting from rules 5 and 4, in relation to rules 1 and 2.

The main results of this section are summarised conveniently in Figure 9. $-\frac{\partial l}{\partial I}$, the slope of the annual labour requirement, investment expenditure relationship, is plotted on the vertical axis of the top half of the figure. n, the *economic* length of life, is plotted on the horizontal axis. As n increases, and $-\frac{\partial l}{\partial I}$ decreases, as I increases, a downward-sloping curve such as AA (drawn, for simplicity, as a straight line), is obtained. Now $-\frac{\partial l}{\partial I}$ is also a function of n in the expressions for the first-order condition for a maximum associated with investment-decision rules 1 and 4, and in the expressions for the first-order condition for a minimum associated with the two variants of investment-decision rule

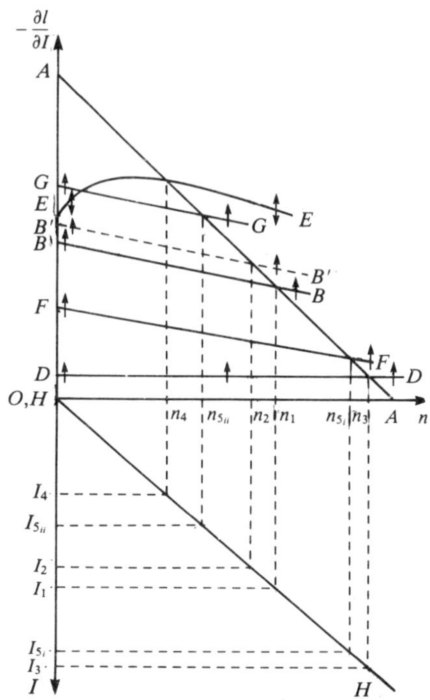

Figure 9: *Choice of technique by rules 1 to 5*

5. These relationships are shown by the curves *BB* (rule 1), *EE* (rule 4), *FF* (rule 5, the variant *excluding* depreciation) and *GG* (rule 5, the variant *including* depreciation). $-\frac{\partial l}{\partial I}$ is a function of b, w_0 and G in the inequality condition associated with investment-decision rule 3; it is shown in the figure as the horizontal straight line, *DD*. Investment expenditure, I, is measured on the vertical axis of the bottom half of the figure. The relationship between I and n is shown by the curve, *HH*.

The economic lengths of life associated with the techniques chosen by each rule are those corresponding to the intersections of the various lines—*BB*, *EE*, and so forth—with *AA* (for example, n_1 is the life associated with the technique chosen by rule 1). The investment expenditures associated with each is found from the investment expenditure, economic length of life relationship, *HH* (for example, I_1 is the expenditure associated with the technique chosen by rule 1). In Figure 9, rule 1 results in the choice of a *more* capital-intensive technique than rule 4 and rule 5 (the variant which includes depreciation); but this is for illustrative purposes only. The length of life and investment expenditure associated with investment-decision rule 2 are also shown (n_2, I_2 in Fig. 9).[31] The arrows attached to the lines, *BB*, *EE*, and so forth, show the influence of the introduction of raw material costs on the techniques chosen by each rule.

4. CONCLUSIONS

Before setting out the main conclusions of this paper, some of the limitations of the analysis are discussed. First, the analysis consists, essentially, of comparisons between different situations where only the investment-decision rules used are allowed to change. It may well be, though, that changes in factor and product prices as between the 'otherwise situations' are such, that the results of the comparisons cannot be applied to situations of *actual change*. Second, *higher* investment expenditures in fact may not be associated with *lower* labour inputs over the entire life of the equipment involved. The greater the investment expenditure, the more complex the equipment is likely to be, and, therefore, the greater may be its maintenance costs (and, thus, indirect labour inputs) in its later years of operation. This point has been guarded against to some extent by supposing that *economic* lives are considerably shorter than *engineering* lives. Third, the expected economic life may be *less* than that determined by the point where q_i first becomes zero, if the expected rate of technical progress is taken into account by businessmen (in a more sophisticated way than is assumed in this paper), or if they operate in an imperfectly competitive situation. However, these considerations probably do not affect the *ordering* of techniques by length of life, which is the relevant factor for the present analysis.

The fourth limitation is that the relative capital-intensities which result from the use of the various rules have been discussed in the context of a situation in which the *level of output* is assumed to be given. However, if, instead, the *level of investment expenditure* is assumed to be given and constant, it can be shown that the pay-off period criterion and, perhaps, the present value rule, will result in the choice of *less* capital-intensive techniques than those indicated by the analysis of this paper. Therefore, if businessmen are in the latter situation, or if they see the problem of the choice of techniques as one of allocating a given amount of investment funds rather than as one of deciding the capital-intensity to be used to produce a given level of output, the orderings of the capital-intensities associated with each rule *may* differ from those suggested by the analysis of this paper.[32]

Bearing in mind the above limitations of the analysis, the analysis of this paper suggests that, with the technology and price and money wage expectations assumed, the *pay-off period* criterion often results in the choice of a technique which is *more* capital-intensive than those resulting from the other four criteria examined: that, is the three other 'capitalist' rules, and the 'socialist' rule, the *recoupment period* criterion, which has two variants. The technology and expectations assumed, though simple, seem plausible. Therefore, as the *pay-off period* criterion is used widely in practice, it may be tentatively concluded that, in many instances, businessmen in the United Kingdom would install *more* capital-intensive techniques than would managers in the socialist countries faced with the same expectations and the same technology. (This conclusion abstracts from the impact of tax provisions on investment decisions.)[33]

The second conclusion (which follows from the first) is that if the use of DCF (Discounted Cash Flow) procedures becomes more widespread in the United Kingdom, as appears to be the aim of both the government and leading business firms, there may well be a switch to investment in *less* capital-intensive techniques than otherwise would have occurred. The adoption of the *internal rate of return* criterion would cause a greater switch than would occur if the *present value* rule were adopted.

The variant of the *recoupment period* criterion which takes no account of depreciation results in a *more* capital-intensive technique being chosen than does the variant which includes depreciation.

In general, the relative capital-intensities of the techniques chosen by the *present value, internal rate of return, accounting rate of profit and recoupment period* criteria, cannot be ordered. With very restrictive assumptions, it can be shown that the variant of the *recoupment period* which takes no account of depreciation results in the choice of a *more* capital-intensive technique than would result from either the *present value* (and, *a fortiori*, the *internal rate of return*) or *accounting rate of profit* criterion. But, even with the same restrictive assumptions, this degree of generalisation is not possible in the case of the variant of the *recoupment period* criterion which includes depreciation.

If raw material costs, as well as labour costs, are considered, the preceding conclusions are not affected. When compared with the results of the 'labour costs only' comparisons, it is found that *less* capital-intensive techniques are chosen by all the rules examined except the *accounting rate of profit* rule, where the outcome is indeterminate.

NOTES

1. This essay first appeared in *Czechoslovak Economic Papers* no. 9, 1967, pp. 65–91. It is reprinted from John T. Dunlop and Nikolay P. Federenko (eds.), *Planning and Markets* (New York: McGraw Hill, 1969), pp. 190–216. The writer is most grateful to Amit Bhaduri, Donald J. Harris, James A. Mirrlees, D. M. Nuti, Graham Pyatt,

R. E. Rowthorn, E. A. Russell, Aubrey Silbertson, Ajit Singh, G. Whittington, K. J. Wigley, F. K. Wright and the members of the Conference at Nice for helpful discussions and comments.

2. See, for example, National Economic Development Council, *Investment Appraisal* (London: HMSO, 1965); A. M. Alfred, 'Discounted Cash Flow and Corporate Planning', *Woolwich Economic Papers*. no. 3, July 1964; A. J. Merrett and Allen Sykes, *The Finance and Analysis of Capital Projects* (London: Longmans, Green and Co. Ltd., 1965).
3. *See*, for example, Tibor Barna, *Investment and Growth Policies in British Industrial Firms* (NIESR *Occasional Paper*, no. 20; Cambridge University Press, 1962); A. S. MacIntosh, *The Development of Firms* (Cambridge University Press, 1963); *Report of the Committee on Turnover Taxation*, Cmnd 2300, 1964; R. R. Neild, 'Replacement Policy,' *National Institute Economic Review*, Nov. 1964, pp. 30–43; D. C. Corner and Alan Williams, 'The Sensitivity of Business to Initial and Investment Allowances,' *Economica*, Feb. 1965, pp. 32–47.
4. *See*, for example, M. S. Feldstein and J. S. Flemming, 'The Problem of Time-Stream Evaluation: Present Value *versus* Internal Rate of Return Rules,' *Bulletin* of the Oxford University Institute of Economics and Statistics, Feb. 1964, pp. 79–85.
5. The paper is essentially an extension of the analyses of Meek and Nuti respectively, to take account of expected inflation and variations in the *economic* life of equipment. *See* Ronald L. Meek, 'Ideal and Reality in the Choice between Alternative Techniques,' *Oxford Economic Papers*, Oct. 1964, pp. 333–54; Domenico Mario Nuti, 'Recoupment Period and Investment Criteria in the Socialist Economies,' unpub., King's College, Cambridge, Dec. 1965.
6. The marginal cost of finance is either the rate which must be paid for additional funds, or the interest foregone when firms use their own funds. It may include elements of imputed psychological cost, for example, those associated with high fixed interest claims on uncertain, fluctuating future profits, or those which take account of the impact of new share issues on the returns to the old shareholders.
7. The initial outlay may also be an estimated value, for example, when a businessman who is considering constructing a new plant within his business estimates its cost. Or, an investment project may contain several stages and take several years to complete, so that the outlays associated with the later stages of necessity must be estimates. An example of a multi-stage project would be the development of a housing estate over a number of years by a speculative builder. The expected rate of profit of a multi-stage project can be found by solving the following equation for ρ:

$$0 = \left\{\sum_{i=1}^{n} \frac{q_i - I_i}{(1+\rho)^i}\right\} + \frac{K}{(1+\rho)^n} \qquad (1.1a)$$

The present value of the same project is:

$$V' = \left\{\sum_{i=1}^{n} \frac{q_i - I_i}{(1+K)^i}\right\} + \frac{K}{(1+R)^n} \qquad (1.2a)$$

where I_1 = capital outlay in year i
and q_i, K, ρ, V' and R are as defined in the text.

8. If factor and product prices are assumed to be independent of the scale of operation of the individual firm, and if the inputs per unit of output of each technique are also independent of scale, the choice of technique can be discussed independently of the other two aspects of the investment decision. The arguments of this paper may be viewed in this way, in which case the problem discussed is the choice of the capital-intensity to be used to produce a *unit* of output.
9. The leading names associated with these alternative views are W. J. Baumol, Robin Marris, Edith Penrose and Herbert A. Simon. For a very useful discussion of the differences in behaviour which result from these differing aims, *see* John Williamson, 'Profit, Growth and Sales Maximization,' *Economica*, Feb. 1966, pp. 1–16.
10. Feldstein and Flemming, 'The Problem of Time-Stream Evaluation', sections I and II, have an excellent discussion of these matters, both with and without the assumption of a budget constraint.
11. 'Replacement Policy', p. 35.
12. Corner and Williams point out that 'The Richardson Committee ... came to the surprising conclusions that firms are not likely to be affected by tax changes because they "look principally at the return before payment of tax" (para. 282)', 'The Sensitivity of Business to Initial and Investment Allowances', p. 34.
13. The writer has discussed some of the implications of the change from initial and investment allowances to cash investment grants, and of the introduction of the corporation tax in place of the old profits tax and standard rate of income tax, for the present values of given investment projects in 'Cash Investment Grants, Corporation Tax and Pay-Out Ratios,' *Bulletin* of the Oxford University Institute of Economics and Statistics, August 1966, pp. 163–79 and February 1967, pp. 87–93.
14. For details of the lengths of the period for various sectors in the two countries, *see* D. M. Nuti, '"Recoupment Period"', p. 16.
15. If it is assumed that factor and product prices, and the inputs per unit of output of each technique are independent of scale (see n. 8), then $x = 1$ in the expressions which follow and l and I should be interpreted as labour requirements and investment expenditures *per unit of output*, respectively.
16. Let $I_2 > I_1$ and:

$$\frac{\sum_{i=1}^{n} C_i^1}{n} < \frac{\sum_{i=1}^{n} C_i^2}{n}$$

Then the recoupment period criterion requires that, for the technique associated with I_2 to be: chosen,

$$\frac{I_2 - I_1}{\frac{\sum_{i=1}^{n} C_i^1}{n} - \frac{\sum_{i=1}^{n} C_i^2}{n}} < \tau.$$

This is equivalent to the instruction to minimise:

$$\frac{I_i}{z} + \frac{\sum_{i=1}^{n} C_i^j}{n}$$

(*see* D. M. Nuti, '"Recoupment Period"', p. 6).

17. I_1 in Fig. 4 is not necessarily the same investment expenditure as I_1 in previous figures. It is assumed that the curvature of ll is such that V_1V_1 is a concave continuous curve so that there is only one maximum value of $(PV - I)$.
18. An alternative explanation of why rule 2 results in the choice of a *less* capital-intensive technique than rule 1 is given in n. 31.
19. *See* D. M. Nuti, '"Recoupment Period"', pp. 11–13.
20. $-\frac{\partial l}{\partial I}$ is shown, in order to have positive values.
21. The writer is indebted to R. E. Rowthorn for this proof.
22. If:

$$\left(p_0 x \frac{\partial B}{\partial n} - w_0 l \frac{\partial A}{\partial n}\right) \leqq 0.$$

and because:

$$\frac{\partial n}{\partial l} < 0, \quad -\frac{\partial n}{\partial l}\left(p_0 x \frac{\partial B}{\partial n} - w_0 l \frac{\partial A}{\partial n}\right) \leqq 0.$$

It therefore is an offset (or, at least, not an addition), to $w_0 A$, which, however, becomes greater as n increases, so *that the value of* $-\frac{\partial l}{\partial I}$ which satisfies (3.2) decreases with n.

23. If $n = b$, rule 4 becomes:

$$P_i = \frac{1}{bI_j}\{p_0 xB' - w_0 l_j A' - I_j\} = max. \qquad (3.6a)$$

The first-order condition for a maximum is:

$$-\frac{\partial l}{\partial I} = \left(\frac{p_0 xB' - w_0 l_j A'}{I}\right)\left(\frac{1}{w_0 A'}\right) \qquad (3.7a)$$

For $P \geqq 0$ (an obvious condition), $p_0 xB' - w_0 lA' \geqq I$, and $\frac{p_0 xB' - w_0 lA'}{I} \geqq 1$. It follows that:

$$(3.7a) > -\frac{\partial l}{\partial I}\left(\leqq \frac{1}{w_0 A'}\right).$$

24. $$w_0 > 0, l > 0, \frac{\partial n}{\partial l} < 0, \left(\frac{\partial A'''}{\partial n} - \frac{A'''}{n}\right) > 0.$$

25. The rule 5, variant 2, condition, with $\bar{n} = z = b$, is:

$$-\frac{\partial l}{\partial I} = \frac{2}{w_0 A'} \tag{3.14a}$$

26. $$V_i' = p_0 x B - w_0 l_j A - r_0 k B - I_j = max. \tag{3.15a}$$

where r_0 = price of raw material input at the beginning of year 1. The first-order condition for a maximum is:

$$-\frac{\partial l}{\partial I} = \frac{1}{w_0 A - \frac{\partial n}{\partial l}\left[(p_0 x - r_0 k)\frac{\partial B}{\partial n} - w_0 l \frac{\partial A}{\partial n}\right]} \tag{3.16a}$$

$$> -\frac{\partial l}{\partial I} = \frac{1}{w_0 A - \frac{\partial n}{\partial l}\left(p_0 x \frac{\partial B}{\partial n} - w_0 l \frac{\partial A}{\partial n}\right)} \tag{3.2}$$

the analogous condition for labour only.

27. The slope of the line analogous to LL in Fig. 7 is the same, but the intercept on the vertical axis

$$\left\{\frac{(p_0 x - r_0 k)B'}{w_0 A'}\right\} \text{ is less.}$$

28. In this case, the rule 4, first-order condition for a maximum is:

$$-\frac{\partial l}{\partial I} = \left[\frac{(p_0 x - r_0 k)B' - w_0 l A'}{I}\right]\left[\frac{1}{w_0 A'}\right] \tag{3.17a}$$

$$-\frac{\partial l}{\partial I} = \left[\frac{p_0 x B' - w_0 l A'}{I}\right]\left(\frac{1}{w_0 A'}\right) \text{ but } -\frac{\partial l}{\partial I} > \frac{1}{w_0 A'}$$

29. The rule 4, first-order condition is:

$$-\frac{\partial l}{\partial I} = \left\{\frac{(p_0 x - r_0 k)B''' - w_0 l A'''}{I}\right\}$$

$$\left\{\frac{1}{w_0 A''' - \frac{I}{n}\frac{\partial n}{\partial l} - \frac{\partial n}{\partial l}\left\{(p_0 x - r_0 k)\left(\frac{\partial B'''}{\partial n} - \frac{B'''}{n}\right) - w_0 l\left(\frac{\partial A'''}{\partial n} - \frac{A'''}{n}\right)\right\}}\right\} \tag{3.18a}$$

This compares with

$$-\frac{\partial l}{\partial I} = \left\{\frac{p_0 x B''' - w_0 l A'''}{I}\right\}$$

$$\left\{\frac{1}{w_0 A''' - \frac{I}{n}\frac{\partial n}{\partial l} - \frac{\partial n}{\partial l}\left\{p_0 x\left(\frac{\partial B'''}{\partial n} - \frac{B'''}{n}\right) - w_0 l\left(\frac{\partial A'''}{\partial n} - \frac{A'''}{n}\right)\right\}}\right\} \tag{3.7}$$

The expression in the first bracket of (3.18a) is less than that of (3.7), but the expression in the second bracket is greater.

30. The rule 5, variant 1, first-order condition for a minimum is:

$$-\frac{\partial l}{\partial I}=\frac{1}{z}\left\{\frac{n}{w_0\left[A'''+l\frac{\partial n}{\partial l}\left(\frac{\partial A'''}{\partial n}-\frac{A'''}{n}\right)\right]+r_0k\frac{\partial n}{\partial l}\left(\frac{\partial B'''}{\partial n}-\frac{B'''}{n}\right)}\right\} \tag{3.19a}$$

$$(3.19a) > -\frac{\partial l}{\partial I}=\left(\frac{1}{z}\right)\left\{\frac{n}{w_0\left[A'''+l\frac{\partial n}{\partial l}\left(\frac{\partial A'''}{\partial n}-\frac{A'''}{n}\right)\right]}\right\}$$

The rule 5, variant 2, first-order condition for a minimum is similar to (3.19a), except that the first bracket becomes: $\left(\frac{1}{z}+\frac{1}{n}\right)$, and the denominator of the second bracket contains an additional term: $-\frac{I}{n}\frac{\partial n}{\partial l}$.

It therefore, is also greater than its 'labour alone' counterpart, equation (3.12).

31. The line, *BB*, shows the relationship between the expression for the first-order condition for a maximum associated with the present value rule (expression [3.2]) and n, *given the* values of R, w_0, G and g. The greater is the value of R, the smaller is the value of A, for *given* values of n, and, therefore, the *greater* is the value of (3.2) (ignoring the other terms in the denominator of [3.2]). Therefore, *BB* will be higher at each value of n, the greater is R, and the intercept of *BB* with *AA* will move to the *left*, implying that a *less* capital-intensive technique will be chosen. Suppose that R is so great that only one technique has a present value of zero, that is $R=\rho$ for this technique, and all the others have *negative* present values. If the *BB* line corresponding to this R is drawn (it is the line, $B'B'$, in Fig. 9), it will intercept *AA* to the left of any of the other *BB* lines associated with lower R's and, therefore, with more than one technique having a positive present value. This is the alternative explanation of why the internal rate of return rule results in the choice of a *less* capital-intensive technique than the present value rule (see n. 18).

32. The writer is indebted to Graham Pyatt for this point. These results can be shown as follows: Let $\bar{I}$ be the fixed amount of investment expenditure and suppose that factor and product prices, and the inputs per unit of output of each technique, are independent of the scale of operations (see n. 8). The pay-off period criterion now requires the investment of I in the technique with the greatest expected net receipts for the pay-off period, subject to the constraint that they at least equal

$\bar{I}$. This may be written as: choose the technique for which:

$$U\{=(p_0B'-w_0lA')x'\}=max. \tag{4.1a}$$

subject to $U \geqq \bar{I}$ where $x' = \dfrac{\bar{I}}{I}$.

The first-order condition for (4.1a) to be a maximum is:

$$-\frac{\partial l}{\partial I}=\left(\frac{p_0B'-w_0A'}{I}\right)\left(\frac{1}{w_0A'}\right) \tag{4.2a}$$

As $(p_0B'-w_0'lA')\geqq I$ (otherwise no technique will be chosen),

$$\frac{p_0B'-w_0lA'}{I}\geqq 1.$$

and

$$(4.2a) \geqq (3.4)\left(-\frac{\partial l}{\partial I}\leqq\frac{1}{w_0A'}\right).$$

the corresponding condition for satisfying the pay-off period criterion with a given level of output. It follows that a *less* capital-intensive technique will be chosen when investment expenditure rather than output is *fixed*. Similarity, *if* the present value rule is interpreted as an instruction to choose that technique, the *present value* of the expected net receipts of which exceeds $\bar{I}$ by the greatest amount, then, again, a *less* capital-intensive technique than that indicated by the analysis of this paper will be chosen. The first-order condition for a maximum in this case is:

$$-\frac{\partial l}{\partial I}=\left(\frac{p_0B-w_0lA}{I}\right)\left(\frac{1}{w_0A-\dfrac{\partial n}{\partial l}\left(p_0\dfrac{\partial B}{\partial n}-w_0l\dfrac{\partial A}{\partial n}\right)}\right) \tag{4.3a}$$

Because $p_0B-w_0lA\geqq I$ (otherwise no technique will be chosen). $\dfrac{p_0B-w_0lA}{I}\geqq 1$ and $(4.5a)\geqq(3.2)$ (for the case of $x=1$ and remembering that l and I are inputs per unit of output).

33. The writer has analysed the impact on the ordering of the capital-intensities associated with rules 1, 3 and 4 of taxation and investment incentives in 'Investment-Decision Criteria, Investment Incentives and the Choice of Techniques', *Economic Journal* LXXVIII (March, 1968), 77–95. While the capital-intensities associated with each rule change as between the *pre-tax* and *post-tax* situations, the *orderings* of the rules do not seem to be affected.

7 Some Cambridge Controversies in the Theory of Capital*[1]

1. MALLEABILITY, FOSSILS AND TECHNICAL PROGRESS

1.1 To begin at the beginning. In 1953 Joan Robinson wrote 'The Production Function and the Theory of Capital' [85], in which she made a number of specific complaints about the state of economic theory and the state of some economic theorists, namely, the latter-day neo-classicals, whose headquarters are now Cambridge, Mass.[2] The response was many articles (some sympathetic, some critical), a number of books (including one of her own [86]) and several new strands of economic analysis. The controversies still rage and judging from one of the more recent exchanges (see [103, 83, 94, 56, 104]), the contestants are as cross with one another as ever and as far away from agreement, even to the extent that one side argues that the other does not know what is being discussed (see, for example, [83, 104]). Part of the trouble is that many of the participants started their working lives on this side of the recent revolution in analytical techniques which has occurred in the teaching of economics, especially in America, so that the possibilities of communicating to practitioners outside the charmed circle of those whose staple diet is the *Review of Economic Studies* or the *International Economic Review* are steadily diminishing. And there are ideological reasons as well. Yet the need for a poet to explain to other poets what is going on is as real as ever because important issues—growth, distribution, accumulation—are being discussed. The aim of this essay is to review the puzzles which were thrown up by Joan Robinson's article and related work—for

* With apologies to Harry Johnson

example, that by Sraffa [117]—and to outline the main streams which have developed from them. Sraffa's *Production of Commodities by Means of Commodities* had an incredibly long gestation period (see the preface to [117]) and Joan Robinson in particular acknowledges her indebtedness, for the development of her own analysis and views, to the hints of what was to come contained in Sraffa's introduction to the volumes of Ricardo's works and correspondence [116].

1.2 Joan Robinson's article was written near the start of the post-war revival of interest in the problems of economic growth and the pattern of income distribution over time. This interest was partly in response to real problems of the post-war era in both developing and developed countries. The great bulk of the modern work in the theory of capital, though, is placed in the context of the analysis of advanced industrial societies, usually capitalist but sometimes treated as socialist.

1.3 Joan Robinson's first complaint related to the fuzzy nature of the capital variable in the aggregate production function, the concept of which, she argued, was used by the neoclassicals to explain the distribution of income between profit-earners and wage-earners in capitalist economies, taking as given the stocks of labour and capital and the knowledge of how one could be substituted for the other, so that their respective marginal productivities were known. She argued that this way of looking at things directed interest away from the forces that determined the growth of capital and labour and how technical progress affected growth, accumulation and income shares. (Her own interest in capital theory was in order to analyse what she regarded as a secondary factor in the list of factors which explained growth and distribution over time; namely, the role of the choice of techniques of production in the investment decision. The main propositions of [86] are established in a model in which there is only one technique of production; see also [124, 47, 35]).[3]

1.4 The first puzzle is to find a unit in which capital may be measured as a *number* (i.e. an index), which is independent of relative prices and distribution, so that it may be inserted in a production function where along with labour, also suitably measured, it may explain the level of national output. Furthermore, in a perfectly competitive economy in which there is perfect foresight (either in fact or for convenience of measurement; see [19]), this unit must be such that the partial derivative of output with respect to capital equals the reward to capital and the corresponding partial derivative of output with respect to labour equals the wage of labour. *If* such a unit can be found, two birds may be killed with one stone; for we may then analyse a system of production in which capital—produced means of production—is an aid to labour, a feature of *any* advanced industrial society, and, simultaneously, we may analyse distribution in a *capitalist* economy in which the institutions are such that property in *value* capital means that its owners share in the distribution of the national income by receiving profits on their invested capital, *where the amount of these profits is related to the technical characteristics of the system of production.* That capital is meant to be measured in such a unit and to serve these two purposes is made explicit, for example, in Champernowne's comment [19] on Joan Robinson's original article and in the appendix to Swan's 1956 article [122].[4]

1.5 Joan Robinson has been concerned to deny that such a unit may be found even in the conditions of a stationary state. The basic reason is that it is impossible to conceive of a quantity of capital in general, the value of which is independent of the rates of interest (or, interchangeably, profit, given the present assumptions) and wages. Yet such independence is necessary if we are to construct an iso-product curve showing the different quantities of labour and capital which produce a given level of national output (or, as is more usual in the theory of economic growth, if we are to construct a unique relationship between national output per man employed and capital per man employed [for any level of *total* national output]; that is, the neoclassical production function, see [106, 33]). The slope of this curve plays a key part in the determination of the relative prices of capital and labour and therefore of factor rewards. However, the curve cannot be constructed and its slope measured unless the prices which it is intended to determine are known beforehand; moreover, because the value of the same physical capital and the slope of the iso-product curve vary with the rates chosen, the construction is unacceptable. Joan Robinson therefore proposed to measure capital in terms of labour time; sets of equipment with known productive capacities (when combined with given amounts of labour) were to be valued in terms of the labour time required to produce them compounded at various given rates of interest. Thus the same sets of equipment would have different values for each rate of profit and different sets would have different values at the same rate of interest. Which set of equipment would actually be used in given *equilibrium* situations may be found by supposing the wage rate to be given and finding the highest rate of profit and therefore set (or sets) of equipment consistent with this wage rate.

1.6 Equilibrium is defined by Joan Robinson [85] as a situation in which expectations are fulfilled so that a given rate of profit has long been ruling and is expected to continue to rule in the future. In such a situation, a given item of capital equipment has the same value whether it be valued at its expected future earnings, discounted back to the present at the ruling rate of profit, or as the work done in order to produce it, cumulated forward to the present at the ruling rate of profit,

i.e.,
$$K = wL_g(1 + r)^t = \frac{O - wL_c}{r} \qquad (1.1)$$

where:

- K = *capital measured in terms of composite commodities;*
- w = *wage rate in terms of commodities;*
- r = *rate of profit;*
- L_g = *input of labour required to produce a unit of equipment t periods ago, where t is the gestation period of investment;*
- O = *output of commodities when L_c men work with a unit of equipment (which is assumed to last for ever).*

Then capital in terms of labour time (K_L) is:

$$K_L = \frac{K}{w} = L_g(1 + r)^t \qquad (1.2)^5$$

Given L_g, K_L is a simple increasing function of r. If, now, all known techniques—equipment producing a final output of commodities—are ordered according to the sizes of their outputs per head (of a constant labour force) and each is 'costed up' at various rates of interest, and expressed as K_L per head, we may derive the *real factor ratio*—the set of equilibrium relationships between output per head, capital in terms of labour time (or 'real capital', as Joan Robinson dubs it) and all conceivable wage rates. Corresponding to each equipment will be the relationship,

$$O = wL_c + rwL_g(1 + r)^t \tag{1.3}$$

so that:

$$w = \frac{O}{L_c + rL_g(1 + r)^t} \tag{1.3a}$$

For any given $w(\leq O/L_c = w_{\max}$, when $r = O$ and is output per head), we find the highest r associated with this w and this equipment. We repeat this process for all equipments, w's and r's and then plot the relationship between real capital and output per head, assuming that competition will lead entrepreneurs to choose those equipments with the highest possible r, given the level of w. This is Joan Robinson's version of the production function. Points on it should be regarded as positions of long-period *stationary* equilibrium which may be compared one with another since capital and output are all measured in units which allow corresponding comparisons. However, movements up and along it may *not* be regarded as processes occurring in historical time, the results of actual accumulation, rises in wage rates and falls in profit rates. Moreover, neither the wage rate nor the reward to capital can be obtained by suitable partial differentiation of the factor-ratio relationship.

1.7 Champernowne [19] accepted the logic of this approach, but objected to the possibility that the same physical capital may have a different value in two situations because it was associated with a different set of equilibrium rates of wages and profits. He felt it offended against the Gertrude Stein dictum (also Solow's, see [105]) that a spade is a spade is a spade. This objection may be valid from the point of view of the theory of production, but it does not hold for capital viewed as property. There is a real difference between the two situations, as far as the distributive shares are concerned, and *value* capital should reflect this. He also felt it would be convenient to have a measure of capital such that the rewards to labour and capital could be obtained by partial differentiation of the relationship between output on the one hand and capital (so measured) and labour on the other. He provided such a measure in a chain index, whereby the usual concave relationship between output per head of a constant labour force and capital could be established, *provided that any one technique having been the most or the equi-most profitable technique at a given rate or range of interest rates could never appear again at another rate or range of rates.*[6]

1.8 Consider an economy (or, rather, a series of possible stationary states) in which the given state of knowledge may be represented by three possible techniques (1, 2 and 3) requiring the investment of a certain amount of labour for certain lengths of time in order to produce the respective equipments; these, in turn, in conjunction with their respective labour forces produce certain amounts of final goods per head. (To avoid index-number problems, let them be one composite good.) Each technique exhibits constant returns to scale, a vital assumption. In Figure 1, we plot the various wage-profit rate trade-offs corresponding to each technique (their respective equations, 1.3a, are above).[7] The w–r trade-off of technique 1 intersects that of technique 2 at P_{12}, and

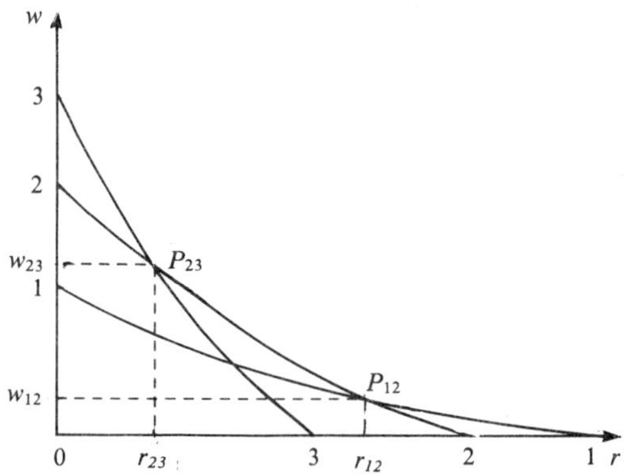

Figure 1

that of technique 2 intersects that of technique 3 at P_{23} (Fig. 1). Suppose that at P_{12}, where techniques 1 and 2 are equi-profitable (at wage rate w_{12}, profit rate r_{12}), the ratio of their capital values in terms of commodities, as given by their respective equations (1.1), is 3 : 10; suppose, further, that at P_{23} the corresponding ratio for the capital values of 2 to 3 is 2 : 3. Then the chain index of capital, whereby consecutive pairs of techniques are comparable one with another, is 3, 10, $10 \cdot \frac{3}{2} (= 15)$, ... This series of index numbers shows changes in the 'quantity' of capital after the effects of different wage and interest rates have been removed. Output may now be expressed as a unique function of labour and capital, so measured, and the rewards of the factors of production correspond to the partial derivatives of the appropriate branches of this function. The partial derivative of output with respect to labour is equal to the wage rate in terms of commodities; the partial derivative of output with respect to capital must equal the rate of profit multiplied by the 'price' of capital,[8] since the chain index has removed, as it were, the 'quantity' of capital from the coefficient of capital term (see [122]). The chain-index method depends on *knowing* the rate of profit (or wage rate) and calculating a price of output which equals the unit cost of producing it. It is therefore not a measure which is independent of prices and distribution.

1.9 In Swan's growth model, capital-labour ratios need to change considerably as accumulation occurs over time, in order that stable equilibrium capital-output ratios may be established following a change in other parameters; for example, the saving ratio. Moreover, he uses a Cobb-Douglas production function and assumes perfect competition, saving determines investment, constant returns to scale and full employment so that the wage of labour equals its marginal product and the rate of profit on capital equals its marginal product. In a 'back foremost' procedure he spells out in the appendix the assumptions that would justify this procedure, the scarecrow that would keep off both 'the index number birds and Joan Robinson herself'. His first line of defence is to suppose that capital consists of meccano sets which can be costlessly and timelessly transformed into any desired form, as given by the latest booklet of instructions (so incorporating technical progress), in order to cooperate with labour in response to the pull of changes in relative factor prices. The relative prices of products (including meccano sets) *never change* no matter how rates of wages, rents and profits do. In this way, aggregation of heterogeneous items of capital, both as a cross-section and over time, where they are both 'infinitely durable and instantaneously adaptable', is possible in terms of their own technical unit, and 'the basic model of (his) text could be rigorously established in a form which deceived nobody'—an answer which proceeds by abolishing the question. This is perhaps the first and certainly the clearest statement of the notorious malleability assumption which underlies many neoclassical growth models (see, for example, [122] and [65]). By measuring capital in terms of its technical unit (and by assuming that the quantity of capital in terms of this unit is uniquely associated with, say, the annual flow of services from it, measured in machine years), it is in the appropriate form for inclusion in a production function viewed as an engineering description of the flow of output which may be expected from the input of certain *flows* of man and machine years. Of course, the marginal product of capital, so measured, is the rate of profit multiplied by the price of the technical unit of capital in terms of product. But if this price does not change when accumulation occurs, as Swan assumes, capital may also be measured in *value* units, in which case its marginal product equals the rate of profit. Thus, *in equilibrium*, $\delta Q/\delta k = rp$, while $\delta Q/p\delta k = r$, where Q = product, k = capital measured in terms of its technical unit, and r = the rate of profit.[9]

1.10 The neoclassical procedure can be regarded as an examination of virtual displacements around an equilibrium point, so that any relative price changes may be ignored, and capital measured in terms of 'an equilibrium dollar's worth'. The trouble is that when either comparisons are made between different economies with different wage and profit rates and factor endowments—'structural comparisons in the large'—or, far worse, when accumulation is analysed, these equilibrium points with all their accompanying rates of change cannot be extended into visible curves associated with the same equilibrium values—an enormous revaluation of existing capital stocks occurs whenever an *actual* change, no matter how small, is contemplated. Hence the need for either meccano sets (and the accompanying unacceptable assumptions of perfectly timeless and costless malleability) or the resort to a chain index, as proposed by Champernowne, which both he and Swan argue also allows an analysis of *slow* accumulation (and, in Champernowne's case, without technical progress). The operative word is *slow* so that it takes a long time to pass between points which are far apart, and the conditions necessary for equilibrium at each point have a 'reasonable' chance of being established as the economy passes from one point to another. This particular act of faith has been a feature of many subsequent growth models constructed by true neoclassical believers, see, for example, [65].

1.11 The use of the malleability assumption and a simple marginal productivity theory of distribution underlies the early post-war work on aggregate production functions and technical progress: the attempts to sort out from actual statistics the increases in output per man which are due to technical progress; (i.e. shifts of an aggregate production function), from those which are due to capital deepening (i.e., movements along a given production function). We use Solow's famous 1957 article [106] to illustrate the approach. Solow assumed a constant-returns-to-scale aggregate production function[10] and competitive conditions so that paying factors their marginal products exhausted the total product, which consisted of a one all-purpose commodity. Technical progress was neutral and completely disembodied, i.e., left all factors unaffected, so that marginal rates of substitution at given factor ratios were unchanged. All capital goods were treated alike, whether they were newly created and incorporated the latest advances in technical knowledge (and the pull of expected changes in relative factor prices), or whether they were the fossils inherited from the past, previous year's investments which in fact would be expected to reflect the *then* prevailing technical conditions, expectations and relative factor prices. It was *as if* we were in Swan's world where, at any moment of time, all existing capital goods could be costlessly and timelessly taken to pieces and, using the latest booklet of instructions as our guide, changed into the latest cost-minimizing form as indicated by expectations of future product prices and relative factor prices. (Indeed, the expectations themselves must be a mirror image of present happenings.)

1.12 With a production function and technical progress of this nature, it is almost inevitable that 'technical progress' will explain most of the growth in output per man. We write the production function as

$$Q = A(t) f(K, L) \tag{1.4}$$

where Q, K and L are measured in appropriate physical units and $A(t)$ is a shift factor which is a function of time and reflects the pull of all the forces of technical change.

With some manipulation we obtain:

$$\frac{dQ}{dt}\cdot\frac{1}{Q}-\frac{dL}{dt}\cdot\frac{1}{L}=\frac{dA}{dt}\cdot\frac{1}{A}\cdot + w_k\left\{\frac{dK}{dt}\cdot\frac{1}{K}-\frac{dL}{dt}\cdot\frac{1}{L}\right\} \tag{1.5}$$

where w_k ($=(\delta Q/\delta K)(K/Q)$) is the share of capital in the national output, *assuming capital to be paid its marginal product.*

Thus the rate of growth of output per head is shown to be a function of the rate of growth of the shift factor ('technical progress') and the rate of growth of capital per man ('deepening') weighted by capital's share in the national ouput. To estimate $(dA/dt)\ 1/A$ we only have to obtain statistics on

$$\frac{dQ}{dt}\cdot\frac{1}{Q}-\frac{dL}{dt}\cdot\frac{1}{L},\ w_k$$

and

$$\frac{dK}{dt}\cdot\frac{1}{K}-\frac{dL}{dt}\cdot\frac{1}{L}.$$

As

$$\frac{dQ}{dt}\cdot\frac{1}{Q}-\frac{dL}{dt}\cdot\frac{1}{L}$$

grows at an order of 2–3 per cent per annum and as w_k is of the order of 1/4 to 1/3, there must be an enormous rate of growth of $(dK/dt)\cdot 1/K$ relative to $(dL/dt)\cdot 1/L$ in order that capital accumulation (and deepening) explain much of the observed growth in output per head. It is therefore no surprise that Solow found (with Hogan's arithmetic help, see [44]) that 90 per cent of the rise in output per head in the United States over the period 1909–49 was due to $(dA/dt)\cdot 1/A$. He then used his estimates of $(dA/dt)\cdot 1/A$ to remove, as it were, the 'effects' of technical progress from the annual series of output per head and this, with his assumption of neutral technical progress, allowed him to estimate an aggregate production function where the effects of deepening on the rise in output per head could be shown. Solow in fact obtained mild curvature. He regarded the analysis as an exercise in empirical aggregation, claimed no rigorous justification for his procedures (though Samuelson later attempted to provide one, see [101] and section 3 below) and regarded any errors as specification errors which ought to be investigated rather than as sins against the Holy Ghost.

1.13 Another famous example where malleability, perfect competition, marginal productivity, disembodied technical progress and constant returns to scale are crucial assumptions is the CES production function which made its debut to a wide audience in an article published in 1961 by Arrow, Chenery, Minhas and Solow [1] (see, also, [70]). The particular empirical findings which led to its debut were the close associations, as confirmed by the appropriate regressions, between the logarithms of labour productivity and money-wage rates in the *same* industries in *different* countries. These observations were treated *as if* they came from a production function characterized by disembodied technical progress and *ex post* variability of factors so that, at any moment of time, the machines in the capital stock could be treated *as if* they had been moulded into the form of the most up-to-date machines, namely, those which would be chosen from the various possibilities currently existing by cost-minimising, profit-maximising, static expectations entrepreneurs in the various countries. With these assumptions, the regression coefficients were shown to be estimates of the elasticity of substitution between capital and labour, were usually less than one and varied as between industries. Many other theoretical and empirical findings were also reported and a considerable new literature was born as a result—a quite fecund debut, in fact.

1.14 The malleability assumption has been removed from the analysis of neoclassical growth models as the embodiment hypothesis with regard to technical progress has replaced the disembodied view. Both patriotism and judgment lead me to select the late W. E. G. Salter's work [96, 97, 98, 99] (which was originally developed in Cambridge, England) as one of the finest—and earliest—examples of the embodiment hypothesis and the attempt to get away from capital measurement puzzles, while, at the same time, recognising the importance of distinguishing between *ex ante* and *ex post* substitutability, the heterogeneity of capital goods, and the distinction between comparisons and processes. Salter accepted Joan Robinson's view that the production function is relevant only in an *ex ante* sense when investment decisions are being made, so that only the margin of the capital stock is affected, both by the additions which are made and by the scrapping of existing machines. The neoclassical assumptions of substitutability, cost-minimisation, and profit-maximisation now relate to the choice from the set of the 'best-practice' techniques available—the *ex ante* production function—of that technique which will minimise costs and maximise profits in the sense of maximising the present value of expected receipts with given (expected) wage rates and profit rates. It comes as no surprise that, in this aspect of the investment decision, the technique which is chosen is that for which the marginal rate of substitution of labour for investment (i.e., the ratio of the respective marginal products) equals the ratio of the factor prices.

1.15 Consider the simplest case in which all investment goods associated with the *ex ante* production function are expected to last for the same length of time and wages and product prices are expected to be constant. The *ex ante* production function, if we assume constant returns to scale and continuity,[11] may be written as:

$$l = f(k) \qquad (1.7),$$

where $f'(k) > 0$, $f''(k) < 0$, and l = labour input per unit of output, and k = investment input per unit of output.

The present value of each 'best-practice' technique per unit of output (V) is:

$$V = \{1 - wf(k)\}A - k$$

where $A = \{(1+r)^n - 1\}/r(1+r)^n$ and r = rate of interest used as the discount factor; that is, the present value of the stream of one dollar per year for n years.

To choose the technique with the highest present value find the condition for which:

$$\frac{\delta V}{\delta k} = -wAf'(k) - 1 = 0.$$

It is:

$$f'(k) = -\frac{A'}{w} \qquad (1.8),$$

where

$$A' = \frac{1}{A}.$$

But A'/w is the ratio of factor prices (for the expected payment on investment each year will be $A'k$) and $f'(k)$ is the slope of the *ex ante* production function.[12] Of course, once we depart from the simple assumptions that all machines have the same length of life and that wages and prices are expected to remain constant (i.e. static expectations), these simple results no longer hold; see, for example, [39, 40, 64].

1.16 With the embodied view of technical progress, the capital stock consists at any moment of time of layers of fossils, or vintages, each set representing the amount of gross investment and the choice of technique under the pull of expected relative factor prices and demand conditions of the time when the investment was made. There are, on this view, *ex ante* substitution possibilities—entrepreneurs have to decide where on the $f(k)$ function they wish to be—but not necessarily *ex post* possibilities. The amount of new investment which is done and the total amount and numbers of vintages that are in use are determined, at the industry level, by demand and supply conditions which allow output to be expanded until the price of the product is such that only the normal rate of profit is expected to be earned on new vintages, and by the condition that only vintages with positive to zero quasi-rents are kept working. The wage level (which is rising over time) therefore determines the scrapping margin in each industry and in the economy as a whole, see [108, 109, 5]. In this way accumulation, technical progress and productivity changes may be analysed as historical processes without any need to measure the capital stock as such, see [111].

1.17 In one paper [107], Solow accepted the embodiment hypothesis but maintained *ex ante* substitution possibilities on existing vintages. Adopting the neoclassical view that full employment is either automatically assured in the short run or contrived by an all-wise government (see [65, 92]), the available labour supply is allocated at each point of time over the existing vintages in such a way that the marginal product of labour on each vintage is the same and equals the overall wage-rate, and output is maximised. Solow repeated again his measurement of technical progress exercise, but this time the pace of investment affects, in a more complex way, the rate at which average productivity improves. He also developed a one-number value measure of the vintage capital stock which depended crucially on the assumption of realised expectations. In a later paper [111], Solow, Tobin, von Weizsäcker and Yaari analysed the case of 'quickening'—that in which there is only one viable 'best practice' technique at any moment of time, and in which there are no *ex post* substitution possibilities. In this model, no use is made of a generalised capital concept, competitive conditions are assumed, and three sorts of technical progress—purely capital-augmenting (i.e. the productivity of capital but not of labour rises), purely labour-augmenting (i.e. the exact opposite of capital-augmenting) and Hicks' neutral (i.e. factor productivities grow at the same rate), and two types of economy—neoclassical, where short-run full employment of labour is automatically assured, and Keynesian, where effective demand determines output—are examined. In both economies, neoclassical modes of analysis are used; quasi-rents on vintages are shown to equal their marginal products and the wage rate to equal the marginal product (equals the average product) of the vintage on the margin of scrapping.

1.18 There are two key features of this model, the significance of which will become clear in the section on the double-switching debate. First, it is a *one* all-purpose commodity model. Second, the capital-augmenting case is dismissed as relatively uninteresting, even though capital-augmenting technical progress has been shown to be the necessary and sufficient condition for the rigorous aggregation of heterogeneous capital goods into one figure to be used in a neoclassical production function in a situation in which there are vintages and embodied technical progress, see [25, 29, 123]. (Solow earlier had spelt out the conditions for aggregation in a simple two malleable capital goods, no technical progress world [105]—a condition akin to the present one in that the rate of substitution of one capital good for another had to be independent of the amount of labour used with each.) Neoclassical vintage models reached their finest hour (to date) in Bliss's recent paper [9] in which there is *ex ante* substitution along the *ex ante* production function but no *ex post* possibilities. It is a rigorous examination of Salter's and Johansen's earlier models [97, 98, 45], and emphasises that there may *not* be a unique choice of technique under competitive profit-maximising assumptions, once very simple factor price expectations are departed from, and the expected *economic* lives of the 'best-practice' techniques differ (see also [19, 96] and, especially, [4], where it is shown that Bliss's result holds *only* if the elasticity of substitution on the *ex ante* production function is greater than unity).

1.19 The embodiment hypothesis has also been used, especially by Solow, to discuss the process of 'deepening' in a world of non-malleable capital goods and therefore no possibility of *ex post* substitution, see [108, 109, 87, 88, 89]. The purpose of these exercises was twofold; first, to show that neoclassical methods could be used and neoclassical results, especially those relating to factor productivities and factor rewards, obtained in such a world; second, to argue that observations taken from *short-run* production functions in which the possibilities of substitution are limited or nil can provide data for good estimates of long-run substitution possibilities as the types of machines installed change in response to changes in factor prices over 'time'; that is, in the long period. The production function which is estimated is a series of isolated islands of long-period equilibria. It is stressed that this is a pure theory of production—the conditions under which short-run full employment output will in fact be demanded are not investigated. Constant returns to scale, competitive conditions and static factor price expectations rule. Specific capital goods require fixed complementary amounts of labour to man them (though this does not stop, at crucial poins, the use of arguments which depend on the ability to employ *one* more man, presumably because machines are divisible; see also [111]), and a simple operating and scrapping rule of positive to zero quasi-rents respectively is used. An approach which is similar in some respects but which is designed for a different purpose, namely, to analyse the development, through accumulation, of an economy from the handicraft industry stage to mechanised capital-intensive industries, industry by industry, is used by Bensusan-Butt [5]. Again factor prices and competition are the means by which this occurs and a slowly falling rate of profit, the values of which are determined within the system plays a key role. Unless there is a shortage of land, the real wage rises as productivity in each industry, in turn, rises.

1.20 A number of criticisms of both malleable capital and vintage models, whether they serve entirely theoretical purposes or are the theoretical scaffolding for econometric exercises, have been made. To my mind, the most damning—and it applies to the whole structure of neoclassical thought—stems from Sraffa's 1960 book [117] and is most conveniently dealt with in section 3 on double-switching. Suffice it to say here that it concerns a view of economic life and especially of the production process, price formation and income distribution which is more akin to that taken by the classical economists—Smith, Ricardo, Marx—than by the neoclassicals—Jevons, Wicksteed, Marshall (though his long-run normal rate of profits is classical) and the present group of 'modern theorists' at M.I.T., *et al.*[13] The second strand of criticism is especially associated with the work of Kaldor (see [51, 52, 53, 54, 55, 56]) and it relates to a denial of the usefulness of the assumptions of perfect competition (as opposed to *some* competition), constant returns to scale, *static* expectations and perfect foresight, and marginal and maximising explanations of the choice of technique and factor rewards. For Kaldor, even the notion of a cost-minimising choice of technique in a vintage model will not hold (see [55]), and he substitutes, instead, a pay-off period criterion. He has kept one strand of the vintage approach, namely, the scrapping rule associated with zero quasi-rents, though this is inconsistent with an assumption of an imperfectly competitive market structure (see [76]).[14] Kaldor also feels that a major contribution by Arrow—his work on learning by doing [2]—puts a shaft through the pure form of neoclassical analysis.

1.21 A third strand, whereby vintages themselves are the medium of criticism, relates to the use of CES aggregate production functions to estimate what in effect is the *ex ante* elasticity of substitution of capital for labour. It has been shown (see [3, 38]) that if the neoclassical game is played in every sense *except* that vintages are taken account of, biases of measurement both enter and cannot be adequately allowed for.

1.22 Finally, mention should be made of what, perhaps, is the most unkindest cut of all, namely, the work of Jorgenson and Griliches on overall factor productivity and technical change [32, 48]. Though neoclassical to their fingertips—they assume perfect competition and constant returns to scale, factors are paid marginal products and price ratios of commodities equal marginal rates of transformation—they argue that the finding that the bulk of the rise in output per man is due to 'technical progress' results from faulty measurement of the input services in the aggregate production function. Correcting for this, they advance the (refutable) hypothesis that the rise in total output is largely explained by the growth of total inputs and not by improvements in them. Their measure of the rate of growth of total factor productivity (which on their hypothesis should be approximately zero) is a quantum index of growth in outputs, each weighted by its value share in total output, *less* a similar index of the rates of growth of input services, similarly weighted. A shift in the aggregate production function occurs if this rate is greater than zero; otherwise all growth is due to movements along a given production function (in *n* dimensional space).

1.23 The estimates of capital services (which in principle should be, say, machine hours) have to be done by chains of inference and the use of assumptions, the most dubious of which are that competitive producer equilibrium conditions were satisfied and that, in effect, all machines worked to the same proportion of their capacities (devastatingly criticised by Denison, [24]). The price of the capital service of each good is the price of each investment good multiplied by the rate of return on *all* capital (to wit, the non-wage share of value added inclusive of capital gains divided by the value of accumulated capital stocks) plus the rate of depreciation and an adjustment for any capital gains on each capital good—a statistical reflection of neoclassical theory as outlined by Champernowne [19] and Swan [122]. This approach makes explicit the important point that flows of services, not stocks of factors, produce output, a point with which no one would disagree. Whether they would accept the method of aggregation of the services is another matter. And the other assumptions which underlie the measurement only have to be read to be disbelieved, or so it seems to me. Lydall [62] has developed a measure of technical progress which is similar to that used by Jorgenson and Griliches but which is statistically tractable and does not depend on assumptions about the natures of producer equilibrium and market structures.

1.24 We have not heard the last of vintage models, the measurement of technical progress nor, indeed, the malleability assumption, see, for example, [57], a paper in which productivity growth in Australia and Argentina are compared using Solow's one-commodity disembodied model. These assumptions have great analytical and mathematical convenience and the hold of them on econometric methodology is still fast. The reasons for this, apart from those already covered, are examined in the section on the rate of return on investment, which is the other main stream which flowed from Joan Robinson's orginal strictures against the production function approach and the impossibility of measuring capital outside worlds of stationary or growing equilibria—her fabulous but mythical Golden Ages [86].

2. SOLOW ON THE RATE OF RETURN: TEASE AND COUNTER-TEASE

2.1 Another offshoot of the criticisms of the use of the concept of malleable capital in the aggregate production function is the work on the social rate of return on investment, which is especially associated with Solow. His views are set out in the 1964 De Vries lectures [110] and in his contribution to the Dobb 'festschrift' [112]. These two sources and Joan Robinson's review article of the former [91] help to crystallise the nature of the approach and to highlight some of the causes of the controversy between Cambridge, Mass., and Cambridge, England.

2.2 Solow wished to analyse the empirical relationship between capital accumulation and economic growth in industrialised countries today. (His two examples are the United States and West Germany.) He argues that the appropriate (or only) theoretical tools are 'a modernised version of neoclassical or late-Wicksellian capital theory', and he starts by stating what he regards as still valid and viable in the theory. The key concept is the rate of return of investment. His own contribution is to introduce technical progress and to consider the relationship between saving and investment and the long-run growth of productive capacity.

2.3 Solow prefaces his analysis with a discussion of why there are recurring controversies in capital theory. He gives two reasons, one of which is ideological—the social function of providing an ideological justification for profit which in the nineteenth century was the non-Marxist backlash; the other reason is analytical—it's difficult. The first reason is not supposed to impugn in any way and by itself either the motives of the economists who provided it or the scientific validity of their doctrines ([110], p. 10). I suspect that here at least some participants in the debate would part company, as they would also over his view that the elegant showpiece of modern economics, the resource allocation implications of a system of prices or shadow prices, is free of ethical overtones (on this see, for example, [26]; [28], p. 162). To escape from the first reason for controversy, all that is necessary, according to Solow, 'is to draw a conceptual distinction between the imputed return to capital and the income of capitalists'. (As the baby said, 'Move over, bathwater, here I come'.) As a corollary of this view, Solow believes that, sometimes, the best way to understand capitalism is to think about socialism. And he goes on to argue that only someone who is naively identifying the many aspects of capitalistic production with one of them (he mentions the Austrians's 'time' as 'an inspired simplification' which did not come off) would believe that the theory could be summed up by defining something called 'capital' and calling the rate of interest the marginal product of 'it'.

2.4 As a self-confessed middlebrow, Solow sees the rate of return on investment as the link between highbrow capital theory—the micro-economic theory of resource allocation and prices which allows for the fact that commodities can be transformed into others over time and which is only complete when it also explains the distribution between factors—and low-brow theory, which is concerned with aggregation and approximation and relates to the empirical implications of saving and investment decisions. He classifies capital theories as either technocratic or descriptive; they are technocratic when planning and allocation questions (and so socialism) are discussed, descriptive when used in an explanation of the workings of capitalism. Finally, Solow warns us that, by dodging the ideological overtones, we may destroy the bridge that leads to descriptive analysis, especially distribution theory, and be left only with answers about the consequences, but not the causes of saving and investment decisions.

2.5 On this view, the central concept of capital theory should be the rate of return on investment; that is, capital theory should be about interest rates, not capital. This make for clarity, while concentrating on 'time' or 'capital' or the 'marginal productivity of capital' (or labour) makes for confusion. What, then, is the rate of return on investment? Consider a planned economy which has a stock of heterogeneous capital goods, produces a certain volume of one consumption good and is at full employment with its inputs efficiently allocated. Compare this situation with a possible neighbourhood efficient arrangement in which there is a little less consumption and therefore more capital goods. Now change over to the alternative arrangement by saving (i.e.

reducing consumption). This allows a one-period gain (the next) in consumption *over what it would have been*. Finally, suppose that in the period after the next the economy reaches the position that it intended to be at by that period anyway. That is, the economy over the three periods has decided on a consumption stream: $C_0 - h$, $C_1 + k$, C_2, . . . instead of one of: C_0, C_1, C_2, ... Then a natural definition of the one-period rate of return of investment (r_1) is:

$$r_1 = \frac{k-h}{h} = \frac{k}{h} - 1 \tag{2.1}$$

At the other extreme is the average rate of return in perpetuity whereby a reduction of consumption now (h) adds p per period extra consumption for ever over what it would have been otherwise, in which case,

$$r_\infty = \frac{p}{h} \tag{2.2}$$

In between these two, we may distinguish 2, 3, . . . , n-period average rates of return. Solow's measure is intimately associated with displacements from basic situations. In the nineteenth century these would have been stationary states from which small displacements were made. The modern equivalent is the balanced growth path.

2.6 Solow claims that calculating the rate of return requires no measure of the stock of capital, nor even necessarily a mention of it, though in some of his theoretical examples and in his empirical work he is unfaithful to himself. He also claims that neoclassical theory, in so far as it centres around the rate of return, can escape from the malleability assumption and 'can accommodate fixity of form and proportions both'. As an aside, but very much related to the malleability assumption, he comments that J. B. Clark's jelly assumption (see [101]) makes the analysis easier; it, moreover, contains the important kernel of truth that substitution possibilities are easier over longer periods of time even though at any moment of time, capital goods are highly specific and substitution possibilities *ex post* (if not *ex ante*), limited. This seems to me to be true only if we are considering the working out in *actual time* of the possibilities which exist at the *beginning* of a Marshallian long period, while not allowing anything to change, other than what was expected to do so at the start of the period. The application of results from this analysis to real world happenings is, therefore, suspect, as Salter [97, 98], for example, has so clearly shown.

2.7 Rates of return are calculated by Solow for two 'poles apart' models of planned economies, the first, a one-commodity model with a smooth, well-behaved constant-returns-to-scale production function, the second Worswick's stockade dictator version of Joan Robinson's one-technique model of accumulation [124]. One-period and perpetuity rates of return are obtained and these are shown, in the neoclassical case, to equal the *net* marginal product of capital.[15] The results in both models are then whipped over to market economies where the only possible outcome of competitive conditions for *both* models is that 'the rate of interest must equal the rate of return on investment'. And these results are offered as the answer to the important question, What is the pay-off to society from an extra bit of saving transformed efficiently into capital formation?

2.8 Joan Robinson [91] interpreted Solow's first lecture as an attempt to justify the marginal productivity theory of distribution and, in particular, the micro-economic proposition that in a competitive capitalist economy labour is paid its *full employment* marginal product. Whether this is so or not—and Solow certainly would deny it—Joan Robinson's argument highlights in a very simple way the heart of the controversy. Especially does it show the difficulties which must develop in post-Keynesian times, when some tackle distribution puzzles within the context of a *full employment* neoclassical model, while others are sceptical of the relevance of these models.[16]

2.9 To illustrate the controversy, consider a very simple one commodity (butter) model with a smooth, well-behaved constant returns-to-scale production function relating butter output to homogeneous labour and butter input. If this were a planned economy and full employment were attained, the wage rate (w_B) would bear the same proportion $(1 - \alpha)$ to the average product of labour (AP_f) as consumption (C) (total butter output less investment, i.e. butter set aside for the next period), does to the total output (B' or prime butter); that is:

$$w_B/AP_f = 1 - \alpha = \frac{(1-\alpha)B'}{B'} \left(= \frac{C}{Y}\right).$$

(Employment devoted to the production of butter for consumption would be $(1-\alpha)$ of the total full employment labour-supply as well.) All butter output produced would then be sold, supposing socialist workers to consume all that they earn and that managers are workers too. The marginal product of labour could be zero (capacity working of the existing stock, if we may momentarily leave the butter world) or equal to the average product (idle machines of the same quality) or it could be equal to the wage, if investment were the 'right' proportion of total output and we have returned to the butter world.

2.10 Now compare the planned economy with a capitalist market economy which has the same level of investment but pays a wage equal to the *full employment* marginal product of labour. Consider, first, a 'low' level of investment so that in the planned economy the real wage rate exceeds the full employment marginal product of labour. Then unless capitalists' consumption were such as to just fill in the gap between the total output produced and the expenditure from the wages bill plus butter put to stock for the next period, there will be unintended stocks, and unemployment will result as output is reduced until aggregate demand matches aggegate supply (Figs. 2a and 2b).

2.11 If investment were very 'large' so that in the socialist state, the wage rate was less than MP_f, in the capitalist economy there would be excess demand for butter and for labour. It is only when, given the consumption functions of the workers and the capitalists, the level of investment is such as to give full employment without excess demand for labour, that the wage rate equals the *full employment* marginal product of labour (and in the butter economy, the rate of profit—a ratio of butter to butter—equals the marginal product of the existing butter stock), see Figure 3. The analysis has been carried out in real terms but it is easy to repeat it with a money wage and price.[17] It brings out the emphasis on effective demand which the neo-Keynesians are

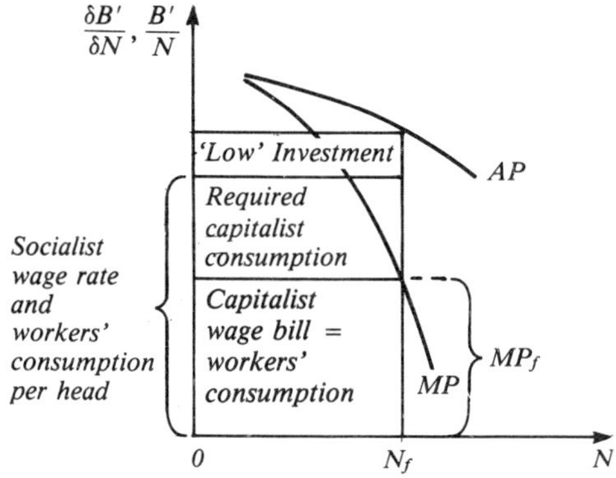

Figure 2a

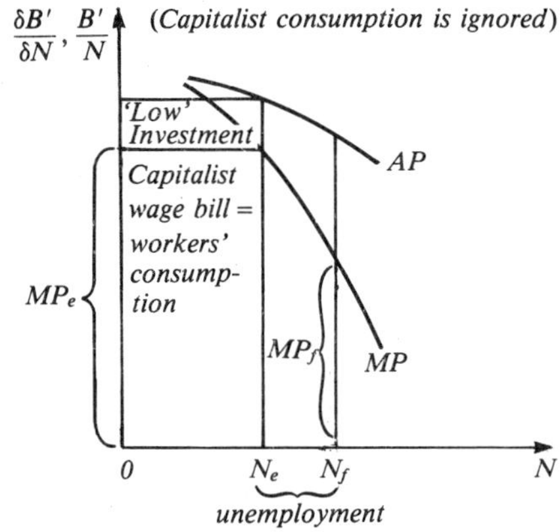

Figure 2b

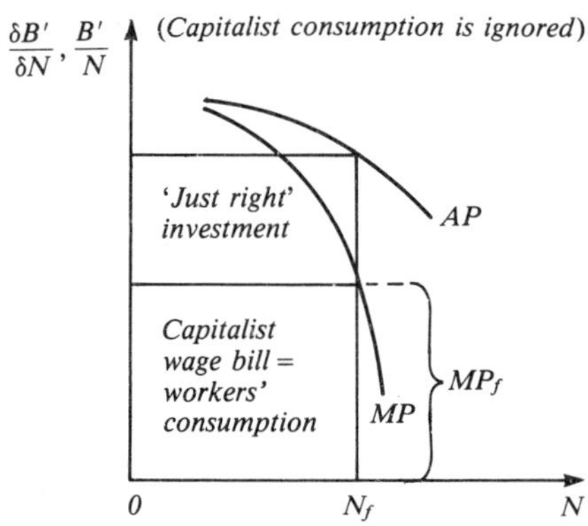

Figure 3

always conscious of but which tends to get lost sight of in the technocratic neoclassical approach to *distribution* theory (on this see also two earlier papers by Solow [108] and [109], and Joan Robinson's comments [90]). Of course, once the real wage is known, *with given technical conditions* and in a non-butter world, the rate of profit, relative prices, and the value of capital may be determined by calculating the 'Sraffa' prices of the system; see [117], Part I.

2.12 The average and marginal product curves in our diagrams are what Joan Robinson calls 'utilisation functions' (i.e. short-run production functions); they show the variations in average and marginal products which occur when varying levels of employment of labour are offered in the short run according to the level of effective demand and given a constant stock of butter capital. However, in a butter economy, they have the additional property that they may also be interpreted as the corresponding aspects of a constant-returns-to-scale production function which shows the average and marginal products associated with changes (due to investment) in the butter capital stock-labour *ratio, when labour is kept fully employed period by period.* (We would now measure B/N on the horizontal axis in Figures 2 and 3.).[18] In Figure 4, I use the *total* product variant of this approach to show that the one-period rate of return on investment in this world equals the marginal product of butter capital. (For simplicity, I assume a constant labour force and

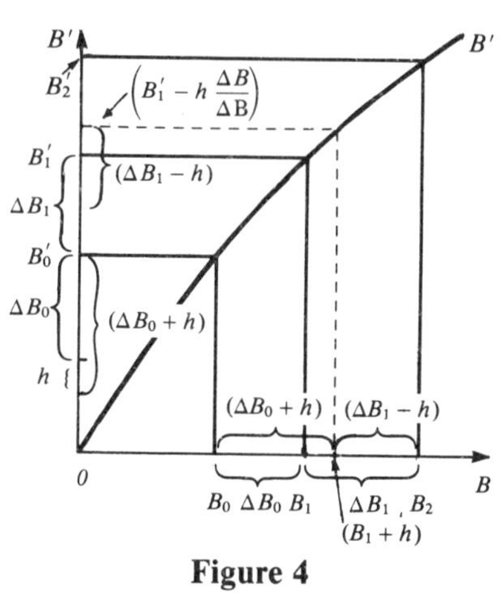

Figure 4

that butter lasts for ever.) A planned economy is examined in order to escape from short-run effective demand puzzles.

2.13 In Figure 4, B_0', B_1' and B_2' are prime butter outputs produced by N_f labour cooperating with butter capital stocks of B_0, B_1 and B_2 respectively in three succeeding periods. ΔB_0, the investment in period 0, establishes the butter capital stock of B_1 in period 1; similarly, ΔB_1 gets the stock to B_2 in period 2. If investment in period 0 were $\Delta B_0 + h$, the capital stock in period 1 would be $B_1 + h$ and total output would be $B_1' + h(\Delta B'/\Delta B)$, where $\Delta B'/\Delta B$ is the marginal product of butter in period 1. Investment in period 1 now need be only $\Delta B_1 - h$, in order that B_2 be the capital stock and B_2' the output, of period 2. The one-period rate of return is $r_1 = (k/h) - 1$ (see para. 2.5 above). We calculate k as follows: In period 1, in the first situation, the consumption of butter, C_1, is:

$$C_1 = B_1 - \Delta B_1 \qquad (2.3)$$

In the second situation, it is:

$$C_1' = B_1' + h\,\frac{\Delta B'}{\Delta B} - (\Delta B_1 - h) \qquad (2.4)$$

$$k = C_1' - C_1 = h\left(\frac{\Delta B'}{\Delta B} + 1\right) \qquad (2.5)$$

so that

$$r_1 = \frac{h\left(\dfrac{\Delta B'}{\Delta B} + 1\right)}{h} - 1 = \frac{\Delta B'}{\Delta B} \qquad (2.6)$$

2.14 Joan Robinson closes her comments on Solow's first lecture by arguing that in a competitive capitalist economy, *expected* rates of profit guide the invesement decisions of individual entrepreneurs and that there will be a Marshallian tendency for them to approach equality. (Presumably they guided the investment expenditure of the utilisation functions of the capitalist economies above.) The expected rate of profit, however, is of no interest to the planner, though the rate of return on investment is, while the latter is of no interest to the capitalist! This bait (which also was dangled by Dobb)[19] was too much for Solow to resist and is the subject of his paper in the Dobb 'festschrift' [112]. Using a Ricardo–Sraffa system with circulating capital, he shows that the rate of interest is an accurate measure of the social rate of return on investment, provided only that the economy is at full employment and uses competitive pricing, and that we are comparing one stationary state with another which has the same labour force, but uses, at the given rate of interest, a different, equiviable technique, namely, one that requires more circulating capital, commodity by commodity. Both stationary states are in long-run competitive equilibrium which implies that their net products are entirely consumption goods. In order for one economy to move (technocratically) from its technology to the other, consumption must be cut in one period (or for a number of periods in more complicated cases). Solow shows that the *extra* consumption per period obtained in perpetuity as a result of this move, when expressed in terms of the common set of prices at the *given* rate of interest and as a proportion of the consumption foregone, similarly measured, equals the rate of interest. This ratio, as we have seen, is Solow's measure of the social rate of return on investment in perpetuity. (In an unpublished paper, Nell [75] has produced counter examples which, he claims, conflict with Solow's demonstration, and has argued that the result depends upon choosing outputs suitably; see also [10].)

2.15 So far we have been discussing deepening, insofar as it is relevant for the rate of return. Now Solow adds his own contribution—the role of technical progress and its effects on the measurement of the rate of return. With technical progress occurring, capital accumulation and saving are twice blest; not only is society's productive capacity raised by saving because it provides more capital, but also because it now provides 'better' capital. This applies to the lot if technical progress is disembodied, and at the margin of the stock if it is embodied. Solow adjusts his measure of the rate of return for both types of technical progress. With disembodied technical progress (which is illustrated by Cobb-Douglas) the possibility that the rate of return—the *net* marginal product of capital at the level of technique ruling in period 1—will get indefinitely large emerges, unless capital deepening is occuring at the same time and at approximately the same rate.

2.16 As a digression Solow derives the factor price frontiers (see paras. 1.8 above and 3.9 below) for the Cobb-Douglas and Worswick cases and analyses the shifts which technical progress causes in these. The analysis is neat, but what is it supposed to teach us? The order of magnitude of the rise in real wages that may be expected if the rate of profit is kept constant while technical progress occurs? Then these neighbourhood islands of long-period equilibria, despite frequent changes in technique, hardly seem the appropriate tools to use (though the Phelps have tried them out [84].)

2.17 Solow's analysis of embodied technical progress uses a model in which both *ex post* and *ex ante* substitution are possible; he argues that something like this happens in a growing economy as one kind of capital good is replaced (slowly) by another. Evidently, for rate of return calculations, you get much the same answer from this as for the *ex ante* substitution, *ex post* none case. Expected obsolescence (absent, of course, in the disembodied case) reduces social and private rates of return below the corresponding marginal products of capital as ordinarily measured. Solow uses a production function with an effective stock of capital as one input—all existing profitable vintages are weighted by their respective productivities. This avoids the need to calculate the output contribution of each layer of 'fossils' in the stock.

2.18 This aggregate production function model is the basis for the empirical estimates given in Lecture 3 of rates of return in the United States and West Germany (East would perhaps have been more appropriate). This ingenious device allows technical progress to affect the rate of growth of output through the product of the rate of growth of the 'effective' capital stock and the elasticity of output with respect to 'capital' as estimated by econometrically fitting the (Cobb-Douglas) production function to the data of each economy. He finds social rates of return of the order of 15 to 20 per cent and comments, 'If the whole economy can be thought of as a bank capable of paying 15 to 20 per cent interest, then it would seem to be in society's interest to find ways of making somewhat larger deposits' ([110], p. 96). With this we could all agree, especially if in the American case it leads to full employment! But, again, his best intentions are not realised, and capital as well as the rate of return is mentioned.

3. A CHILD'S GUIDE TO THE DOUBLE-SWITCHING DEBATE

3.1 As we have seen, both sides of the debate have examined heterogeneous capital models in which any *one* technique of production does not allow substitution between factors (i.e. fixed input–output coefficients prevail), and proportions of factors may vary only by going over to another technique as a result of changing factor prices. The objects of these exercises differed as between the two groups. To the neo-Keynesians they represented an attack on the marginal method, an attack which has been led, in spirit anyway, by Sraffa who subtitled his book [117] *Prelude to a Critique of Economic Theory,* by which he meant marginal theory. To the other side, the object was to justify neoclassical marginalist procedures. A puzzle that arises is whether the stories associated with smooth, one-commodity malleable capital models can 'stand in' as analogies for comparisons using these more 'realistic' models.[20] The aggregate production function must now refer to the relationship between value capital and other variables within the whole set of techniques (though Bruno, Burmeister and Sheshinski [17] have recently argued that the term, production function, should be confined to the engineering aspects of *each* technique, which seems to me a fudge based on hindsight). If the neoclassical stories as told, for example, by Swan [122] and Solow [106] did in fact hold for heterogeneous capital models, this would be an enormous simplification which would be most helpful for econometric specification and economic theory alike; see [14, 15]. It is to this question that the double-switching debate is especially addressed.

3.2 The neoclassical tradition, like the Christian tradition, believes that profound truths can be told be way of parable. The neoclassical parables are intended to enlighten believers and non-believers concerning the forces which determine the distribution of income between profit-earners and wage-earners, the pattern of capital accumulation and economic growth over time, and the choice of the techniques of production associated with these developments. Four truths which, before the revelations of the false and true prophets in the course of the recent debate on double-switching, were thought to be established were:

(1) An association between lower rates of profit and higher values of capital per man employed;
(2) An association between lower rates of profit and higher capital-output ratios;
(3) An association between lower rates of profit and (through investment in more 'mechanised' or 'round-about methods of production') higher sustainable steady states of consumption per head (up to a maximum);
(4) that, in competitive conditions, the distribution of income between profit-earners and wage-earners can be explained by a knowledge of marginal products and factor supplies.[21]

3.3 I have avoided the temptation to write these as, for example, falling rates of profit lead to higher values of capital per head—a temptation which is not always avoided in the literature. Following Joan Robinson's stricture [85] that it is most important not to apply theorems obtained from the analysis of differences to situations of change (or, at least, to be aware of the act of faith involved in doing this), modern writers have usually been most careful to stress that their analysis is essentially the comparison of different equilibrium situations one with another and that they are not analysing processes.[22] Nevertheless, in their asides, they sometimes speak as if their results were applicable to a world of change and as if 'back of an envelope' excursions into the statistics can provide 'realistic' orders of magnitude to try out in their theorems.[23] Moreover, Samuelson's 1962 paper on the surrogate production function [101], which is a watershed on the way to the main debate, was written partly as a defence of the methodology and analysis used by Solow in his work on the aggregate production function and technological change [106] (see above, para. 1.11–1.14). One might also ask, what is the point of these exercises if they are *not* meant to throw some light on the second way of phrasing the propositions. Be that as it may, the outcome of the double-switching debate is to put a shaft through the above four propositions. Even as parables, they must be expunged from the Bible proper (or at least 1 to 3 must), though no doubt they will continue to be told in the commentaries and Sunday School lessons for a long time to come.

3.4 The phenomena of double-switching and capital-reversing were first noticed in the modern literature by Joan Robinson [85, 86], Champernowne [19, 21] and Sraffa [117] (but see the proviso in para. 1.1 above). Double-switching is essentially associated with the possibility that the same method of production may be the most profitable of a number of methods of production at more than one rate of profit (r), even though other methods are more profitable at values of r in between; capital-reversing is the value of capital moving in the *same* direction as the rate of interest. Both imply that the same physical capital goods will have more than one value, because a different real wage rate and set of relative prices will be associated with each rate of profit and the capital goods associated with the method have to be valued at their appropriate set of prices. Double-switching and capital-reversing may occur in an industry (Sraffa's example, [117], Ch. XII) and in an economy (the original cases discussed by Joan Robinson [85, 86] and Champernowne [19]). Levhari's article [59] claimed to show that, while the industry case was a possibility, the economy example was not.[24] This latter proposition was conclusively shown to be false (except under very special conditions, see [16, 119]) in a series of papers in the 1966 and 1967 issues of the *Quarterly Journal of Economics* [82, 60, 71, 16, 30, 102, 95].[25]

3.5 The analysis has been conducted in terms of equilibrium comparisons at different, arbitrarily given rates of profit, of Ricardo-Sraffa[26] systems in which labour and commodities are used to produce commodities, one commodity being produced by each activity or method of production. Suppose that there is more than one method available for producing directly or indirectly a commodity which will be in surplus and therefore form part of the net product of the year's production after account has been taken of the amount of commodities used up as means of production in the production process.[27] Suppose, further, that the forces of competition ensure that the same rates of profit and wages will be paid in all industries (notice that this implies *nothing* about what determines their actual sizes or the distribution of income). We assume that the method which makes possible the payment of the highest real wage rate at a given rate of profit will in fact be chosen.[28] Then the neoclassical parables lead us to believe that as we consider (arbitrarily) a lower and lower rate of profit, the methods which are associated with a higher and higher output per head will become eligible, that the value of capital per head and per unit of output will be greater and that the distribution of income can be obtained by multiplying the respective quantities of factors, labour and 'capital', by their marginal products which may be treated *as if* they were equal to the equilibrium real wage and rate of profit.

3.6 Indeed, it was exactly these stories which Samuelson told in his 1962 article [101]. He started with a heterogeneous capital model whereby there were many different ways of producing a consumption good which required different inputs of direct and indirect labour and therefore different inputs of the same good, *treated as a capital good,* into itself. (When producing itself, its form varied from method to method, so that we have in effect heterogeneous capital goods.) Taking each method in turn, he 'costed' them up at different rates of profit, in order to find the maximum equilibrium real wage rate that could be associated with each. The range of rates of profit is from zero to a maximum which is determined by the commodity's own rate of growth when the real wage rate is zero and radioactive depreciation is allowed for. (We ignore the latter in what follows.)

3.7 We may illustrate this procedure in the most general sense by using the general example given by Joan Robinson and Naqvi ([95], pp. 585–6). Consider the two activities, 1 and 2, each producing a quantity (gross output) of one commodity (X_1 and X_2 respectively) and using in its production the other commodity and direct labour.[29]

If we let commodity 1 be the *numéraire,* we may write the price equations for a given rate of profit (r) as:

$$(1 + r)(x_{11}X_1 + p_2x_{21}X_1) + wl_{01}X_1 = X_1 \qquad (3.1)$$

$$(1 + \mathrm{r})(x_{12}X_2 + p_2x_{22}X_2) + wl_{02}X_2 = p_2X_2 \qquad (3.2)$$

where x_{ij} is the input per unit of output of commodity i into commodity j ($i = 1, 2$). Equations (3.1) and (3.2) may be rearranged so that each forms an expression for p_2. Equating these expressions, we derive the expression for w as a function of r, as in equation (3.3).[30]

$$w = \frac{(x_{11}X_1x_{22}X_2 - x_{21}X_1x_{12}X_2)(1 + \mathrm{r})^2 - (X_2x_{11}X_1 + X_1x_{22}X_2)(1 + r) + X_1X_2}{(l_{02}X_2x_{21}X_1 - l_{01}X_1x_{22}X_2)(1 + r) + l_{01}X_1X_2} \qquad (3.3)$$

3.8 Expression (3.3) is the basic relationship of the analysis. In general, all that can be said of it is that the greater is w, the smaller is r.[31] (Nuti [77] has shown that if there are limitations to the choice of the length of gestation of a process, then under certain conditions not even the monotonicity of the relation between w and r is granted.) Joan Robinson and Naqvi (and other writers, see [14, 31, 42, 115]) have systematically examined the conditions under which (3.3) (which we may call the w—r relationship) is convex or concave to the origin, or a straight line (a very special but crucial case, as we see below). The w—r relationship is a straight line if, when $r = 0$, the ratio of the labour value of the means of production to the direct labour used in the production of commodity 1 is the same as the corresponding ratio associated with the production of commodity 2 and the time patterns of the inputs are uniform, so that the *relative* prices of the two commodities are independent of the rate of profit (even when it is positive). Students of Marx will prick up their ears here for this is, if you like, the pure labour theory of value case.[32]

3.9 Samuelson in fact made this assumption and, as a

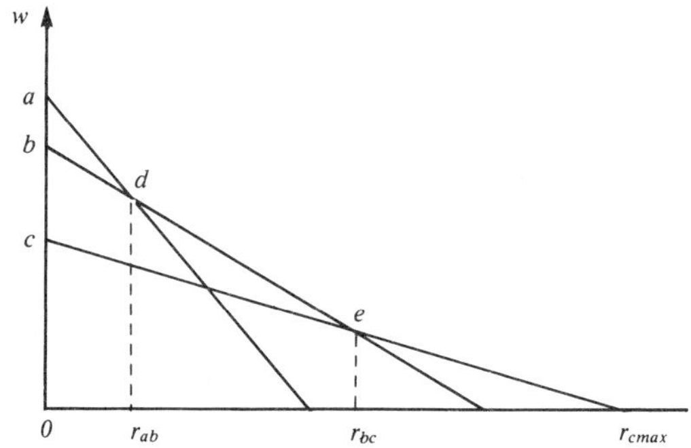

Figure 5

result, he could order techniques according to their maximum real wage rate (physical outputs per head when $r = 0$). The three w—r relationships corresponding to techniques a, b and c are shown in Figure 5. Then, for any given value of r, that method which offers the highest w will be chosen; for example, c will be chosen for rates of profit between r_{cmax} and r_{bc}. The switch points are $e(r_{bc})$ and $d(r_{ab})$ for, there, two methods are equiprofitable. Notice that as r gets smaller, one method may either survive or at a critical value of r (a switch point, e.g., r_{bc}) swap over to another, *but it can never reappear.* Samuelson christened the outer envelope, $ader_{c\ max}$, the factor price frontier (the individual w—r relationships are the factor price frontiers of each method). Clearly, by increasing the density of techniques, 'increasing the number of pages in our book of blueprints', a virtually continuous change from one method to another will occur, though each point on the envelope is associated with a specific method of production in which there is no substitutability of commodities—'capital'—for labour.

3.10 Samuelson then shows that this frontier may be approximated to, as close as we like, by using a simple, one-commodity model in which 'capital' and output are jelly,[33] the production function showing the various combinations of labour and jelly which produce jelly is homogeneous of order one, and factors are paid, through the workings of competition, their marginal products measured in jelly. In Figures 6a and 6b we show the relationships between these rates and the jelly capital–labour ratio.[34] Corresponding to each J/L ratio are an equilibrium wage and profit rate which make up a point on a factor price frontier (see r_1, w_1 and r_2, w_2 in Fig. 6c).

3.11 It can easily be shown that the simple Marshallian elasticity at each point on this frontier measures the distribution of income. Corresponding to any point on the frontier it will always be true that:

$$y = rk + w \qquad (3.4)$$

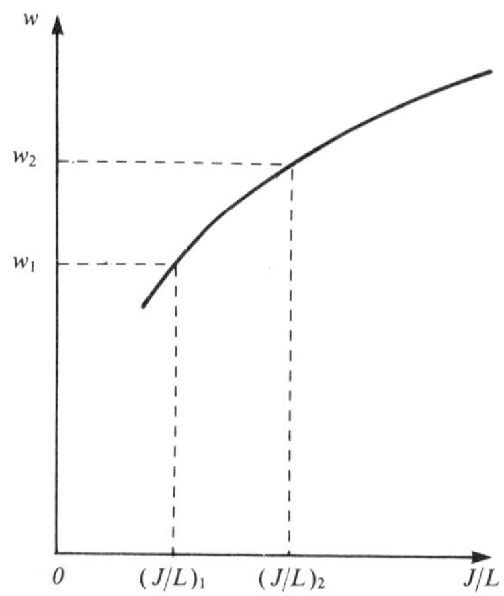

Figure 6a

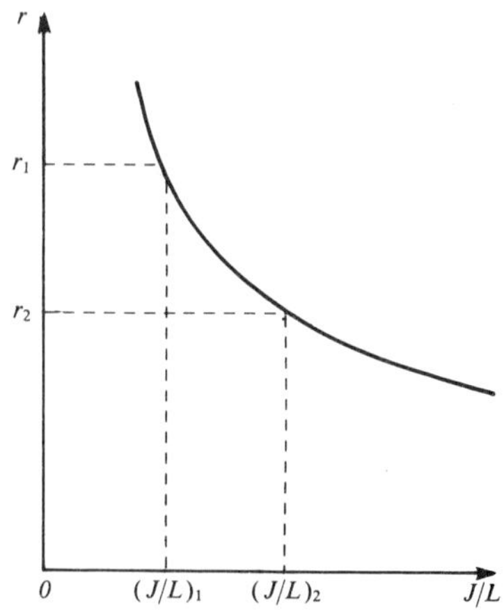

Figure 6b

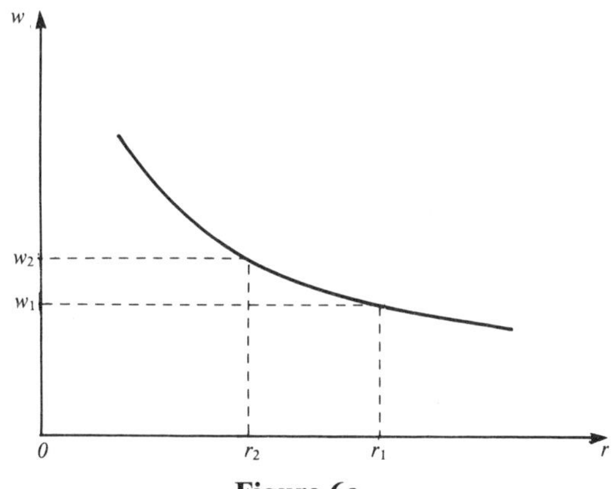

Figure 6c

where y = output per head, k = capital per head and w = real wage per head, all measured in jelly, and that

$$dy = rdk + kdr + dw \qquad (3.5)$$

Divide (3.5) by dy, and *remember that* $r = dy/dk$ *by assumption,* to obtain $1 = 1 + (kdr + dw)/dy$.

This implies that:

$$k = -\frac{dw}{dr} \qquad (3.6)$$

where $-dw/dr$ is the slope of the factor price frontier. The elasticity of the frontier at each point (E) is

$$E = -\frac{r}{w}\frac{dw}{dr} = \frac{rk}{w} \qquad (3.7)$$

which is the distribution of income.[35]

3.12 It may also be shown that lower rates of profit are associated with higher values of 'capital' per head and per unit of output, and with higher sustainable states of consumption per head. Moreover, the correspondence between the jelly world of parable and the 'real world' of heterogeneous capital goods may be made as close as we like by choosing the suitable brand of jelly to use in the surrogate '*as if*' production function, the name given by Samuelson to the function from which the Figures 6 are derived.

3.13 Unfortunately for the neoclassical revivalists, all these results disappear when we drop our very special assumption (which is, however, related to that in Marx, Vols. I and II) that each w—r relationship is a straight line.[36] For now the *possibility* that the same method will be the most profitable at *two* (or more) values of r, while others are the most profitable at the values in between, becomes inevitable, see Figure 7, where the w—r relationships of two methods, one a straight line, the other a curved one, are shown. For rates of profit greater than r_{ba} or less than r_{ab} method a is the more profitable; for rates between r_{ba} and r_{ab}, method b is; there is, therefore, double-switching at r_{ba} and r_{ab} where the two are equiprofitable. It will be noticed that output per man of $a(O_a)$ exceeds that of $b(O_b)$. If, therefore, we were to compare the sustainable states of consumption at different

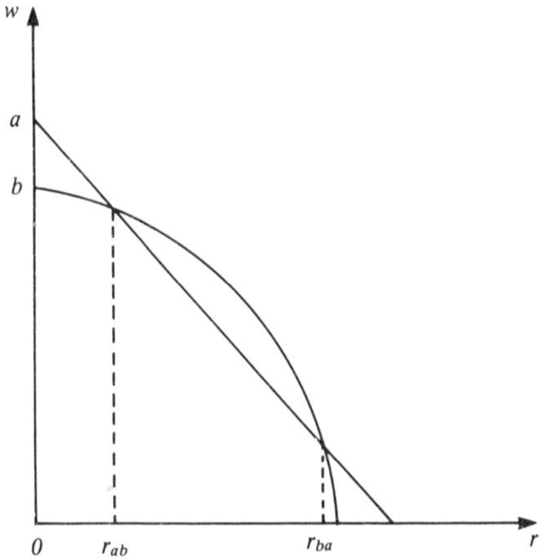

Figure 7

rates of profit, instead of obtaining the steady increase of the neoclassical parable—investment in more roundabout methods of production as r falls allows higher sustainable standards of living in the long run—we would instead have a 'dip' over the range of $r_{ba} - r_{ab}$ (Fig. 8).[37]

3.14 It may also be shown that the elasticities of points on the factor price frontier envelope no longer give the distribution of income, essentially because nonstraight line w—r relationships for methods of production are inconsistent with the neoclassical parable that $r = dy/dk$. It follows that the 'as if' production function will not in general do the

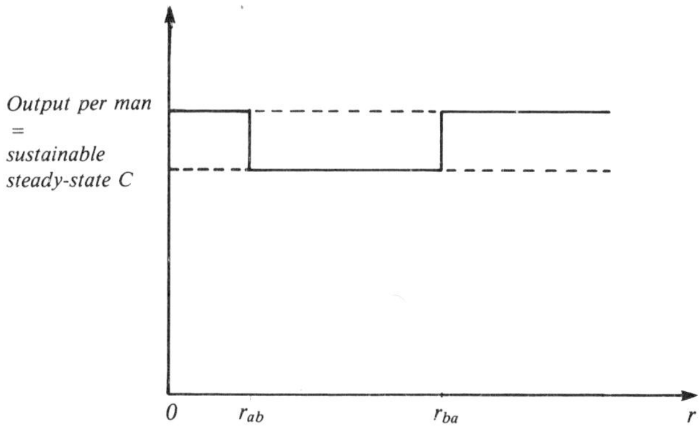

Figure 8

trick. Thus it is always true that income per head and its distribution may be written as:

$$y = rk + w \tag{3.4}$$

and, therefore, by definition, that

$$k = \frac{y - w}{r} \tag{3.8}$$

We have already seen that when $r = dy/dk$,

$$k = -\frac{dw}{dr} \tag{3.6}$$

But k cannot equal both $(y - w)/r$ and $-dw/dr$ *unless* the factor price frontier of each method is a straight line. Consider any point P on a concave w—r relationship (Fig. 9). Tan θ measures $(y - w)/r$ and tan ψ measures $-dw/dr$. Tan θ and Tan ψ are only equal when the relationship is a straight line. As the former is always true, by definition, the latter cannot also equal the value of capital, r is *not* equal to dy/dk and the value of E at P is *not* a measure of the distribution of income.[38] When $k = -dw/dr$ so that each w—r relationship is a straight line, we have, in effect, a measure of capital within each technique which *is* independent of distribution and prices. But as each technique produces the *same* all-purpose commodity, using *itself* and labour, albeit with different proportions *as* between techniques, though not

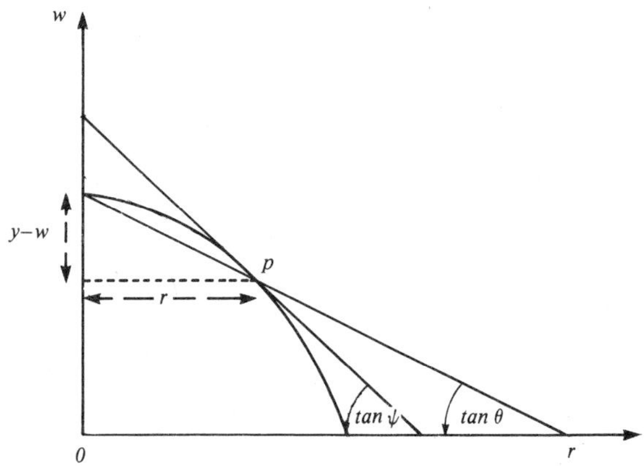

Figure 9

within them, *we have never really left the malleable capital or jelly world* (on this, see especially [31, 115]).

3.15 Why did the original neoclassical parables omit the double-switching possibilities and why, essentially, must they be supposed to occur in comparisons of technologies such as those actually used? In the simplest Austrian schemes of production, labour is applied *uniformly* through time to produce, say, a unit of output, and it is assumed that the greater is the time that is taken for production, the smaller is the total amount of labour that is needed overall.[39] It follows that at very high rates of profit (and low real wage rates), techniques which use more total labour but less time will be cheapest; while at low rates of profit the more time-intensive methods will be the most profitable. With discreetness in technology, one technique may be the most profitable for a range of values of *r*; but once it disappears it never reappears again.[40]

3.16 Now consider the case where we compare two methods, in *neither* of which is labour applied uniformly over time. Then it is clear that the ratio of the costs of the methods for producing a unit of net output at different values of *r* can fall below and rise above unity. Suppose, for example, that one—method A—has a large input of labour at the start of its gestation period, which extends over two periods of time, while the other—B—has a larger gestation period than A, a small input of labour at the start and a large one towards the end of the period, which is, however, *less* than the total input in A. The total input of labour in A is less than that in B. Then at very high values of *r*, interest on the cost of labour employed at the start of method B must outweigh the wage and interest costs of method A, so that A is preferred to B. At very low or zero values of *r*, A will also be preferred because it has the lower total input of labour. But there is an intermediate range of values of *r* where the investment of most of B's labour for a shorter period than A's at moderate rates of interest makes B's total cost *less* than A's. Hence B is preferred. (The analogy between this result and the possibility of multiple internal rates of return whenever there are negative quasi-rents in an investment project has been noticed by several writers, see, for example [16].)

3.17 Joan Robinson and Sraffa used this uneven distribution of labour through 'horizontal' time to describe the possibility of double-switching. Sraffa used his reduction to 'dated' labour examples to make the point (see [117], p. 81) and Joan Robinson described the phenomenon as the Ruth Cohen curiosum (see [85], [86], p. 109). However, as is clear in Sraffa's description of the *timelessness* of the concept of 'dated' labour and has been made quite explicit by Champernowne [19, 21], Morishima [71] and Joan Robinson and Naqvi [95], it is the *heterogeneity of capital goods* (whether fixed or circulating) *as well as the time pattern of production* which gives rise to the possibility of double-switching. As Morishima points out, a process involving a lapse of time from input to output can be regarded as an instantaneous process requiring heterogeneous capital goods by introducing as many fictitious intermediate goods and sectors as we require.[41]

3.18 Morishima gives the following example: suppose that we have two types of machines, M_1 and M_2, which can be made by the following methods of production:

M_1

1. $0.5\,M_1 + 0.1\,M_2 + 0.5\,L \rightarrow 1\,M_1$
2. $1\,M_2 + 0.2\,L \rightarrow 1\,M_1$

M_2

$$0.2\,M_1 + 1L \rightarrow 1M_2$$

At low levels of w the second method of producing M_1 is preferred. As the value of w (notionally) gets greater, 1 takes over until at very high levels 2 comes back again. For with either very high wages *or* very high rentals of M_1, 2 is obviously preferable to 1; while, at very high rentals of M_2, 1 is preferred to 2.[42]

3.19 Using comparisons of equilibrium positions, we have seen that, once heterogeneity of capital goods is introduced, the parables based on jelly no longer apply. In particular, it can no longer be argued that 'capital' is paid a marginal product which equals r (even in an equilibrium situation), which has led some writers to look elsewhere than to the concept and properties of a production function ('as if' or real) to explain the distribution of income. Furthermore, Garegnani in particular argues that the finding (that lower *r*'s do not necessarily relatively cheapen the more capital-intensive, greater output per head techniques) destroys the foundations of the traditional demand and supply approach to the theory of distribution (see [31], section V). Some writers, for example, Bhaduri [6, 7], Joan Robinson [93] and Nell [73], look to Marx's theory of exploitation, brought up to date in the guise of relative bargaining strengths, to explain the distribution of the product, treated as a surplus, between profit-earners and wage-earners. Competition's role then is to ensure equality of profit rates in all activities, and this together with the technical coefficients of production determine relative prices. In this way capital in its role of aid to labour—a role common to all societies, capitalist or socialist—can be separated from capital in its role of investible funds, belonging to those who own—have property in—the means of production and who obtain a share in the distribution of product because of their property rights. The trouble with jelly is that it was meant to serve both purposes (it is after all the ideal medium by which the two concepts may be merged into one), and the theory of production relations was meant to be independent of the institutions of society; that is, relations between men were treated as irrelevant for an explanation of distribution. It was Marx's insight that this separation is invalid, even in the world of pure logic, and the significance of this distinction for the case of more than one capital good has been emphasised by the modern critics of the neoclassical parables. If, then, the distribution of income cannot be explained within the system of production alone, factors and forces elsewhere in the economic system must be introduced. Sraffa himself has suggested that the rate of profit may be related to the money rate of interest; other writers—Kaldor, Joan Robinson, Pasinetti—have suggested the rate of growth allied with the coefficients of the capitalists' saving function (and, latterly, their borrowing function, see [56]). Which is correct seems to me a still unsettled question. What is clear is that the neo-Keynesians regard the marginal productivity parable, as set out, for example, by Samuelson in [101], as bankrupt in a world of heterogeneous capital goods and so have advanced these alternatives. Brown [13] has suggested neoclassical exploitation, as he still wants to include maximising behaviour which Nell [73] and Kaldor [56] and possibly Sraffa would exclude. Finally, Bliss [10, 11] argues that *if* we assume equilibrium (a most important proviso) and price-taking, profit-maximising behaviour under perfectly competitive conditions in linear models, factors *as a matter of logic* must receive their marginal products, *suitably defined,* even though an aggregate production function may not be shown to exist. He argues that marginal product relations in distribution theory and the existence of a production function (in the sense of a unique relationship between output per head and capital per head) are *not* one and the same thing, as Champernowne showed long ago in [19]. (None of these comments affects the criticisms of parables 1 to 3, which both sides accept, but which the neoclassicals tend to dismiss, *ex post*, as not very interesting.)

3.20 In postscript, it should be added that if double-switching is ruled out by assumption and if the rate of profit or real wage rate is a *parameter, given from outside*, the Champernowne chain index method of measuring capital [19] will allow *rp* to equal the marginal product of capital (this is always true), and higher values of capital will be associated with lower rates of profit.[43] But, even so, the conclusion that the rate of profit and distribution of income cannot be solved for from within the production system itself still holds.

4. THE RATE OF PROFIT IN CAPITALIST SOCIETY

4.1 We concluded the section on double-switching by arguing that, in order to determine the rate of profit, further factors have to be introduced from outside the production system. Certain economists—Kaldor, Pasinetti, Joan Robinson[44]—have argued that the factors were the saving propensities associated with different classes of income-receivers in the community and the rate of growth of the economic system (as given by the rate of growth of the labour force and Harrod netural technical progress). These veiws have been discussed in a series of articles which appeared, principally, in the *Review of Economic Studies* and the *Economic Journal* [53, 54, 78, 66, 79, 67, 81, 68, 103, 83, 94, 56, 104, 12, 22, 23, 74, 58].[45]

4.2 Kaldor's statement of the problem in 1959 [53, 54] contains, in essence, the principal features. He showed that the rate of profit in a growing economy which had attained long-run, steady-state equilibrium at full employment was equal to the rate of growth of the economy divided by the profit-earners' marginal propensity to save. He linked this result to an earlier one of his own (in an analysis of a slave state) and to von Neumann's famous model of an expanding economy, in which the rate of interest is equal to the *net* productivity of the whole system.[46] And he developed it further to obtain the same expression for the marginal efficiency of investment, in order to explain investment demand in an expanding capitalist economy. An integral part of the result was his view that the share of profits in full employment national income may be explained by the share of investment in national output, provided only that this was determined by long-run growth forces, that the saving propensities of profit-earners were greater than those of wage-earners, and that industrial market structures were sufficiently competitive to allow prices to respond to changes in demand.

4.3 Pasinetti's 1962 paper [78], which arose partly as a critique of one aspect of Kaldor's theory of distribution and partly from his own work on a multi-sector growth model [80], precipitated the remaining papers. The debate is intricate and fierce, and one despairs of giving its full flavour.[47] It concerns the characteristics and values of certain key economic variables and ratios associated with long-run, steady-state equilibria, *if the latter exist.*[48] The simplest statement of the issues in the controversy will be found in Meade's taxonomic note, which uses one simple diagram to show how the key economic variables of the analysis—P/K, Y/K, P/Y, I/Y, s_w, s_c and g_n—interact.

4.4 Though the level of analysis is highly abstract, the debate is nevertheless concerned with important empirical characteristics of capitalist economies, in particular, with the role of the class which accumulates capital, both by making investment decisions and by organising the saving (either their own or borrowed) to finance investment. This class, whom Meade calls 'pure' capitalists, receive income—profits—*only* from their ownership of capital.[49] Other groups in the community—Pasinetti's 'workers'—may receive two classes of income, wages and profits on the *financial* capital which they own. It is financial capital because it results from lending their savings as they accrue to the pure capitalists who invest them in real physical capital assets. Both classes are assumed to have simple proportional saving functions—$S_w = s_w\,(W + P_w)$ and $S_c = s_c P_c$; they are permanent classes of income receivers—once there always there, otherwise the respective property holdings will not grow at the rates assumed in the model (see [66], pp. 671–2). This assumption is easier to accept for the pure capitalists, where companies as going concerns immediately spring to mind, than for workers.

4.5 Pasinetti first got into the act by pointing out that Kaldor in his Keynesian theory of distribution, which explained P/Y and P/K by use of the Keynesian saving investment relationship [51], forgot that workers' saving would also lead to them accumulating financial capital and receiving profits. By allowing for this, and by assuming that in long-run steady-state equilibrium, the rate of interest will be equal to the rate of profit,[50] so that all classes receive the *same* return on their savings, Pasinetti shows that $P/K = 1/s_c \cdot I/K = g_n/s_c$ (and that $P/Y = 1/s_c \cdot I/Y$). These are remarkable results because the steady-state values of P/K and P/Y are *independent* of the workers' saving propensities and of any factors connected with the production function and are general, not special cases as Kaldor's were. A further important point which emerges is that Pasinetti has explained the income shares (i.e. P/Y) which now differ from the distribution of income between *persons* (which is also explained in his paper).

4.6 In long-run equilibrium, the ratio of saving to profits of all classes must be the same—otherwise the proportions of financial property owned by each class would be changing. The ratio is determined by the ratio of the 'pure' capitalists who directly control their own accumulation, both saving and investing; i.e. $s_c P_c/P_c$ is a key, independent ratio and $s_w(W + P_w)/P_w$ $(= S_w/P_w)$ adapts to it. This in turn implies that if workers save they must receive enough profits to make *their* savings what they would have been had the capitalists received the workers' profits and saved them at the *capitalists'* rate.[51]

4.7 A crucial assumption on the way to Pasinetti's results is that $s_w < I/Y$ (and, by implication, $s_c > I/Y$), which when written in its equivalent saving terms, is $s_w < g_n \cdot (K/Y)$ or $s_w Y < s_c rK$.[52] Pasinetti justifies this assumption on empirical grounds; namely, that the inequality, $s_w < I/Y$, is the economically relevant range of s_w to investigate in advanced capitalist economies. A subsidiary justification is that the share of profits in national income, *as given by Kaldor's theory of distribution* [51], would be < 0 if $s_w > I/Y$. This second justification is of value to Kaldor but not necessarily to Pasinetti, who was investigating the characteristics which are associated with full employment which has been attained by having the correct value of I/Y, i.e., for Pasinetti, the level of I is what is dictated by g_n, not because endogenous forces make it so (as Kaldor argues), but because he wishes to investigate the characteristics of long-period equilibrium when it has been *made* so.

4.8 Samuelson and Modigliani [103] try to show that s_w has to be less than a 'modest 0.05' in order that the Pasinetti result holds. However, this value depends upon the choice of unrealistically low values of s_c and I/Y (see [83], p. 304, and [104], p. 329). Nevertheless, much of the critics' space is devoted to analysing what happens when s_w is outside the Pasinetti-Kaldor range, where the steady-rate output–capital ratio = g_n/s_w, the dual of Pasinetti's result, and the steady state value of P/K does depend on the production function. Meade [66, 68] and Samuelson and Modigliani [103] have exhaustively investigated these possibilities. As I see it, they are examining the characteristics of a world where workers' savings dominate the accumulation process (capitalists' property relative to the workers' approaches zero), a world of bloodless revolution in which socialism in the guise of a workers' state has been painlessly ushered in and the characteristics of which, though fascinating in their own right, are irrelevant for a debate about what determines the rate of profit in capitalist societies.[53]

5. CONCLUSION

5.1 We break off in midstream and few issues are settled. A key one relates to marginal productivity and its role in distribution, about which, as we have seen, there is a complete cleavage of opinion on the significance of the double-switching results for this issue. I suspect, though, that in the future, the battles will centre more around the *relevance* of equilibrium analysis and of maximising behaviour, for it is *the general methodology* of neoclassical analysis, rather than any particular result, which basically is under attack (see, for example, [56, 114]).[54] As a betting man, I know on whom I'd put my money; but then as a God-man, I have never expected virtue to triumph this side of the grave. In closing, I might say that some of my best friends are neoclassicals and I hope that they remain so!

TECHNICAL ADDENDUM: WICKSELL EFFECTS—REAL AND PRICE, POSITIVE, NEUTRAL AND NEGATIVE—EXPOSED

A1. Running through the literature of modern capital theory are frequent mentions of Wicksell effects (see, for example [6, 7, 85, 86, 87, 95, 103, 104, 122). The apparatus of the double-switching debate allows a simple discussion of them. *Price Wicksell effects* relate to changes in the value of capital as w and r change but techniques do not; that is, they are associated with the w—r relationship corresponding to one technique. *Real Wicksell effects* relate to changes in the value of capital associated with a change in techniques as w and r take on different values; that is, they are the differences in the value of capital at switch points on the factor-price envelope frontier. Both effects[55] reflect the influence, through w and r, of the 'time' pattern of inputs of production, but the real effects reflect in addition changes in production methods, changes which affect real production potential, not just its market value. In this addendum, we use Bhaduri's definitional relation (see [6, 7] and sect. 3 above) to examine the links between the shapes of the w—r relationship of given techniques, price Wicksell effects and values of capital.

A2. Consider an economy-wide technique which has a net output per head of a consumption good, y.

We known that:

$$y = rk + w \tag{A1}$$

where all values are measured in consumption good units per head of labour, and that:

$$k = \frac{y - w}{r} \tag{A2}$$

when $r = 0$, $y = w_{\max}$, the maximum wage rate per head.

The simplest way that we may write the w—r relationship is:

$$w = w_{\max} + f(r) \tag{A3}$$

where $f'(r) < 0$.

It follows from (A2) and (A3) that

$$k = -\frac{f(r)}{r} \tag{A4}$$

A3. If (A3) is a straight line, $f(r) = f'(r)r = (dw/dr)r$ and $k = -dw/dr$, a result which we have already met in section 3.11. In this case, of course, the price Wicksell effect is *zero* or *neutral,* using Joan Robinson and Naqvi's terminology (see [95]), and any changes in capital values along an *envelope* of straight-line w—r relationships must be pure *real* Wicksell effects, reflecting switches from one technique to another with a different but *constant* value of capital. A neutral price Wicksell effect implies that the input time patterns are such that changes in the value of k associated with r are exactly offset by those associated with w.

A4. Now consider the general case:

$$k = -\frac{f(r)}{r}$$

and remember that $f'(r) < 0$.

$$\frac{dk}{dr} = -\left[\frac{1}{r^2}\left(f'(r)r - f(r)\right)\right] \tag{A5}$$

and is $\gtrless 0$ if $f(r)/rf'(r) \lesseqgtr 1$ (A6). Consider a w—r relationship which is concave to the origin with $w_{\max} = OS$, and any

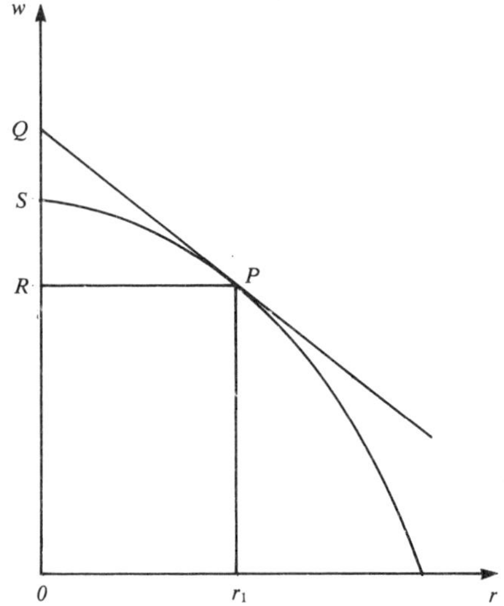

Figure A1

value of r, say r_1 (Fig. A1). Draw a tangent to the curve at P, the point on the w—r curve corresponding to r_1, and extend it to meet the vertical axis at Q. Draw a horizontal line from P to join the vertical axis at R. Then $RS = f(r_1)$ and $RQ = r_1 f'(r)$ (as the slope of the tangent to the curve at P is $f'(r_1)$). $RS/RQ < 1$, which by (A6) implies that $dk/dr > 0$, that is, a *concave* w—r relationship implies a *negative* price Wicksell effect—the value of capital is *lower*, the lower is the value of r. By exactly analagous reasoning we may show that a w—r relationship which is convex to the origin implies a positive price Wicksell effect so that the value of capital is higher, the lower is the value of r. Readers may also check the result for the straight-line w—r relationship. An economic interpretation of these results is given in [42, 95, and 115]. It relates the means of production-labour ratios of the different activities of each technique to shapes of curves and, therefore, to price Wicksell effects.

A5. Finally, we may identify a *positive* real Wicksell effect as one at which a technique with a higher output per head is chosen at a *lower* rate of profit, e.g., at $r = r_{ba}$ or just $< r_{ba}$ in Figure A2. A negative real Wicksell effect is exactly the opposite—in Figure A2, it occurs at $r =$ or just $< r_{ab}$.

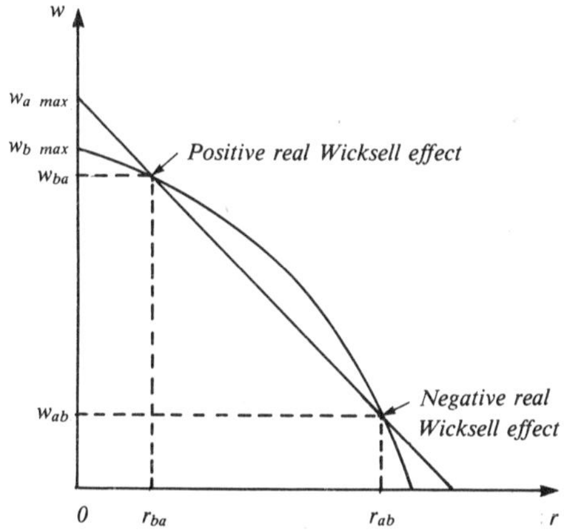

Figure A2

Notice that at r_{ab},

$$k_b = \frac{w_{b\ max} - w_{ab}}{r_{ab}} < k_a = \frac{w_{a\ max} - w_{ab}}{r_{ab}},$$

while at r_{ba},

$$k'_b = \frac{w_{b\ max} - w_{ba}}{r_{ba}.} < k'_a = \frac{w_{a\ max} - w_{ba}}{r_{ba}}$$

(Of course, $k'_a = k_a$ [neutral price Wicksell effect] and $k'_b < k_b$ [negative price Wicksell effect].) But, as Joan Robinson has remarked, all this is very much economics for the economists.

NOTES

1. This essay was originally published in the *Journal of Economic Literature*, June 1969, pp. 369–405. It is reprinted in Italian in G. Nardozzi and V. Valli (eds.), *Teori Dello Sviluppo Economico* (Etas Kompass, 1971). In writing the survey I have benefited from the comments of a number of economists, none of whom—and the usual caveat really is necessary—is responsible for any views stated, or errors and libels committed. I would especially like to thank Joan Robinson for her great encouragement. I am also extremely grateful to P. K. Bardhan, A. K. Bagchi, C. J. Bliss, Murray Brown, W. M. Corden, M. H. Dobb, J. H. Hatch, N. F. Laing, A. Lowe, James A. Mirrlees, Edward J. Nell, D. M. Nuto, Luigi L. Pasinetti, A. A. L. Powell, E.

A. Russell, Robert M. Solow, L. Spaventa, Joseph E. Stiglitz, R. H. Wallace and A. S. Watson. Finally, I especially thank Pippa Simpson for her expert mathematical advice, without which I would have been even more lost than I obviously have been in the jungle of squiggles that characterises most modern economic theory.

2. It has been said that time is a device to stop everything happening at once—to which Dr Dharma Kumar quipped that space was a device to stop everything happening in Cambridge. If we include both places, space has not had much effect on the modern theory of capital, though Cambridge, Mass., has had useful allies in Israeli economists on sabbaticals and Cambridge, England, useful allies in visiting or permanent Indian and Italian economists. Joan Robinson did not specifically name the economists that she had in mind, and some of those who subsequently stood up to be counted, including Samuelson and Solow, had not yet published papers on these specific topics.
3. This does not necessarily place Joan Robinson in the group of economists whom Hicks has, loosely and dangerously, labelled 'the accelerationists', but it certainly puts her apart from the aggregate production function boys who, Hicks argues, armed with MIT-type techniques, are providing a strong backlash for the role of the rate of interest in an explanation of long-run accumulation and distribution (see [41]). For convenience, but just as loosely and dangerously, I shall refer to the two groups, in what follows, as the neo-Keynesians and the neoclassicals. I take it that the leaders of each group are so well known that a Who's Who is unnecessary.
4. Solow, however, would deny this view—for him, capital as a unit only has significance in empirical work, not in rigorous theory; *see also* [101] and section 3.1 below.
5. The simplest possible gestation period and pattern of input of labour to build machines has been chosen for illustrative purposes only.
6. The significance of this proviso will emerge in the discussion of the double-switching debate, *see* section 3 below. Champernowne examined the case where the proviso does not hold in the appendix to his article [19].
7. *See* section 3 below, where they are also described as *w—r* relationships and factor price frontiers.
8. This 'price' is itself a chain-index price.
9. As Hicks has pointed out [42], outside a one-commodity world the price of capital services is the rate of profits multiplied by the price per unit of capital goods. It is only in a one-commodity world that the rate of profits—a pure number—and the marginal product of capital—an instantaneous rate of change—can be equal in size and the valuation problem dodged. Malleability cannot, however, because we must suppose that capital can change its form (or be viewed 'as if' it could) in order to identify its marginal product (see [101] and section 3 below). In a world of heterogeneous capital goods, valuation is needed so that we have a sum to which to apply the rate of profits and obtain the amount of profits. As we shall see below in section 3, this rate of profits is not in general equal to the marginal product of 'capital'.

10. Solow did not specify the form of the function until after he made his empirical fittings, when Cobb-Douglas gave the best fit.
11. A feature of Joan Robinson's analysis is discontinuities—gaps between the output per head of one technique and another. This does not imply, though, gaps in the realtionship between real capital and output per head, as two techniques may be equi-profitable, see [85, 86].
12. That cost-minimisation gives the same result is easily shown. Write

$$C = wl + A'k \tag{1.i}$$

where

$$C = \text{total annual cost per unit.}$$

Then

$$\frac{\delta C}{\delta k} \; (= wf'(k) + A') = 0$$

when

$$f'(k) = -\frac{A'}{w} \tag{1.ii}$$

13. That much of the *technical* analysis in this field has been done by the attacked themselves, *see* especially Samuelson's work on linear programming, [118], Part V, the economics of Ricardo and Marx, [118], Part IV, and nonsubstitution theorems, [118], Part VI is a seeming paradox which disappears when the *objects* of the two groups are examined, see [8, 37, 69, 73].
14. Kaldor is in excellent company with this one, see, for example, [100, 39, 40].
15. This is illustrated for the neoclassical case in paragraphs 2.12 and 2.13 below.
16. Solow and Stiglitz return to these issues in [113], where they argue that the essential difference between the two approaches is that the real wage rate is regarded by neoclassicals as a *labour* market clearing price while, for the neo-Keynesians, it is a *goods* market clearing price—a view which is consistent with Joan Robinson's criticisms.
17. Let the money wage be w, ignore capitalists' consumption, and let wage-earners consume all that they earn. The price charged for butter consumption (P) will be the total wages bill divided by butter available for consumption:

i.e., $$P = \frac{wN_f}{(1-\alpha)B_f'} = \frac{w}{AP_f}\left(\frac{1}{1-\alpha}\right) \tag{2i}$$

(Notice that this implies that firms may be thought of as using a markup, $\alpha/1-\alpha$, equal to the ratio of employment (and production) in the two sectors.) It is easy to show that the *full employment* value of the marginal product, VMP_f, is less than w, so that $MC_f > P$, which implies that ouput and employment must fall.

Thus:

$$\frac{VMP_f}{w} = \frac{P \cdot MP_f}{w} = \frac{MP_f}{AP_f}\left(\frac{1}{1-\alpha}\right) \tag{2ii}$$

Now (2ii) < 1, if

$$\frac{MP_f}{AP_f} < \frac{1-\alpha}{1}.$$

But

$$\frac{1-\alpha}{1}$$

is the ratio of the full employment production of butter not set aside for the next period to the full employment production of butter, which, because investment is 'low', we know exceeds MP_f/AP_f. Therefore, $VMP_f/w < 1$.

18. It is this property which makes this particular form of production function so attractive to econometricians in their work on aggregate production functions and which explains the tenacious grip of its users in the face of considerable onslaughts by the critics. For if real world observations could be regarded 'as if' they came from such a function, there is available actual data—observations from short-run utilization functions—which allow estimates of the characteristics of the 'as if' longer-run production functions, see [106, 1, 70, 101]. Technical progress, of course, complicates the methodology—destroys it, some might say—but there are no shortages of ingenious suggestions for coping with this puzzle, also.
19. Dobb [27] argued that there is a gap between the (private) profitability of investment and the (social) marginal productivity of investment, because the former excludes payment to factors other than capital, while the latter should reflect the *total* resulting addition to national output without any deductions of the values of other factors. He was, of course, discussing the case of surplus labour and changing employment levels and explicitly conceded the point, which Solow tries to establish rigorously, that there is no gap when all other factor supplies are constant and the real wage does not change. The rate of return on investment is, of course, an important concept in both types of economy and can stand alone without any need to connect it to the rate of return on private capital.
20. Both Samuelson and Solow have argued that heterogeneous capital models analysed by modern programming techniques are the appropriate tools for a rigorous development of capital theory. As a communication problem then arises, and because of the nature of economic statistics, the simpler stories (and empirical exercises) have, now and then, to be indulged in, if only for the sake of the more peasantish, albeit poetic, members of the trade; see [101]. The econometric methodology then becomes: we know we've been naughty but we don't think it makes much difference to our estimates of the values of key concepts; if it does, it's up to the critics to tell us the orders of magnitude involved, rather than smack our bottoms for our lack of principle.
21. The explanation relates to expressions for the equilibrium values of

factor prices and supplies in a general equilibrium situation in which demand factors, e.g., consumer tastes, also play a role.

22. They do, of course, analyse processes in other contexts and the spate of phase diagrams and dynamic processes now so common in the literature owes something surely to Joan Robinson's original paper, see, for example [18, 34], which are typicai members of a rapidly growing tribe.
23. See, for example, [16], n. 2, p. 545; [67], n. 1, p. 448; [104], p. 329.
24. Levhari claimed to have demonstrated that double-switching was impossible in an 'indecomposable' or 'irreducible' technique—a situation in which every single output requires directly or indirectly as an input for its production, something of every other single output, [60] pp. 518–9. Pasinetti [82] was the first to provide a counter example, originally in his paper to the Rome Congress of the Econometric Society of 1965.
25. Following the Symposium in the *Quarterly Journal of Economics,* further excellent papers have been written, see [14, 15, 31, 115].
26. Sraffa was concerned to analyse, in the classical tradition, those properties of an economic system that are independent of changes in scale and proportions of factors. The production process is regarded as a circular one in which intermediate goods get star billing rather than as 'a one-way avenue' from 'Factors of Production' to 'Consumption Goods' [117], p. 93. An important consequence of Sraffa's view is that the marginal product is ruled out—'it just would not be there to be found' ([117], p.v; on this, see also [8, 37].)
27. Those who find this an unfamiliar way of looking at the economic system may like to read an outstanding article by Edward J. Nell [73]. They might also find helpful two papers [36, 37] by the present writer and Vincent G. Massaro, and a paper by Adolph Lowe [61].
28. Samuelson [102] attributes this result to the workings of ruthless competition, (allied with geometry.)
29. We may also suppose, as Joan Robinson and Naqvi do (also Garegnani [31] and Samuelson [102]), that the activities are in such a proportion to one another that they form a sub-system with *a net* product of one unit of commodity 1.
30. I have corrected a printing slip in the version of (3.3) shown in [95], p. 586. My definition of x_{ij} differs from that of Joan Robinson and Naqvi, and I have not cancelled X_1, X_2 in expression (3.3) so that readers may translate my version into theirs. Brown [14], Garegnani [31], Hicks [42], and Spaventa [115] use a simpler formulation of (3.3), namely, that capital and labour are inputs into consumption and capital goods respectively in the two activities, but this obscures some of the technological factors made explicit here. Brown has a most interesting analysis of the double-switching issues in terms of a composite production coefficient—the amount of labour required to produce a machine which in turn produces one unit of consumption good; see [14].
31. Samuelson [102] uses this result to poke fun at Marx for backing one horse too many. I suspect that they went to different race tracks.

32. In the Hicks, Brown, Garegnani and Spaventa versions, we get a straight line if each activity has the *same* capital input to labour input ratio. See, also, the Technical Addendum to this essay.
33. The list of homogeneous, all-purpose commodities in the literature now includes corn, treacle, meccano sets, putty and clay, steel, leets, ectoplasm, butter and jelly. I have often been tempted to suggest toffee meccano sets on the principle of something for nearly everyone, i.e. treacle-putty-clay-steel-meccano sets.
34. The factor payments are obtained by differentiating the expression for the production function with respect to L and jelly and putting the resulting marginal products equal to w and r respectively.
35. This section draws heavily on two excellent papers by Bhaduri [6] and [7], papers which are marked by great clarity and insight.
36. It is ironic that, nearly a hundred years later, the rival theory of value and distribution to that of Ricardo and Marx should founder on the assumption which Böhm-Bawerk found objectionable in Marx's theory. On this, see [26] n. 1, p. 74 and generally for a brilliant account of the historical and analytical background to the present debate.
37. Solow analysed the relationship between the dip, the neoclassical parable case and the social rate of return on investment in [112]; see also [16]. While reswitching makes it possible, curved w—r relationships are all that is needed to allow it to happen; *see* [16], p. 549.
38. Figure 9 is according to Garegnani [31] and is used by Bhaduri in [7]. Champernowne has shown that in the general case the distribution of income is:

$$E_{rw} + E_{yw} = -\left(\frac{w}{r}\frac{dr}{dw} + \frac{p}{r}\frac{dp}{dw}\right),$$

where p is the (Champernowne) price index of capital (chain index) in terms of consumer goods.
39. This is the basis of the Austrian measurement of 'capital' in terms of an average period of production. The next two paragraphs owe much to Samuelson's excellent 'summing up' of the debate; see [102].
40. Notice the subtle way all our stories have been told so far. Though we are only making comparisons of equilibrium positions, we nevertheless always start with a high rate of profit and move to situations with low ones, and it is sometimes hard to remember that we are not being told about a process—for example, how an economy may move, through accumulation and deepening, from a high rate of profit, scarce capital position to a low rate of profit, abundant capital one—and what we may hope to achieve by this process.
41. This, as I understand it, is the essence of Sraffa's concept of 'dated' labour. It should be remembered that Sraffa is always dealing at an instant of time with those properties of an economic system which are independent of change. It is also natural for anyone thinking, as Sraffa is, in the Ricardian-Marxian mould, of 'divergences of prices from values' changing as the rate of profits changes, to sense the possibility

of such double substitutions of machines for labour. I am indebted to M. H. Dobb for this comment.

42. Champernowne has discussed in an unpublished note [21] his reasons for ruling out double-switching by assumption in his original article [19]. He argues that his intuition as the time was that the probability of the input per unit of output coefficients being such as to allow it, i.e. to be consistent with ranges of r which allow positive real wages, was low. However, the very restrictive assumptions needed to rule it out, as established by Bruno, Burmeister and Sheshinski [16], pp. 538–46, suggest that this intuition was wrong.
43. If capital is measured in terms of commodities and r and w are given from outside as $\bar{r}$ and $\bar{w}$, totally differentiating $y = \bar{r}k + \bar{w}$ gives $dy = \bar{r}\,dk$, so that $\bar{r} = dy/dk$, see [6]. Differentiation here is to be interpreted as the procedure by which two equiprofitable techniques are compared side by side, using a *common set of prices*. In a general equilibrium model with fixed, i.e., equilibrium prices, the marginal product of aggregate capital is equal to the rate of interest (determined in conjunction with either consumers' or the government's rate of time preference), but this relates only to *one* point, *see*, for example, [122]. A possible reconciliation between this view and Sraffa's view that the marginal product does not exist in linear models will be found in [37], pp. 442–43.
44. Pasinetti adds Champernowne [20], Kahn [49] and von Neumann [125]. All would, I am sure, acknowledge the prior inspiration of Kalecki's work; *see* [50], pp. 76–7, and the comments by Dobb in [27], p. 91.
45. An alternative view which 'closes' the system in a more traditional manner by using time preference will be found in an article by J. Hirshleifer [43].
46. *See also* [72] in which Wicksell's *natural* rate of interest is interpreted in these terms.
47. Readers studying it should divide their approach. First, read the exchanged abuse for the sheer pleasure of savouring its savagery; second, ignore the abuse, and try to follow the analysis.
48. Meade [68] especially has dealt with the existence problem and shown the limits outside of which the various possible steady-state equilibria cannot exist. Much of Samuelson and Modigliani's paper [103] is concerned with the existence and stability of the various equilibria.
49. It is in the spirit of the analysis to regard the class as profit-retaining companies organised by, say, Mr. Marris's managers [63], as Kaldor does in his reply to Samuelson and Modigliani, *see* [56]. The managers might well have the saving behaviour of workers in their private lives yet, simultaneously, organise the saving of companies in their role of good organisation men, Bagger-Daggers all, (in honour of that really great BBC offering, 'The Diary of a Young Man').
50. This assumption does not seem to have been much commented on in the literature, (but see [22], [58]). It *may* be a clue to the meaning of Sraffa's throw-away remark that the rate of profit is related to the

money rate of interest (*see* sect. 3 above, and also [93]) in which case there is little conflict between Pasinetti, Kaldor and Joan Robinson, on the one hand, and Sraffa, on the other.

51. Kaldor's neo-Pasinetti theorem allows this assumption to be dropped and introduces a role for companies' borowing behaviour and that 'with it' statistic, the valuation ratio, *see* [56], pp. 316–19.
52. In Golden Age equilibrium, $I/K = g_n$ and $r = g_n/s_c$, implying that $rs_c = g_n$. It follows that $I/Y = g_n \cdot K/Y$ so that the Kaldor-Pasinetti-Robinson condition is $s_w < g_n \cdot K/Y$ or $s_w Y < g_n K = s_c r K$ (*see*[67], p. 447 and [94], p. 307.).
53. One attraction of this case is supposed to be that there is in effect only one saving coefficient and no classes, or anyway, none of significance for economic analysis; see [121], Lecture 4. This is regarded as more 'realistic', which prompts one to ask whether labour economics is taught at either Cambridge.
54. A recent rereading of Dobb's *Political Economy and Capitalism* [26] (which seems as fresh and relevant now as it was in 1937) convinces me that divergent views concerning the nature of economic analysis and its relationship to the existing stages, classes and institutions of societies are still central to the controversies.
55. As Joan Robinson and Naqvi [95] point out, 'effect' is an unfortunate word to use because we are only discussing differences—comparisons of equilibrium situations—not changes. Joan Robinson has herself examined, in [87], the two types of Wicksell effects when an economy experiences change.

REFERENCES

[1] K. J. Arrow, H. B. Chenery, B. S. Minhas and R. M. Solow. 'Capital–Labour Substitution and Economic Efficiency.' *Rev. Econ. Statist.* XLIII, 3 (1961), 225–50

[2] K. J. Arrow. 'The Economic Implications of Learning by Doing'. *Rev. Econ. Stud.*, XXIX (3), 80 (1962), 155–73

[3] P. K. Bardhan. 'On Estimation of Production Functions from International Cross-Section Data.' *Econ. J.* LXXVII, 306 (1967), 328–37

[4] —— 'Equilibrium Growth in a Model with Economic Obsolescence of Machines.' *Quart. J. Econ.*, 83 (Nov.), 312–23

[5] D. M. Bensusan-Butt. *On Economic Growth. An Essay in Pure Theory.* Oxford, Clarendon Press, 1960

[6] Amit Bhaduri. 'The Concept of the Marginal Productivity of Capital and the Wicksell Effect'. *Oxford Econ. Pap.*, XVIII, 3 (1966), 284–88

[7] —— 'On the Significance of Recent Controversies on Capital Theory: A Marxian View'. *Econ. J.*, LXXIX., 115, (1969), 532–9

[8] Krishna R. Bharadwaj. 'Value through Exogenous Distribution.' *Econ. Weekly*, 24 August 1963, pp. 1450–4

[9] C. J. Bliss. 'On Putty-Clay' *Rev. Econ. Stud.* XXXV (2), 102 (1968), pp. 105–32
[10] —— 'Rates of Return in a Linear Model' Cambridge, 1968, unpublished paper
[11] —— Letter to author, 1968
[12] R. Britto, 'A Study in Equilibrium Dynamics in Two Types of Growing Economies.' *Econ. J.* LXXXVIII, 311 (1968), 624–40
[13] Murray Brown. 'A Measure of the Change in Relative Exploitation of Capital and Labour'. *Rev. Econ. Statist.* XLVIII, 2 (1966), 182–92
[14] —— 'Substitution–Composition Effects, Capital Intensity Uniqueness and Growth.' *Econ. J.* LXXIX 314 (1969) 334–47
[15] —— 'A Respecification of the Neoclassical Production Model in the Heterogeneous Capital Case.' Discussion Paper No. 29, State University of New York at Buffalo, 1968
[16] Michael Bruno, Edwin Burmeister and Eytan Sheshinski. 'Nature and Implications of the Reswitching of Techniques.' *Quart. J. Econ.* LXXX, 4 (1966), 526–53
[17] ——, —— and ——. 'The Badly Behaved Production Function: Comment.' *Quart. J. Econ.* LXXXII, 3 (1968), 524–5
[18] David Cass and Joseph E. Stiglitz. 'The Implications of Alternative Saving and Expectations Hypotheses for Choices of Technique and Patterns of Growth', 1967, unpublished paper
[19] D. G. Champernowne. 'The Production Function and the Theory of Capital: Comment.' *Rev. Econ. Stud.* XXI (2), 55 (1953–4), 112–35
[20] —— 'Capital Accumulation and the Maintenance of Full Employment' *Econ. J.* LXVIII, 270 (1958), 211–44
[21] ——'Luigi Pasinetti's Note on "Changes in the Rate of Profit, etc."' Cambridge, Feb. 1966, unpublished note
[22] Perry P. Chang. 'Rate of Profit and Income Distribution in Relation to the Rate of Economic Growth: A Comment' *Rev. Econ. Stud.* XXXI (1), 86 (1964), 103–5
[23] Paul Davidson. 'The Demand and Supply of Securities and Economic Growth and its Implications for the Kaldor–Pasinetti versus Samuelson–Modigliani Controversy.' *Amer. Econ. Rev.* LVIII, 2, (May 1968), 252–69
[24] E. F. Denison. 'Capital Theory: Technical Progress and Capital Structure—Discussion.' *Amer. Econ. Rev.* LVI, 2 (May 1966), 76–82
[25] P.A. Diamond. 'Technical Change and the Measurement of Capital and Output' *Rev. Econ. Stud.* XXXII (4), 92 (1965), 289–98
[26] M. H. Dobb. *Political Economy and Capitalism. Some Essays in Economic Tradition.* London, Geo. Routledge, rev. ed., 1940
[27] —— *An Essay on Economic Growth and Planning.* London, Routledge and Kegan Paul, 1960
[28] —— *Papers on Capitalism, Development and Planning.* London, Routledge and Kegan Paul, 1967

[29] F. M. Fisher. 'Embodied Technical Change and the Existence of An Aggregate Capital Stock.' *Rev. Econ. Stud.* XXXII (4), 92 (1965), 263–88
[30] P. Garegnani. 'Switching of Techniques.' *Quart. J. Econ.* LXXX, 4 (1966), 555–67
[31] —— 'Heterogeneous Capital, the Production Function and the Theory of Distribution.' *Rev. Econ. Stud.* XXXVII (3), (1970), 407–36
[32] Z. Griliches and D. W. Jorgenson. 'Sources of Measured Productivity Change: Capital Input.' *Amer. Econ. Rev.* LVI, 2 (1966), 50–61
[33] F. H. Hahn and R. C. O. Matthews. 'The Theory of Economic Growth: A Survey.' *Econ. J.* LXXIV, 296 (1964), 779–902.
[34] F. H. Hahn. 'Equilibrium Dynamics with Heterogeneous Capital Goods.' *Quart. J. Econ.*, LXXX (1966), 633–46
[35] G. C. Harcourt. 'A Simple Joan Robinson Model of Accumulation with One Technique: A Comment.' *Osaka Econ. Pap.*, XI (2), 21 (1963), 24–28
[36] —— and Vincent G. Massaro. 'A Note on Mr Sraffa's Sub-Systems.' *Econ. J.* LXXIV, 295 (1964), 715–22
[37] —— and Vincent G. Massaro. 'Mr Sraffa's Production of Commodities.' *Econ. Rec.* XL, 91 (1964), 442–54
[38] —— 'Biases in Empirical Estimates of the Elasticities of Substitution of CES Production Functions.' *Rev. Econ. Stud.* XXXIII (3), 95 (1966), 227–34
[39] —— 'Investment-Decision Criteria, Capital-Intensity and the Choice of Techniques.' *Czech. Econ. Pap., No.* 9 (1967), 65–91
[40] —— 'Investment-Decision Criteria, Investment Incentives and the Choice of Technique.' *Econ. J.* LXXVIII, 309 (1968), 77–95
[41] John Hicks. 'Thoughts on the Theory of Capital—the Corfu Conference.' *Oxford Econ. Pap., XII*, 2 (1960), 123–32
[42] —— *Capital and Growth.* Oxford, Clarendon Press, 1965
[43] J. Hirshleifer. 'A Note on the Böhm-Bawerk/Wicksell Theory of Interest.' *Rev. Econ. Stud.* XXXIV (2), 98 (1967), 191–9
[44] W. P. Hogan. 'Technical Progress and Production Functions.' *Rev. Econ. Statist.* XL, 4 (1958), 407–11
[45] L. Johansen. 'Substitution versus Fixed Production Coefficients in the Theory of Economic Growth: A Synthesis.' *Econometrica XXVII*, 2 (1959), pp. 157–76
[46] —— 'A Method for Separating the Effects of Capital Accumulation and Shifts in Production Functions upon Growth in Labour Productivity.' *Econ. J.* LXXI, 284 (1961), 775–82
[47] H. G. Johnson. 'A Simple Joan Robinson Model of Accumulation with One Technique.'*Osaka Econ. Pap.* X (1/2), 19 (1962), 28–33
[48] D. W. Jorgenson and Z. Griliches. 'The Explanation of Productivity Change.' *Rev. Econ. Stud.* XXXIV (3), 99 (1967), 249–83
[49] R. F. Kahn. 'Exercises in the Analysis of Growth.' *Oxford Econ. Pap.*, XI, 2 (1959), 143–56

[50] Michal Kalecki. *Essays in the Theory of Economic Fluctuations.* London, Allen and Unwin, 1939

[51] N. Kaldor. 'Alternative Theories of Distribution.' *Rev. Econ. Stud.* XXIII (2), 61 (1956), 83–100

[52] —— 'A Model of Economic Growth.' *Econ. J.* LXVII, 268 (1957), 591–624

[53] —— 'Economic Growth and the Problem of Inflation—Part I.' *Economica* XXVI, 103 (1959), 212–26

[54] —— 'Economic Growth and the Problem of Inflation—Part II.' *Economica* XXVI, 104 (1959), 287–98

[55] —— and James A. Mirrlees. 'A New Model of Economic Growth.' *Rev. Econ. Stud.* XXIX (3), 80 (1962), 174–92

[56] —— 'Marginal Productivity and the Macro-economic Theories of Distribution.' *Rev. Econ. Stud.* XXXII (4), 96 (1966), 309–19

[57] J. M. Katz. 'The Sources of Manufacturing Growth in Australia and Argentine in the Period 1946–60.' *Econ. Rec.* XLIV, 107 (1968) 377–81

[58] N. F. Laing. 'Two Notes on Pasinetti's Theorem.' *Econ. Rec.* XLV, 111 (1969) 373–85

[59] David Levhari. 'A Non-Substitution Theorem and Switching of Techniques.' *Quart. J. Econ.* LXXXIX, 1 (1965), 98–105

[60] —— and Paul A. Samuelson. 'The Non-Switching Theorem is False.' *Quart. J. Econ.* LXXX, 4 (1966), 518–19

[61] Adolph Lowe. 'The Classical Theory of Economic Growth.' *Soc. Res.* XXI (1954), 127–58

[62] H. F. Lydall. 'On Measuring Technical Progress.' *Australian Econ. Pap.* VIII, 12 (1969), 1–12

[63] R. L. Marris. *The Economic Theory of 'Managerial' Capitalism.* London, Macmillan, 1964

[64] R. C. O. Matthews. 'The New View of Investment: A Comment.' *Quart J. Econ.* LXXVIII, 1 (1964) 164–72

[65] J. E. Meade. *A Neo-classical Theory of Economic Growth.* London, Allen and Unwin, 1961

[66] —— 'The Rate of Profit in a Growing Economy.' *Econ. J.* LXXIII, 292 (1963), 665–74

[67] —— and F. H. Hahn. 'The Rate of Profit in a Growing Economy.' *Econ. J.* LXXV, 298 (1965), 445–8

[68] —— 'The Outcome of the Pasinetti-Process: A Note.' *Econ. J.* LXXVI, 301 (1966), 161–5

[69] R. L. Meek. 'Mr Sraffa's Rehabilitation of Classical Economics.' *Scottish J. Polit. Econ.* VIII, 8 (1961), 119–36

[70] B. S. Minhas. *An International Comparison of Factor Costs and Factor Use.* Amsterdam, North-Holland, 1963

[71] Michio Morishima. 'Refutation of the Non-Switching Theorem.' *Quart. J. Econ.* LXXX, 4 (1966), 520–5

[72] Edward J. Nell. 'Wicksell's Theory of Circulation.' *J. Polit. Econ.* LXXV, 4 (1967), 386–96

[73] —— 'Theories of Growth and Theories of Value'. *Econ. Develop., Cult. Change.* XVI, 1 (1967), 15–26
[74] —— 'A Note on Neo-Keynesian Distribution Theories.' East Anglia, 1968, unpublished paper
[75] —— 'A Note on the Social Rate of Return and the Switching Rate of Profit.' East Anglia, 1968, unpublished paper
[76] D. M Nuti. 'The Degree of Monopoly in the Kaldor-Mirrlees Growth Model.' *Rev. Econ. Stud. Vol.* XXXVI, 106, 257–60
[77] —— 'Capitalism, Socialism and Steady Growth.' *Econ. J.* LXXX, 317, (1970), 32–57
[78] Luigi L. Pasinetti. 'Rate of Profit and Income Distribution in Relation to the Rate of Economic Growth.' *Rev. Econ. Stud.* XXIX (4), 81 (1962), 267–79
[79] —— 'A Comment on Professor Meade's "Rate of Proft in a Growing Economy.' *Econ. J.* LXXIV, 294 (1964), 488–9
[80] —— 'A New Theoretical Approach to the Problems of Economic Growth.' Pontificiae Academiae Scientiarum, *Scripta Varia,* 1965
[81] —— 'The Rate of Profit in a Growing Economy: A Reply.' *Econ. J.* LXXVI, 301 (1966), 158–60
[82] —— 'Changes in the Rate of Profit and Switches of Techniques.' *Quart. J. Econ.* LXXX, (1966), 503–17
[83] —— 'New Results in an Old Framework.' *Rev. Econ. Stud.* XXXII (4), 96 (1966), 303–6
[84] E. S. Phelps and C. Phelps. 'Factor-Price-Frontier Estimation of a "Vintage" Production Model of the Postwar United States Non-farm Business Sector.' *Rev. Econ. Statist.* XLVIII, 3 (1966), 251–65
[85] Joan Robinson. 'The Production Function and the Theory of Capital.' *Rev. Econ. Stud.* XXI (2), 55 (1953–4) 81–106
[86] —— *The Accumulation of Capital.* London, Macmillan, 1956
[87] —— 'The Real Wicksell Effect.' *Econ. J.* LXVIII, 271 (1958), 600–5
[88] —— 'Accumulation and the Production Function.' *Econ. J.* LXIX, 275 (1959), 433–42
[89] —— *Exercises in Economic Analysis.* London, Macmillan, 1960
[90] —— 'Symposium on Production Functions and Economic Growth: Comment.' *Rev. Econ. Stud.* XXIX, 79 (1962), 258–66
[91] —— 'Solow on the Rate of Return.' *Econ. J.* LXXIV, 294 (1964), 410–17
[92] —— 'Equilibrium Growth Models.' *Collected Economic Papers,* Vol. III Oxford, Basil Blackwell, 1965, pp. 15–29.
[93] —— 'A Reconsideration of the Theory of Value.' *Collected Economic Papers,* Vol. III. Oxford, Basil Blackwell, 1965, pp. 173–81
[94] —— 'Comment on Samuelson and Modigliani.' *Rev. Econ. Stud.* XXXIII (4), 96 (1966), 307–8
[95] —— and K. A. Naqvi. 'The Badly Behaved Production Function.' *Quart. J. Econ.,* LXXXI, 4 (1967), 579–91

[96] W. E. G. Salter. 'The Production Function and the Durability of Capital.' *Econ. Rec.* XXXV, 70 (1959), 47–66
[97] —— *Productivity and Technical Change.* Cambridge, Cambridge University Press, 1960
[98] —— 'Productivity Growth and Accumulation as Historical Processes.' *Problems in Economic Development,* ed. by E. A. G. Robinson. London, Macmillan, 1965, pp. 266–91
[99] —— 'Marginal Labour and Investment Coefficients of Australian Manufacturing Industry.' *Econ. Rec.,* XXXVIII, 82 (1962), 137–56
[100] J. R. Sargent. 'Recent Growth Experience in the Economy of the United Kingdom.' *Econ. J.* LXXVIII, 309 (1968), 19–42
[101] P. A. Samuelson. 'Parable and Realism in Capital Theory: The Surrogate Production Function.' *Rev. Econ. Stud.*, XXXIX (3), 80 (1962), 193–206
[102] —— 'A Summing Up.' *Quart. J. Econ.* LXXX, 4 (1966) 568–83
[103] —— and F. Modigliani. 'The Pasinetti Paradox in Neoclassical and More General Models.' *Rev. Econ. Stud.* XXXIII (4), 96 (1966), 269–301
[104] —— and —— 'Reply to Pasinetti and Robinson.' *Rev. Econ. Stud.,* XXXIII (4), 96 (1966), 321–30
[105] R. M. Solow, 'The Production Function and the Theory of Capital'. *Rev. Econ. Stud.* XXIII (2), 61 (1956), 101–8
[106] —— 'Technical Change and the Aggregate Production Function.' *Rev. Econ. Statist. XXXIX, 3 (1957), 312–20*
[107] —— 'Investment and Technical Progress'. *Mathematical Methods in the Social Sciences 1959: Proceedings of the First Stanford Symposium,* ed. by K. J. Arrow, S. Karlin and P. Suppes. Stanford, Stanford University Press, 1960
[108] —— 'Substitution and Fixed Proportions in the Theory of Capital.' *Rev. Econ. Stud.* XXLX (3), 80 (1962), 207–18
[109] —— 'Heterogeneous Capital and Smooth Production Functions: An Experimental Study.' *Econometrica,* XXXI, 4 (1963), 623–45
[110] —— *Capital Theory and the Rate of Return.* (Professor Dr F. De Vries Lectures). Amsterdam, North-Holland, 1963
[111] ——, J. Tobin, C. C. von Weizsäcker and M. Yaari. 'Neoclassical Growth with Fixed Factor Proportions.' *Rev. Econ. Stud.* XXXIII (2), 94 (1966), 79–115
[112] R. M. Solow. 'The Interest Rate and Transition between Techniques'. *Socialism, Capitalism and Economic Growth. Essays presented to Maurice Dobb,* ed. by C. H. Feinstein. Cambridge, Cambridge University Press, 1967
[113] —— and Joseph E. Stiglitz. 'Output, Employment and Wages in the Short Run.' *Quart J. Econ.* LXXXII, 4 (1968), 537–60
[114] R. M. Solow. 'Distribution in the Long and Short Run.' *The Distribution of National Income,* ed. by Jean Marshal and Bernard Ducros. London; Macmillan, 1968, pp. 449–75
[115] L. Spaventa. 'Realism without Parables in Capital Theory.'

Recherches récentes sur la Fonction de Production. Centre D'Études et de Récherches Universitaire de Namur, 1968, pp. 15–45

[116] P. Sraffa (ed.), with the collaboration of M. H. Dobb. *Works and Correspondence of David Ricardo*, 10 Vols, Cambridge. Cambridge University Press, 1950–55

[117] P. Sraffa. *Production of Commodities by Means of Commodities. Prelude to a Critique of Economic Theory.* Cambridge, Cambridge University Press, 1960

[118] Joseph E. Stiglitz (ed.). *The Collected Scientific Papers of Paul A. Samuelson,* Vol. 1. Cambridge, Mass., MIT Press, 1966

[119] Joseph E. Stiglitz. 'Notes on the Switching of Techniques.' Cambridge, 1966, unpublished paper

[120] —— 'A Two-sector Two Class Model of Economic Growth.' *Rev. Econ. Stud.* XXXIV (2), 98 (1967), 227–38

[121] —— *Lectures on Economic Theory.* University of Canterbury, New Zealand, 1967

[122] T. W. Swan. 'Economic Growth and Capital Accumulation.' *Econ. Rec.* XXXII, 63 (1956), 334–61

[123] J. K. Whitaker. 'Vintage Capital Models and Econometric Production Functions.' *Rev. Econ. Stud.* XXXIII (1), 93 (1966), 1–18

[124] G. D. N. Worswick. 'Mrs. Robinson on Simple Accumulation, A Comment with Algebra.' *Oxford Econ. Pap.* XI, 2 (1959), 125–41

[125] J. von Neumann. 'A Model of General Economic Equilibrium.' *Rev. Econ. Stud.* XIII, 33 (1945–46), 1–9

8 The Rate of Profits in Equilibrium Growth Models: A Review Article[1]

Dr Kregel is convinced that a viable theory of the rate of profits is a prerequisite for the theory of long-run equilibrium growth. The rate of profits which he has in mind is a classical macro-economic concept, the ratio of the values of total profits to total 'capital' in the economy.[2] It is important in this context also to distinguish between the expected rate of profits and the realised rate of profits. The former is an *ex ante* concept associated with investment decisions. It is a viable concept in either equilibrium or disequilibrium situations. The latter can be defined rigorously and logically only in an equilibrium state in which expectations are realised and risk and uncertainty are absent. Kregel is mainly concerned in *Two Views* with equilibrium situations in which the two concepts merge into one.

The processes of distribution and growth intertwine through saving and investment. The rate of profits affects them both and, of course, the stability properties of growth models are related to both investment and saving behaviour.

The object of Kregel's book is to examine the theories of the rate of profits in a number of growth models. The first group are those in the neoclassical (now neo-neoclassical) tradition, represented by Meade (1961),[3] Solow (1963), Tobin (1965) and Samuelson and Modigliani (1966*a*, 1966*b*). The second are those in the neo-Keynesian, neo-Marxian tradition, represented by Kalecki (1935, 1937, 1954, 1962, 1966, 1968, 1969), Kaldor (1955–56, 1957, 1959*a*, 1959*b*, 1961, 1962, 1966, 1970), Pasinetti (1962) and Joan Robinson (1956, 1962, 1971). Kregel adds his own contribution in the last chapter. He argues, conclusively in my view and in contradiction to at least the neo-neoclassical viewpoint, that the key difference between the two approaches lies in the treatment and status of investment expenditure, in particular its independence of saving decisions, rather than in the constitution and differing saving behaviour of particular social classes in the community.

In order to assess the contributions of the two groups of authors Kregel provides himself with criteria that derive mainly from the path-breaking work of Piero Sraffa in *Production of Commodites by Means of Commodities* (1960). The subtitle of this book is *Prelude to a Critique of Economic Theory*, by which is meant the neoclassical marginal theory of value and distribution. Kregel draws on two strands of Sraffa's implied critique. The first is positive in the sense that it provides an alternative theory of value and distribution to that of the marginalists. The second is negative in the sense of exposing logical flaws in the currently received paradigm, neoclassical theory.

By solving the problem of the transformation of Marxian values into long-run competitive prices, Sraffa provides a viable labour theory of value in a setting in which 'the marginal product... just would not be there to be found', that is, we are concerned with 'such properties of an economic system' from which 'changes in the scale of production or in the proportion of "factors" have been excluded' (Sraffa, 1960, p. v). It is a labour theory of value in the limited sense that relative prices can be shown to be determined by amounts of direct and indirect embodied labour. Included in the amounts are those associated with the maximum rate of profits of the system as a whole. The maximum rate of profits itself can be shown to be determined by the technical conditions of actual economic systems; this is the unique and most satisfying feature of Sraffa's solution (see Meek, 1967, pp. 175–78; Hunt, 1971). A by-product of his solution is the demonstration that it is impossible to conceive of a quantity of 'capital' which is measured in a unit which is independent of distribution and prices—'an independent measure ... which could be used, without arguing in a circle, for the determination of prices and of the shares in distribution' (Sraffa, 1960, p. 38). The demonstration consists essentially of showing that the relative prices of two products which are produced by given methods of production change in relation to one another as alternative values of the rate of profits and the wage rate are considered. (The prices of the products are expressed in terms of their 'dated' labour components [see Sraffa, 1960, pp. 37–40]). This proposition is a central part of Kregel's critique of the neo-neoclassical models in Chapters 3–6.

For the second strand of his critique, Kregel uses Sraffa's account of the switching of techniques in order to dismiss the *invariant* association between higher values of 'capital' and lower rates of profits. This association is crucial to *all* traditional versions of the neoclassical theory of distribution; that is, to those theories which depend on a supply and demand approach to distribution (see Garegnani, 1970, p. 422). Thus in Part 3 of his book, Sraffa had shown that the same technique may be adopted by profit-maximising businessmen at two widely different rates of profits, even though other techniques were the profit-maximising ones at rates of profits in between. (It was this demonstration that precipitated Levhari's 1965 article and the 1966 *Quarterly Journal*'s symposium on reswitching.) Moreover, Champernowne (1953–4) and Joan Robinson (1953–4, 1956) had shown that it did not follow invariably that the more 'capital'-intensive, more productive (in the sense of output per head) technique of two possibilities may be chosen at a lower rate of profits (see Harcourt, 1972, pp. 124–8). Subsequent analysis has shown that far from being theoretical *curiosa* or perverse cases, both these possibilities are as likely to occur as not. Furthermore, because they are essentially propositions about alternative equilibrium states, they are not subject to empirical falsification as some econometricians and neoclassical exponents have argued (see Brown, 1969; Ferguson, 1969).

The main analysis of Kregel's book is preceded by a historical excursion which, in a potted form, goes something like this. Ricardo's theory of the rate of profits was logical as long as he confined himself to the corn model. There, given competition and a long-run tendency to equality of rates of profit in all industries, the technically determined rate of profits in agriculture of corn over corn ruled the roost (no pun intended). However, when Ricardo attempted to deal with a real wage that contained commodities other than corn, he needed a measure of value which was invariant to changes in distribution, a measure that he himself never found. Sraffa has shown that, nevertheless, such a measure, namely the Standard commodity, was embedded in the Ricardian system. The Standard commodity consists of a particular combination of *all* the basics—price-determining commodities as opposed to price-determined non-basics—in the system. The combination is such that each commodity is in the same proportion to all others in the net product of the Standard system as it is in the means of production. The Standard commodity may be shown to be akin to a labour commanded measure of value, a result which Ricardo, no doubt, would have thought rather shocking (see Sraffa, 1960, p. 94).

Marx also had a persuasive theory of distribution. It stressed the capitalists' role in organising the conditions of production and drew on the exploitive characteristics of the system of production under capitalist institutions whereby ownership of the means of production enabled capitalists to expropriate the net product (defined in the classical sense as excluding wages) so created. But he, too, never fully succeeded in coping with the transformation problem in the general case where commodities are produced by commodities. Sraffa, strand one, has now sown this one up also (see Meek, 1967, pp. 175–78; Hunt, 1971).[4]

The early neoclassicals are represented in the present book by Walras and Marshall. In Kregel's (and Joan Robinson's) view, they rejected the classical, especially the Marxian, theory whereby profits arose from capital's power to exploit labour but had no satisfactory theory of the rate of profits for the economy as a whole to put in its place. Walras is pictured as considering given stocks and a market period and assuming perfect foresight and no uncertainty. His auctioneer obtains a set of market-clearing prices. There is, however, no adequate explanation of who owns the stock, or why, or what the rate of profits is, or how it could arise.[5] We deal more with the characteristics of an exchange economy than with those of a producing, accumulating one. (Joan Robinson's reference to the economics of a POW camp is to the point at this juncture [see Robinson, 1971, p. 4].) Kregel's principal complaint is concisely stated: 'The system cannot be used to distribute the output once the value is determined' (1971, p. 4). (Exponents of the MIT neo-neoclassical model would argue that there is no need to obtain an aggregate rate of profits anyway [see Solow, 1970*b*, pp. 427–8]. They would add that from the earliest days it has been recognized that the assumption of profit maximisation implies imputed rentals equal to the 'notional' marginal products of each input in the individual production functions, see Hahn and Matthews, 1964, p. 888.)

Marshall[6] was tempted to extend the Malthusian-Ricardian theory of rent to all 'factors' of the production (or 'agents', as he generally would have called them when taking an overall view). However, he was well aware that 'capital' was not a primary factor like 'labour' and 'land'; that there was no technical unit independent of distribution and prices in which it could be measured; that capital goods were intermediate goods and so not a long-run constraint on economic development; and that free or money capital would be invested in specific capital goods in the expectation of earning a rate of return, a pure number.[7] Marshall wanted to explain, perhaps also to justify, rentiers' incomes as the return to waiting. He also had long-run normal rates of profit in long-run normal prices. He knew perfectly well that expected rates of profit guided businessmen's investment decisions in particular lines of production, but he also treated any returns to existing capital goods, themselves not capable rigorously of being valued, as quasi-rents. But, because he was reluctant ever completely to use either a stationary state or a Golden Age (see Pigou, 1925, p. 16), he was prevented from spelling out explicitly a fully fledged marginal productivity theory, using an aggregate production function. He got pretty close. Thus: 'By far the most important use of the term Capital in general, i.e. from the social point of view, is in the inquiry how the three agents of production, land (that is, natural agents), labour and capital, contribute to producing the national income . . .; and how that income is distributed among the three agents' (Marshall, 1961, p. 78). As a result, the normal rate of profits as a macro concept in Marshallian thought, towards which all rates of profit would tend in long-run competitive equilibrium, and viewed in the perspective of the post-war developments of the theory of growth, was left 'hanging in the air', unable to be exlained by the marginal product of 'capital', since 'capital' could not itself be valued until the rate of profits it was meant to help explain was itself known.

So ends the historical excursion. Kregel's discussion of the contributions of von Neumann, Kalecki, Keynes and Sraffa himself fits more properly into the modern period.

Later neoclassical economists—J. B. Clark, Hicks (in *The Theory of Wages*, 1932) and, today, Swan (1956), Meade (1961), Ferguson (1969) and H. G. Johnson (1971)—'overcame' the puzzle by assuming that 'capital' is a primary factor which may be treated 'as if' it were a malleable quantity measurable in its own technical unit.[8] Its marginal product, labour's marginal product, both of which are obtained form the production function or functions, and the preferences of individuals combine together in a general equilbrium system to give equilibrium solutions for all 'prices' and quantities. In this way, 'capital' as investable funds on which a rate of return must be expected to be paid and capital goods are boiled down into one. The same concept, 'capital' may then be used, simultaneously, to help to predict output levels and to determine, via the principle of substitution, the distribution of income in terms of the technical conditions of production. (In the one commodity case, technical conditions alone determine distribution; in the general case, it is individual preferences and the technical conditions of production combined [see H. G. Johnson, 1971, pp. 15–16].)

'Sraffa's system is beyond doubt competitive and general equilibrium in nature', yet nowhere are demand or change (i.e. marginal products) mentioned. This leads Kregel to comment: 'His conclusions raise serious questions about the contribution of marginal theory to economics' (p. 39)—and also to an analysis of modern capitalism and its prices where in Kregel's view, demand plays little part in setting prices (p. 38). Thus Sraffa's expression for the wage-rate–rate-of-profits trade-off relationship, $r = R(1 - w)$ [or $w = 1 - (r/R)$], where w is the proportion of the national income[9] Standard commodity which is accounted for by the wage bill and R is the maximum rate of profits, allows us to determine prices and value 'capital' once we have, from elsewhere, an acceptable theory of the rate of profits (Sraffa's view) or share of wages (Marx's and/or von Neumann's and/or Kalecki's solutions).

The questions then are: Are the two theories of value rivals or complements? Which isolates the more fundamental determinants of relative prices? The stands taken on these issues categorise neatly the leading practitioners of our trade. The neo-neoclassicals treat the theories as complements so that the question of fundamentals does not arise. (If pressed, though, they seem to have more fondness for preferences and time than for labour [see Samuelson, 1971].) Of the neo-Keynesians, the neo-Marxians treat them as rivals and deem Sraffa's view the more fundamental (see Dobb, 1970; Harcourt, 1972, appendix to Ch. 4).

Von Neumann (1945–46) provided a theory of the rate of profits in a classical model in which there was a technically determined subsistence wage and all profits were reinvested. The rate of profits (r) is technically determined and equals the rate of growth of the system (g). This result ceases to hold once the wage ceases to be a subsistence one, or some part of profits is consumed. Nevertheless, von Neumann's is a remarkable paper because it is the first modern paper (it was originally written in the 1930s) in which it is shown rigorously that the rate of profits is a function of the dynamic rate of growth of the economy rather than of the relative scarcity of 'capital'.[10] Kalecki's solution is in terms of the degree of monopoly, which is related to Marx's theory of exploitation, and the classical link between the income receipts of broad social classes and expenditure on broad groups of commodities. Thus Kalecki's neat phrase, 'The workers spend what they get and the capitalists get what they spend' (Robinson, 1971, p. 119, n. 8), makes one think of the Ricardian categories of rent, profits and wages, on the one hand, and luxuries, means of production and wage goods, on the other; of Marxian schemes of reproduction with three sectors producing the means of production, consumption goods, and luxuries, respectively, to be bought by the income flows of advanced wages and profits; and, in more modern times, of wages and profits spent, respectively, on consumption and investment goods ('available' and 'unavailable goods' in the terminology of Keynes of the *Treatise* [1930]). In the *Treatise*, Keynes explained both the overall level of prices and distribution, in the sense of the relationship of prices to money wages, by a relationship between saving and investment, and the links between broad expenditure patterns and broad groups of income. Saving and investment are equal at equilibrium when the rate of change of the overall level of prices ceased. In the *Treatise* as in *The General Theory*, investment played the dominant and saving the passive role in their relationship.

The contributions of Keynes and Kalecki relate basically to the share of profits rather than to the rate of profits. Kaldor (1955–56, 1957, 1959*a*, 1959*b*, 1961, 1962, 1966, 1970) has drawn on them in order to show that if we assume steady growth and ignore rentier's expenditure and wage-earners' saving, von Neumann's result that $r = g$ follows immediately.[11] The result is not one, however, that I think Kalecki would have found interesting; a world of capitalist Golden Ages, of realised expectations and of rigorously defined measures of 'capital' and the rate of profits is not the natural habitat of a practising Marxist. Kalecki, like Goodwin, regarded the trend and cycle as indissolubly mixed (see Dobb, 1972, p. 216). However, neither the majority of writers whose work is surveyed in this book nor, possibly, the author himself, would share this view. We have therefore to work with a model of realised expectations, that is to say, of one akin to perfect foresight, for only in this world can a rigorous meaning be given to the rate of profits (equals the rate of interest) *ex post* as well as *ex ante* and 'capital' be valued in terms of long-run normal (i.e. equilibrium) prices.

Kregel criticises Meade, Tobin, and Samuelson and Modigliani for either implicitly or explicitly depending on the malleability assumption and/or an inverse relationship between the value of 'capital' and rate of profits in order to introduce the marginal product of 'capital' as part of the distributive mechanisms in their growth models. For example, Meade (1961) goes over classical ground but wishes in addition to include in the story the principle of substitution of 'capital' for labour and the influence of technical progress (so, too, did Marx) and the influence of the relative scarcities of factors on wages and profits. As he also supposes that saving determines—is—investment, in most places he needs a theory of distribution in order to determine aggregate saving and discuss the possibility of stable growth and full employment over time. Meade looks for a harmonious outcome—steady growth at full employment and an efficient allocation of resources. He does not necessarily approve of the resulting personal distribution of income, being a lib-lab, planning-through-the-price-mechanism man.[12] Marx, by contrast, looked for contradiction, conflict and crisis. It has been left to Joan Robinson to emphasise the basically Marxian (but also Keynesian) view that if it is investment, done in anticipation of profits, which creates saving (rather than saving which creates investment), then the theory of profits, indeed, their very existence, are no longer a justification for rentiers' incomes. Marshall was certainly aware of this but avoided making it explicit. Hence, perhaps, the rationale of Joan Robinson's celebrated statement, 'The more I learn about economics the more I admire Marshall's intellect and the less I like his character' (1953, p. 14), which is rather freely deployed by Kregel on page 4 as 'the more she learns about economics the more she respects Marshall as an economist and the less as a man'.

Kregel, drawing on Sraffa's arguments, considers Meade's theory of stable growth to be deficient once the existence and ownership of heterogeneous capital goods are recognised. If capital goods are not malleable, the rate of growth cannot be reconciled with the saving rate except by a fluke. Moreover, the saving rate cannot be changed by changing the distribution of income if either there are no differences in the saving propensities of different classes or distribution itself is indeterminate because the marginal product of 'capital' does not exist. Indeed, in the absence of substitution possibilities, Meade is forced to fall back on something very like the Kalecki-Keynes-Kaldor distributive mechanism (see Kregel, 1971, pp. 62–3). The same sort of critique is made of Tobin's

'Keynesian' model where an association between a declining marginal product of 'capital' and a rising stock of 'capital' both unmeasured, plays a key role.

In their controversy with Pasinetti, Samuelson and Modigliani (1966*a*, 1966*b*) claim that the only assumption that they need make is that of an inverse relationship between the ratio of the value of 'capital' to labour and the rate of profits. As a general proposition, this, too, is denied to them by the Sraffa critique and the outcome of the reswitching and capital-reversing debate (see Harcourt, 1972, Ch. 4). Essentially, such a relationship is a 'must' if a downward-sloping demand curve for 'capital' is to be constructed. While we may live quite happily with Giffen goods as a minor exception to the general theory of demand, it is an entirely different proposition to view 'capital' as possibly a Giffen good, especially when its price is meant to be an index of scarcity (see Pasinetti, 1969; Garegnani, 1970).

Previously, Samuelson, in his 1962 surrogate production function article, tried to provide some sort of rationalisation for the use of malleable capital models to illustrate phenomena in a world of heterogeneous capital goods. However, as is now well known, his results are confined, ironically, to worlds with technologies in which, in the general case, the organic composition of capital is uniform in all uses (see Robinson and Naqvi, 1967), and, in the special neoclassical case, the physical capital-labour ratios of all sectors are identical (see Samuelson, 1962). These assumptions ensure that long-run competitive relative prices are identical with Marxian values and thus that the value of 'capital' of each technique is independent of changes in distribution. Within this world, a pseudo-production function seemingly behaves 'as if' processes of, for example, the substitution of 'capital' for labour were occurring in a malleable capital world (see Harcourt, 1972, pp. 131–44). (A pseudo-production function consists of a set of long-run stationary states, each with its own 'history' and 'future' and equilibrium rate of profits, real wage and value of 'capital' and output per head. With Samuelson's assumptions, as we move up the factor-price frontier, it is found that the states associated with lower rates of profits and higher real wages have higher values of output and 'capital' per head.)

Two other criticisms of marginal theory, one of which Kregel stresses, may be mentioned in passing. The first concerns the inapplicability of the law of variable proportions, especially in the short run, to manufacturing industry. This has been well discussed by Nell (1972), who concludes as follows: 'In the three-quarters of a century that this theory has ruled in classrooms, no one has produced a simple but detailed and convincing real-life example drawn from industry' (p. 447). The second criticism relates to the supposed equality of the marginal product of labour with the real wage. Leaving aside all the other objections that may be made against this proposition, both Kregel and Joan Robinson argue that the equality should be between the marginal product of labour, on the one hand, and the wage *plus* interest on the additional finance required to advance the wages of the additional man, on the other. This view reflects the essence of the Marxist insight that the ability to advance wages by having property in the means of production, including the wages fund, ensures that the capitalists can expropriate the net product of the next round of production. However, it is not really a knockdown blow, for, following Sraffa, we may regard the wage as paid, like the profits, out of the surplus at the end of the period of production. Moreover, in a continuous process the point may be ignored. In any event, even if the simple equality be destroyed, the maximising principle which is basic to the marginalist view, far from being refuted by the proposition, is in fact consistent with it.

In Chapter 5, Kregel reviews Solow's contribution (in the 1963 De Vries Lectures [Solow, 1963]) whereby 'capital' and 'its' marginal product are seemingly vanished from the analysis, and the rate of return on investment becomes the central variable of the theory of capital. The latter itself becomes 'a modern amalgamation of Wicksell and Irving Fisher' (Solow, 1963, p. 17). Solow argues that the concept of the rate of return on investment (R), which is the ratio of extra consumption gained in the future (a period which may vary from next year to eternity) to consumption given up now, is as applicable to the neoclassical world of infinite substitutability and production functions as it is to one of fixed coefficients. The example that Solow uses is Worswick's stockade-dictator version of Joan Robinson's 1956 model of accumulation with one technique (see Worswick, 1959). In the former world, the main result is that $MP_K = r = R$, where MP_K is the marginal product of 'capital'. In the latter (and contrary to what Kregel says on p. 82) only $r = R$—the marginal product of 'capital' is 'just ... not there to be found'. (The proof of the latter equality in Worswick's example founders on the second point raised in the preceding paragraph, unless the wage is paid out of the surplus, as Sraffa has it, rather than advanced.) Most of Solow's theoretical and empirical work, however, draws on the neoclassical model and so is vulnerable to the criticisms of that model which stem from Sraffa and the neo-Keynesian critique in general (see Harcourt, 1972, Ch. 3).

Surprisingly, Kregel refers only in passing to Solow's contribution to the Dobb *Festschrift* (1967), Pasinetti's important article (1969) and the subsequent exchanges between Solow and Pasinetti (Solow, 1970*b*; Pasinetti, 1970). In these articles and critiques, a Fisherian theory of the aggregate rate of profits and of its equality with the rate of return on investment, which is derived in part from Solow's analysis in the De Vries Lectures, once again is shown to founder on the results of the reswitching and capital-reversing debates. In order to show that $r = R = (\Delta Q/\Delta K)$, where ΔQ is the increment in output and ΔK is the increment in the value of 'capital', Solow concentrates on the comparisons of two economies at a switch point and on processes of technocratic accumulation whereby one economy has its characteristics changed to that of another over one or more periods. A switch point is a configuration of the rate of profits and real wage such that the techniques of production of the two economies are equiprofitable, and their relative price systems are identical. However, in Pasinetti's view, this case is not truly analogous to the traditional neoclassical case in which it is (infinitesimal) changes in the rate of profits which bring about changes in techniques. In order, then, to identify the $\Delta Q/\Delta K$s which are associated with these changes, 'capital' (K) needs must be measured in a unit that is independent of distribution and prices. The seeming independence of K of distribution and prices in Solow's analysis is achieved only by having the common rate of profits, wage and relative price systems. This ensures that $\Delta Q/\Delta K$ and R are defined as equal to r. Pasinetti goes on to argue that differing values of an externally given r sweep out an inverse relationship between r and K only if an 'unobtrusive postulate' which rules out capital reversing and reswitching by assumption is introduced into the analysis. Moreover, although Solow explicitly denies it (see Solow, 1970*b*, pp. 427–8), the equality of R and r is thought by Kregel and other neo-Keynesians to have some bearing on both the efficiency of the functioning of competitive capitalist economies, whereby private choices and social choices are shown to coincide, and the justification of the payment of profits, presumably because the return to the capitalist has guided satisfactorily the use of the societies' resources between the present and the future.

We come now to the neo-Keynesian contributions, all of which derive from the extraordinarily powerful Keynesian tool of the equality of planned saving and investment.[13] Distribution is seen not as a resultant of substitution, technology, and individual preferences, but of aggregate expenditures, incomes, and overall saving behviour. With the exception of Harrod (1939, 1948), who usually ignores theories of distribution and the rate of profits, all the neo-Keynesian growth models incorporate a Keynesian (of the *Treatise*) theory of distribution. The models of Kaldor and Pasinetti are confined to a long-run full-employment state. Kaldor believes that there are forces which make the long-run equilibrium position of a growing economy a full-employment one, whereas Pasinetti wished to investigate the existence and stability of the equilibrium relationships of an economy when investment had been constrained to a level which ensured full employment over time. Joan Robinson's classification is more flexible. As Asimakopulos (1969, 1970) has shown, she uses either a monopolistic-type economy with fixed margins, which may imply unemployment of both the existing capital stock and of labour, or a competitive-type economy within which there is sufficient price flexibility always to ensure short-run full employment of the capital stock. She highlights the two-edged relationship between the rate of profits and investment, namely, that high expected profits are required to encourage investment but that profits themselves cannot be high unless investment is. Joan Robinson, more than any other writer, has provided the framework within which *The General Theory* may itself be generalised in order to tackle long-run growth and distribution puzzles. As a by-product she has attacked existing neoclassical theory within, as she sees it, its own confines, providing analyses which are meant to show up logical flaws within the system itself rather than to solve practical problems. Kregel's review of her contributions in Chapter 11 is one of the best and most helpful sections of the book.

If in the neo-Keynesian models we suppose that the economy is in a Golden Age (i.e. a state of realised expectations and steady growth at a constant rate of profits), rigorous meanings can be given to both the rate of profits and the value of 'capital', and the rate of profits can itself be shown to equal the rate of growth divided by the capitalists' marginal propensity to save. This follows directly from the multiplier-like relationship between investments and profits. The relative prices of the commodities of the economies concerned are 'Sraffa' prices, and the system is 'closed' by the expression for the rate of profits above. In the Kaldor and Joan Robinson versions (also Kahn's [see Kahn, 1959]), if workers save, this is an approximate result only. It is an exact one in Pasinetti's model, where account is taken of the fact that if workers save they earn interest on their accumulated savings. (If we assume a long-run steady state with risk and uncertainty absent, the equilibrium rate of interest naturally equals the equilibrium rate of profits.)[14]

Pasinetti's 1962 article led to the controversy about the orders of magnitude that the saving propensities of the workers may take in relation to the share of investment in income. It is here that Samuelson and Modigliani (1966*a*, 1966*b*; also Meade, 1963, 1966; and Meade and Hahn, 1965) enter the scene with the 'dual' to the Pasinetti result that if $s_w \geq \bar{I}/Y$, where s_w is the marginal propensity to save of the 'workers' and $\bar{I}/Y$ is the share of investment in national income, $K/Y = g/s_w$, rather than $r = g/s_c = MP_K$ (in the neoclassical case) when $s_w < \bar{I}/Y$ and s_c is the marginal propensity to save of the 'capitalists'. Kregel argues in his last chapter (see p. 148), that the distinguishing marks of the two approaches lie not so much in the different assumptions about the saving propensities of different social groups and the permanency of these groups, as is contended in these controversies, but in, rather, the treatment of investment as independent of saving. (Saving *is* investment in the neoclassical approach.) In order to make his point and also to mark out the range of implications of different saving assumptions, he examines a property-owning democracy model in which, initially, the saving behaviour of all citizens is the same but investment is independent of saving. (He subsequently allows the saving behaviour of firms and the market-clearing prices of the markets for securities to enter the analysis.) He examines both the theory of the rate of profits and the stability conditions of equilibrium growth models in this context and obtains neo-Keynesian type results of varying degrees of complexity.[15]

All of Kregel's results depend upon the economy finding its way to the equilibrium position where *ex ante* saving equals autonomous investment expenditure. Since the world, especially when it experiences high levels of activity, cannot be trusted always to behave in this manner, it is Kaldor alone of this group of writers who has argued that these sorts of models are useful as a description of actual events, albeit stylized ones.[16] We may adapt Joan Robinson's recent comment on the validity and limitations of the Kahn-Keynes short-run multiplier relationship (see Robinson, 1969, p. xiv) in order to make the point. 'When time-lags are not negligible, the [distribution of] income appropriate to one level of investment cannot, in general, be reached before the level of investment has changed, so that the exact equality between the rate of investment and the *appropriate* rate of saving would never be established.' As long ago as 1962, Meade (in the preface to the second edition of his *Neo-classical Theory of Economic Growth*) pointed out that the Kaldor model was more 'appropriate for the explanation of short-run inflation than of long-run growth' (p. x). I argued in 1963 that Kaldor's 'representative firm' model (which is reproduced by Kregel on pp. 122–6) does not imply that full employment is the long-run equilibrium position of a growing economy. Rather, it implies that capitalist economies are either caught in a deep underemployment equilibrium slump or are exhibiting full-employment growth with wage and price inflation; that is, a disequilibrium process (see Harcourt, 1963, pp. 33–36).

In Chapter 12, Kregel sorts out in a helpful fashion the equilibrium relationships between investment, saving and the monetary and stock-market sectors of neo-Keynesian models. He shows explicitly the effects of income flows and social classes ceasing to coincide and the link between the level of investment and past and present methods of financing it. He also attempts to deal with the determination of the price levels of consumption goods and investment goods in macro-distribution models. I am not sure that he has satisfactorily overcome a puzzle which is implicit in Kaldor's model; namely, that in order to obtain a determinate solution for the price of investment goods in a two-sector model, we must have either an *ad hoc* mark-up theory of prices or use a neoclassical-type solution of equality of expected rates of profits on the investment goods destined for the two sectors.[17] His models, like other neo-Keynesian models, assume a long-run rigidity in the values of the saving propensities of the different social classes and from different sorts of incomes, despite the fact that capital gains and losses may be made on financial assets on the way to equilibrium positions.

In any event, it is doubtful whether these particular exercises really take us that much closer to an understanding of the actual processes of growth and distribution over time. This is a pity, for, in his preface, Kregel pays a generous tribute to Joan Robinson's influence, and one could argue that the book may well have been inspired by her views,[18] as snappily expressed in the following passage:

> Presumably, no one would deny that there is more hope of understanding what is going on in the world when we recognize that the wage bargain is made in terms of money; that the level of prices is influenced by effective demand and the degree of imperfection of competition; that accumulation is controlled by the policy of firms and governments, not by the propensity to consume of private citizens, and that today is an ever moving break in time between an irrevocable past and an uncertain future.
>
> To understand is not easy, but at least we could try. [1965, p. 68]

Spurred on to read by such expectations, one must express a slight disappointment by the end of the book. Nevertheless,

Kregel has written a thoroughly worthwhile book, even though *Two Views* is not always an easy book to read and the exposition itself is variable. Thus, for example, I found the chapters on Sraffa, Harrod and Joan Robinson excellent, those on von Neumann, Meade and Tobin less so, and the one on Solow misleading in places. Readers of the book get a useful introduction to the modern theories of long-run equilibrium growth. The theories themselves are put in perspective and thoroughly evaluated in the light of the implied critique of Sraffa's classic. Those who agree already with the critique will have their views reinforced; those who disagree now have the task of refuting the arguments.

NOTES

1. This essay is a review of J. A. Kregel, *Rate of Profit, Distribution and Growth: Two Views* (London: Macmillan, 1971). It is reprinted here from the *Journal of Political Economy* 81, no. 5 (Sept./Oct. 1973), 1261–77. It is also published in French in C. Berthomieu and J. Cartelier (eds.), *Ricardiens, Keynesiens et Marxistes* (Nice: CORDES, 1974), pp. 51–74.

   I am indebted to J. H. Hatch, T. R. Hastings, N. F. Laing, Allen Oakley and E. A. Russell for helpful discussions and comments on a draft of this article.
2. It is no accident that Sraffa uses the phrase 'rate of profits' in his *Production of Commodities* (1960).
3. Kregel refers to the revised second edition of Meade's book (1962).
4. This particular point of Meek's, which is absolutely central to the discussion, is not discussed explicitly by Samuelson in his recent survey of the transformation problem (1971, 1972).
5. Much the same criticism may be applied to the modern neo-neoclassicals' version of a general equilibrium system, for a succinct account of which *see* Solow (1970*a*), pp. 33–34.
6. In writing the section on Marshall, I benefited greatly from discussion with Allen Oakley and from reading his Honours thesis (Oakley 1972). I have attempted to set out the evidence that lies behind the rather bald statements of Kregel (and Joan Robinson).
7. 'The income derived from capital already invested in particular things . . . is properly a quasi-rent and can be regarded as interest only on the assumption that the capital value of the investment has remained unaltered' (Marshall, 1961, p. 533). '"The general rate of interest" applies in strictness only to the anticipated net earnings from new investments of free capital' (Marshall, 1961, p. 533).
8. 'Problems of the nature of capital can be evaded by identifying capital as a malleable physical stock of productive equipment' (H. G. Johnson, 1971, p. 16).

9. I.e., the amount of Standard commodity that would be produced when the Standard system employed the actual amount of labour in the economy.
10. In the 1950s, Samuelson and Solow fitted the neoclassical concept of production functions (as engineering data, not aggregate) into von Neumann and Ramsey models (*see* Kregel, 1971, p. 6).
11. The same ideas, more properly and less ambitiously confined to their rightful theoretical context, are beautifully expressed in a rare Kahn article (1959). Understandably, Kaldor always wants to say something about the real world and, in the process, he often strays from the strictly logical confines of his analysis.
12. As is well known, Meade admires the price mechanism because of the scope that it offers for both consumers' choice and individual and political freedoms, but loathes the existing distribution of property. He therefore has long advocated policies which tend to preserve one while smashing the other.
13. This equality serves to illuminate many other facets of economic life apart from those of distribution and employment. Recently, for example, Eatwell, following some hints of Kahn (1959), has applied it to the area of fiscal incidence (see Eatwell, 1971).
14. Kregel's proof on p. 144 gets the right result but is surely wrong in depending upon the equality, $S_w = K_w$. How can the current saving of the workers (S_w), a *flow* per period, equal their capital (K_w), an accumulated *stock* of their past savings?
15. We have not the space to mention in this paper Kregel's treatment of Kaldor's technical progress function model, Kaldor's arguments that full employment is the natural equilibrium level of a growing capitalist economy, and the many strands of Joan Robinson's approach to growth and distribution.
16. Sometimes Kregel and Joan Robinson go so far as to say that if we assume very sluggish but compatible expectations and behaviour on the part of businessmen, the economy *may* enter a state of tranquility, in which case the exact relationships of Golden Ages may serve as surrogates for the approximate relationships of tranquility (*see* Kregel, 1972, pp. 3–7).
17. In his Louvain Lectures (1972), Kregel adopts a solution of equality of rates of profit as between the two *producing* sectors in his exposition of Joan Robinson's contributions to the theory of economic growth.
18. Coach Paul Davidson should also get a guernsey, as we say in Australia.

REFERENCES

Asimakopulos, A. 'A Robinsonian Growth Model in One-Sector Notation.' *Australian Econ. Papers* 8 (June 1969), 41–58

——— 'A Robinsonian Growth Model in One-Sector Notation—an Amendment.' *Australian Econ. Papers* 9 (Dec. 1970), 171–6

Brown, Murray. 'Substitution—Composition Effects, Capital Intensity Uniqueness and Growth'. *Econ. J.* 79 (June 1969), 334–47

Champernowne, D. G. 'The Production Function and the Theory of Capital: A Comment.' *Rev. Econ. Studies* 21 (Feb. 1953–54), 112–35

Dobb, M. H. 'The Sraffa System and Critique of the Neo-classical Theory of Distribution'. *De economist* 118 (July–Aug. 1970), 347–62

——— 'Review of Michal Kalecki, *Selected Essays in the Dynamics of the Capitalist Economy, 1971*'. *Econ. J.* 82 (Mar. 1972), 215–17

Eatwell, John. 'On the Proposed Reform of Corporation Tax'. *Bull. Oxford Univ. Inst. Econ. and Statis.* 33 (Nov. 1971), 267–74

Ferguson, C. E. *The Neoclassical Theory of Production and Distribution*. Cambridge, Cambridge Univ. Press, 1969

Ferguson, C. E., and Nell, E. J. 'Two Books on the Theory of Income Distribution: A Review Article'. *J. Econ. Literature* 10 (June 1972), 437–53

Geragnani, P. 'Heterogeneous Capital, The Production Function and the Theory of Distribution'. *Rev. Econ. Studies* 37 (July 1970), 407–36

Hahn, F. H., and Matthews, R. C. O. 'The Theory of Economic Growth: A Survey'. *Econ. J.* 74 (Dec. 1964), 779–902

Harcourt, G. C. 'A Critique of Mr. Kaldor's Model of Income Distribution and Economic Growth'. *Australian Econ. Papers* 2 (June 1963), 20–36

——— *Some Cambridge Controversies in the Theory of Capital*. Cambridge, Cambridge Univ. Press, 1972

Harrod, R. F. 'An Essay in Dynamic Theory'. *Econ. J.* 49 (Mar. 1939), 14–33

——— *Towards a Dynamic Economics: Some Recent Developments of Economic Theory and Their Applications to Policy*. London, Macmillan, 1948

Hicks, J. R. *The Theory of Wages*. London, Macmillan, 1932

Hunt, E. K. 'Religious Parables versus Economic Logic: An Analysis of the Recent Controversy in Value, Capital Distribution Theory'. *Intermountain Econ. Rev.* 2 (Fall 1971), 1–14

Johnson, H. G. *The Two-Sector Model of General Equilibrium*. The Yrjö Jahnsson Lectures, 1970. London, Allen & Unwin, 1971

Kahn, R. F. 'Exercises in the Analysis of Growth'. *Oxford Econ. Papers* 11 (June 1959), 143–56

Kaldor, N. 'Alternative Theories of Distribution'. *Rev. Econ. Studies* 23 (June 1955–56), 83–100

——— 'A Model of Economic Growth'. *Econ. J.* 67 (Dec. 1957), 591–624

——— 'Economic Growth and the Problem of Inflation. Part I'. *Economica* 26 (Aug. 1959), 212–26. (*a*)

——— 'Economic Growth and the Problem of Inflation. Part II.' *Economica* 26 (Nov. 1959), 287–98. (*b*)

——— 'Capital Accumulation and Economic Growth'. In *The Theory of*

Capital, edited by F. A. Lutz and D. C. Hague. London, Macmillan, 1961
—— 'Marginal Productivity and the Macro-economic Theories of Distribution'. *Rev. Econ. Studies* 33 (Oct. 1966), 309–19
—— 'Some Fallacies in the Interpretation of Kaldor'. *Rev. Econ. Studies* 37 (Jan. 1970), 1–7
Kaldor, N. and Mirrlees, J. A. 'A New Model of Economic Growth'. *Rev. Econ. Studies* 29 (June 1962), 174–92
Kalecki, M. 'A Macrodynamic Theory of Business Cycles'. *Econometrica* 3 (July 1935), 327–44
—— 'A Theory of the Business Cycle'. *Rev. Econ. Studies* 4 (Feb. 1937), 77–97
—— *Theory of Economic Dynamics*. London: Allen & Unwin, 1954
—— 'Observations on the Theory of Growth'. *Econ. J.* 72 (Mar. 1962), 134–53
—— *Studies in the Theory of Business Cycles, 1933–39*. New York, Kelley, 1966
—— 'Trends and Business Cycles Reconsidered'. *Econ. J.* 78 (June 1968), 263–76
—— *Introduction to the Theory of Growth in a Socialist Economy*. Oxford, Blackwell, 1969
Keynes, J. M. *A Treatise on Money*. 2 vols. London, Macmillan, 1930
—— *The General Theory of Employment, Interest and Money*. London, Macmillan, 1936
Kregel, J. A. *Rate of Profit, Distribution and Growth: Two Views*. London, Macmillan, 1971
—— *Lectures*. Louvain, Spring 1972
Levhari, D. 'A Non-Substitution Theorem and Switching of Techniques'. *Q.J.E.* 79 (Feb. 1965), 98–105
Marshall, A. *Principles of Economics*. 9th (variorum) edn with annotations by C. W. Guillebaud. 2 vols. London, Macmillan, 1961
Meade, J. E. *A Neo-classical Theory of Economic Growth*. London, Allen & Unwin, 1961
—— *A Neo-classical Theory of Economic Growth*, rev. 2nd edn. London, Allen & Unwin, 1962
—— 'The Rate of Profit in a Growing Economy'. *Econ. J.* 73 (Dec. 1963), 665–74
—— 'The Outcome of the Pasinetti-Process: A Note'. *Econ. J.* 76 (Mar. 1966), 161–5
Meade, J. E. and Hahn, F. H. 'The Rate of Profit in a Growing Economy'. *Econ. J.* 75 (June 1965), 445–8
Meek, R. L. *Economics and Ideology and Other Essays. Studies in the Development of Economic Thought*. London, Chapman & Hall, 1967
Oakley, A. 'The Theory of the Rate of Profits in English Economic Thought'. B.Ec. (Hons) thesis, Univ. Adelaide, 1972
Pasinetti, L. L. 'Rate of Profit and Income Distribution in Relation to the Rate of Economic Growth'. *Rev. Econ. Studies* 29 (Oct. 1962), 267–79

——'Switches of Technique and the "Rate of Return" in Capital Theory'. *Econ. J.* 79 (Sept. 1969), 508–31

——'Again on Capital Theory and Solow's "Rate of Return".' *Econ. J.* 80 (June 1970), 428–31

Pigou, A. C., ed. *Memorials of Alfred Marshall*. London, Macmillan, 1925

Robinson, Joan. *On Re-reading Marx*. Cambridge, Students Bookshop, 1953

——'The Production Function and the Theory of Capital'. *Rev. Econ. Studies* 21 (Feb. 1953–54), 81–106

——*The Accumulation of Capital*. London, Macmillan, 1956

——*Essays in the Theory of Economic Growth*. London, Macmillan, 1962

——*Introduction to the Theory of Employment*, 2nd edn. London, Macmillan, 1969

——*Economic Heresies: Some Old-fashioned Questions in Economic Theory*. New York, Basic, 1971

Robinson, Joan, and Naqvi, K. A. 'The Badly Behaved Production Function'. *Q.J.E.* 81 (Nov. 1967), 579–91

Samuelson, P. A. 'Parable and Realism in Capital Theory: The Surrogate Production Function'. *Rev. Econ. Studies* 33 (Oct. 1962), 193–206

——'Understanding the Marxian Notion of Exploitation: A Summary of the So-called Transformation Problem between Marxian Values and Competitive Prices'. *J. Econ. Literature* 9 (June 1971), 399–431

——'The Economics of Marx: An Ecumenical Reply'. *J. Econ. Literature* 10 (Mar. 1972), 51–57

Samuelson, P. A. and Modigliani, F. 'The Pasinetti Paradox in Neoclassical and More General Models'. *Rev. Econ. Studies* 33 (Oct. 1966), 269–301. (*a*)

——'Reply to Pasinetti and Robinson'. *Rev. Econ. Studies* 33 (October 1966), 321–30 (*b*)

Solow, R. M. *Capital Theory and the Rate of Return*. Professor Dr F. De Vries Lectures, 1963, Amsterdam, North-Holland, 1963

——'The Interest Rate and the Transition between Techniques'. In *Socialism, Capitalism and Economic Growth, Essays Presented to Maurice Dobb*, edited by C. H. Feinstein. Cambridge, Cambridge Univ. Press, 1967

——'Microeconomic Theory'. In *Economics*, edited by Nancy D. Ruggles. Englewood Cliffs, NJ, Prentice-Hall, 1970 (*a*)

——'On the Rate of Return: Reply to Pasinetti'. *Econ. J.* 80 (June 1970), 423–28 (*b*)

Sraffa, P. *Production of Commodities by Means of Commodities. Prelude to a Critique of Economic Theory*. Cambridge, Cambridge Univ. Press, 1960

Swan, T. W. 'Economic Growth and Capital Accumulation'. *Econ. Rec.* 32 (Nov. 1956), 334–61

Tobin J. 'Money and Economic Growth'. *Econometrica* 33 (Oct. 1965), 671–84 von Neumann, J. 'A Model of General Economic Equilibrium'. *Rev. Econ. Studies* 13 (Feb. 1945–46), 1–9

Worswick, G. D. N. 'Mrs. Robinson on Simple Accumulation. A Comment with Algebra'. *Oxford Econ. Papers* 11 (June 1959), 125–41

PART IV
Policy Issues

9 The Social Consequences of Inflation[1]

EXPLANATIONS OF INFLATION: WHY IS IT SO?

Following Keynes's analysis in *The General Theory* of the causes of prolonged recessions, economists (including Keynes himself in *How to Pay for the War*) have adapted his analysis in order to tackle the puzzle of inflation. Just as recessions were seen to result from the inability of a decentralised capitalist economy automatically to provide sufficient overall demands with which to absorb the total supplies of goods and services that would be forthcoming *if* the potential workforces and existing stocks of capital goods were fully employed at each point in time, so inflation was seen to be due to an excess of total demands in real terms over available supplies of goods and service *when* the potential workforces and existing stocks of capital goods *were* fully employed. The resulting 'inflationary gap', the tendency for planned investment expenditure to exceed full employment saving, generated tendencies for stocks of goods to be run down, queues to form, order books to lengthen and prices to rise. (The exact mixture of these ingredients depended upon the nature of the market structures of the economy concerned.)

The theory did not predict the *rate* at which prices rose, only that they would tend to rise. It did suggest that rising prices themselves could cure an inflationary situation *only* if their impact on planned real expenditures was to reduce them. Unlike the market for a single good, where an initial imbalance between demand and supply may be removed by a rise in the price of the good, an imbalance between total demands and supplies is not necessarily removed by rises in the general price level. For the other side of overall rising prices is rising money incomes of the same amount (abstracting from overseas transactions and the government for the moment), so that the capacity to buy at the higher price levels is not impaired in real terms. (In the market for an individual good, it is reasonable to suppose that the incomes of its purchasers are in the main independent of those of its suppliers, a supposition that is patently false for the economy as a whole.) It *might* be that, in an inflationary situation, there would be a tendency for prices to rise faster than money wages. Real income then would be redistributed by the inflationary process from a class which tends to spend much of its income, both on average and at the margin (the wage-earners), to one which does not (the profit-receivers), so that the overall level of planned spending in real terms on consumption goods could be reduced. If, also, the level of planned investment in real terms is not raised by the inflationary situation, there may be a level of prices overall that would be consistent with 'full employment without inflation'. But there is no guarantee that this will be achieved—money wages may not, for example, continue to lag behind prices—and, in any event, as it is the fall in the level of planned spending that is the key, it may be better consciously to bring this about rather than to depend on (and wait for) 'automatic' market forces to do so. Especially is this so in an open economy trading with the rest of the world; in this case the general price level that is consistent with full employment without inflation at home may be associated with a level of demand for imports which *vis-à-vis* export earnings and desired borrowing from, or lending abroad may imply serious balance of payments difficulties. Implicit in this discussion is the assumption of a flexible money supply. Otherwise, rising prices may have such an impact on rates of interest through the rise in the demand for money that expenditures in real terms are sooner or later choked off by higher rates of interest and the accompanying lower supplies of funds.

Also implicit in the preceding discussion is an assumption about the nature of the markets for individual commodities and productive services, namely, that they are competitive ones in which each individual, whether supplying or demanding a good or a service, is a price-taker. That is to say, prices are set by the automatic market forces and individuals lack discretionary power over the prices that they receive or pay for products and services. Clearly this is an unreal assumption to make about most markets in the manufacturing sectors of the economy (where, typically, administered pricing rules in oligopolistic settings) and, possibly, even in most sections of primary production as well. Moreover, most segments of the labour market are now unionised, at least to some extent; money wage levels therefore are not the outcome of automatic market forces but of bargaining processes which reflect relative bargaining strengths and social, historical, institutional and conventional processes.

The above factors imply that over quite a large range of fluctuations in overall activity, the general price level may be independent of the *actual* level of activity (and changes in it). (In the simple Keynesian model discussed above, the general price level (up to full employment) reflected the outcome of the intersections of individual demand and supply relationships, that is to say, their positions relative to one another and their elasticities and shifts over time.) In the present case we are arguing that the *same* level of activity *over time* may continue to be associated with a rising general level of prices, as autonomous rises in (say) money wages, or profit margins by price-makers using their discretionary power, or the prices of imported goods used as inputs into the domestic production process, feed through to the overall price level in the now familiar process of cost-push inflation. Because businessmen and wage-earners have come to believe that governments are committed to the maintenance of full employment, or, at least, high levels of activity, price-makers are not deterred either from seeking higher monetary awards and/or passing on *in full* autonomous rises in costs. The resulting higher money incomes tend to provide, together with sustained levels of autonomous expenditures (because of confident expectations about sustained activity levels), sufficient demands in real terms to maintain existing levels of activity. (We continue to assume a flexible money supply with which to support at the higher price levels and at least unchanged real rates of interest, the same level of activity.) In an open economy, with a fixed exchange rate, there are limits to the rate of increase which are dictated by movements in the prices of our exports and imports. But, given that inflation has tended to be a world-wide phenomenon for a considerable period of time, it is clear that cost-push inflation could be a self-sustaining process also for a considerable period of time. (Notice that this analysis is consistent with the 'Keynesian Revolution', at least as seen by the original Keynesians. Thus, Joan Robinson 'summarised [the 'Keynesian Revolution'] in the propositions that the rate of saving is governed by the rate of investment, that the level of prices is governed by the level of money wage rates, and [that] the level of interest rates is governed by the supply and demand of money.' (Introduction to Michal Kalecki, *Studies in the Theory of Business Cycles 1933–39*, Blackwell, Oxford 1969, pp. viii–ix.)

Both 'demand-pull' (as the orthodox 'Keynesian' theory is dubbed) and 'cost-push' elements obviously are present in the inflationary process that we are experiencing at the moment. Even when taken together, though, they are inadequate as a complete explanation. (I hasten to add that economists generally, unlike some politicians, are perplexed by the modern inflations and that no completely satisfactory explanation, widely accepted, has yet been formulated.) Underlying both theories is an assumption, based upon the experience of the nineteenth and first third of the twentieth century, that while price levels may fluctuate over time, the long-run trend through the cycles is at a pretty constant level; that is, that there is no obvious tendency for price levels either to go up or down over long stretches of time. This view in turn reflects those periods of capitalism where there was considerably more flexibility *in both directions* in money wages and prices. That it was not an unreasonable assumption for long periods of historical time may be checked by examining the levels of prices (and also the levels of the money rate of interest) over much of the nineteenth century and in the inter-war years.

With the commitment of the capitalist world in the post-war period to high levels of activity and growth, coupled with both the will and the power to attain them (if only by using defence spending as a base), the widely held expectation of a continuing long-run steady level of prices has been, at first gradually, and, recently, rapidly and virtually completely eroded. In its place have come very widely spread expectations of continuously rising price levels. These have carried with them in turn, attempts to compensate for past rises and, indeed, anticipate future ones when individual money-wage bargains are struck, either by arbitration procedures or, directly, by collective bargaining processes. Since individual money-wage bargains (that is, within firms or industries or trades) in a decentralised capitalist economy have also the aims of both protecting established (and hallowed) relativities and enabling wage-earners to share in the trend rise in overall national productivity, there has been in recent years a cumulative tendency for previously established sociological 'norms' as to what constitute reasonable rates of increases in money wages, acceptable both to wage-earners and employers, to break down. This is a world-wide phenomenon, observable (though with time lags) in the United States, the United Kingdom, Western Europe, Japan and, now, in Australia.

Since there has also been a relative relaxation of 'stop-go' policies, at least in their severity (and excluding the United Kingdom under the second Wilson administration and Australia after the first Snedden budget), the outcome has been accelerating rates of increases in money wages and, thus, prices, both internally and externally, because of the interlocking of countries through international trade. This has been accompanied by a great increase in the quantity of money in most capitalist countries, emanating from the United States and, in the Australian case, exacerbated (until recently) by a large amount of capital inflow together with the reflation of the economy following the 1971–72 recession. The result, world-wide, has been the discrediting of the Phillips curve relationship—the belief in the existence of a discernible stable trade-off between rates of increase of money wages and levels of, and rates of change in, unemployment. In the Australian case the prices of our imports and exports also have had an effect on the domestic cost level, both directly and indirectly, insofar as they consist of wage goods and so affect the demands made by wage-earners for increases in money wages.

As long as we live in a world of relatively fixed exchange rates, it is impossible completely to isolate trading nations from price changes that occur elsewhere in the world. Moreover, there is no guarantee that a floating exchange rate would be any protection. With expectations of accelerating inflation widely held, a floating exchange rate may well prove to be destabilising, either starting or continuing a cumulative process to which there is no foreseeable end. Especially is this so when there are strong cost-push forces at work associated with rising import prices and widely held expectations of a continuing rise in the general level of prices.

I hope that it is obvious from the above sketches that all the elements that have been identified with inflationary situations are recognisable in the present Australian experience. First of all, it is clear that there are excess demand elements present; these are shown not only by rapidly rising prices in various sectors, especially in certain key manufacturing sectors associated with the supplies of intermediate goods from other sectors, but also in the widespread phenomenon of shortages, accompanied by lengthening order books. The shortages themselves are a combination of a sustained boom not only in Australia but in the industrialized world as a whole, so that the usual outlet of extra imported supplies is not available as it would be if Australia were experiencing excess demand on its own. As far as excess demand is concerned, it is not possible to pin-point any particular segment of expenditure as responsible—it is the inconsistency in the total of planned real expenditures, some autonomous, some induced, in relation to total supplies that is the key.

Second, there are cost-push elements that are associated both with the prices of 'importable' and 'exportable' wage goods and inputs into domestic production and money wage increases. The latter reflect not only demand-pull forces due to the shortages of labour in general and special skills in particular (which belong, of course, under the first head) but also the responses of discretionary price-makers under conditions of extreme uncertainty coupled with expected price increases so that old established sociological 'norms' go by the board. The rise in militant union pressures and the accompanying increase in industrial unrest reflect both the anxieties of an inflationary situation and the basic class conflicts over the distribution of income which continuously high levels of activity increasingly have brought to the surface. Imposing excess demand on such a situation invariably runs a capitalist economy into what Joan Robinson has graphically called the 'inflation barrier'—the situation in which trade unions and wage-earners generally fight back via rising money wages against the attempt by other sectors of the community to use resources, for purposes other than the production of wage goods, in such proportions as to imply an intolerable level of real wages.

There is also a strongly entrenched desire to maintain well-established relativities. Here key sectors—for example, certain sectors of the public service—can be vital in giving the initial autonomous push, with other sectors attempting to achieve a flow-on that maintains their relative positions, if only after a lag. The actual increases in money wages aimed for and attained are influenced increasingly by the impact of unrevised progressive income tax schedules, set originally with much lower levels of *average* money incomes in mind, on effective levels of take-home pay. Thus larger and larger pre-tax incomes have to be bargained for in order to protect and /or improve, at a constant rate, post-tax real incomes. These factors help to account for the phenomenon of stagflation—sustained or even accelerating rates of increases in prices associated with rising levels of unemployment. There no longer seems to be (if there ever was) any simple stable trade-off between unemployment levels and rates of increase of money–wage rates and thus prices. Therefore, though reducing excess demand may be necessary as a measure of economic control, if excess demand features prominently in an inflationary situation, it is certainly not sufficient to remove inflationary pressures because of the other sets of factors that are independent of expenditure cuts and activity levels, at least over those ranges of activity that are politically possible in modern capitalist economies. Moreover, to get rid of *all* excess demand would require intolerably high levels of unemployment. Finally, the very large expansion in the monetary base, until recently, was also responsible for total spending being brought to a level where accelerating (and absolutely very large) rises in prices, especially in certain key sectors—for example, building and construction—were inevitable.

CONSEQUENCES FOR THE REDISTRIBUTION OF INCOME AND WEALTH: NEVER A LENDER BUT A BORROWER BE

Apart from the inefficiencies and shortages that are associated with the inflationary process, the waste of energy that goes into stock-exchange speculation, tax avoidance and fly-by-night schemes designed to make a quick profit for their initiators, there occur major redistributions of real income and wealth holdings for which there is no economic, political or social justification. The most obvious examples are people on fixed money incomes, or in receipt of money incomes, the adjustments to which take place only after very considerable time lags. By squeezing the real purchasing power of these groups—pensioners, teachers, nurses, weakly unionised groups—the community is using them as safety valves which allow more favourably placed groups—businessmen who can maintain or increase their profit margins, wage-earners who quickly can obtain compensating increases in money wages—to maintain or increase their own spending in real terms. Within the squeezable groups are those who even if they can adjust their money incomes relatively quickly are nevertheless in occupations where all or most of their recorded incomes come within the tax man's orbit and are subject to rates of taxation that were designed, as we saw above, for considerably lower levels of average money incomes. The scope for avoidance and evasion is most unequally distributed through the community and, as a general rule, those who can least afford to, get the highest proportion of their earnings caught within the tax man's net. (I am not arguing against either progressive or high rates of taxation as such but for equal treatment for all those with equal economic power.) At the best of times, there is only rough justice, especially in the Australian case where legal tax avoidance has been designed especially to favour the middle and upper income groups, the cumulative result of twenty-three years of unchanged perspectives in government taxation policies. But in a severe inflationary situation these built-in dodges are compounded, so adding considerably to social unrest and bitterness.

Another group which is at risk when rates of inflation (in

the sense of domestic cost levels) differ as between countries are those whose costs are largely determined at home and whose revenues are determined abroad, principally exporters and importers (where, in the main, in the latter case, it is the other way around). We are all familiar with the phenomenon of the cost-price squeeze in the rural exporting sector whereby, in effect, real income is redistributed from the export sector to workers and manufacturers in the domestic manufacturing sector. (This abstracts from the many current and capital subsidies and other schemes that were devised in order to redistribute income back again through the taxation system and government intervention generally.)

Perhaps the most serious redistributions that occur are not on income account but on capital account. A feature of inflation, especially when it 'hots up' and is expected to get worse, is a flight from liquid assets, especially money, into real goods. If, moreover, interest rates are kept artificially low, in the sense that Reserve Bank interference in the money market does not allow the pattern of rates of interest to attain their 'natural' levels in the market, people attempt to change the composition of their wealth portfolios by increasing their holdings of land, pictures, jewelry, and, possibly also, shares, in order to hedge against inflation. What may be prudent and rational for the individual turns out to be anti-social for the community as a whole, for the combined efforts of people to so change their portfolios bring about the very sectional price changes which they individually are at pains either to avoid or to protect themselves against. Appreciation in the prices of real assets creates arbitrary pockets of increased wealth which only very imperfectly, if at all, come within the tax man's orbit and which basically do not reflect any particular productive contribution to society at all.

In the economy as a whole there is a large-scale redistribution from creditors to debtors. In practice, this often means a redistribution of the money saving of low income earners and negligible wealth holders to those whose income and wealth positions are such as to make them credit-worthy and therefore able to borrow considerable amounts. No more so than in an inflationary situation is the biblical maxim, 'To him that hath shall be given and from him that hath not even that little which he hath shall be taken away', applicable. These effects are greatly added to if there is simultaneously an attempt by the central government and the Reserve Bank to keep down the levels of money rates of interest so that what little money-returns lenders receive in the form of interest payments are effectively made low or even negative by accelerating rates of increases in prices.

Another aspect of inflation, to which accountants increasingly have addressed themselves in recent years, is the problem of accounting for different rates of price increase of the products which their firms sell, on the one hand, and of the assets that are used in the productive process, on the other. As is well known, historical-cost accounting procedures are especially deficient in these situations, both for assessing incomes earned and guiding pricing, investment and financing decisions. Moreover, tax rates that are levied on incomes as conventionally measured are designed for a world in which the monetary unit is stable over the long haul, result in very different incidences of taxation on current or economic incomes. Incidentally, it was Keynes and his 'true' followers who always stressed that the monetary unit, the money wage (in relation to productivity) and therefore the general price level needed to be relatively stable in order to preserve democratic capitalist institutions, of which Keynes was a great defender. Events in recent years all round the capitalist world show how correct his intuition was. The bitterness that is inevitably associated with a class society of competing and often irreconcilable interests is greatly enhanced when the arbitrariness of rewards to different groups is greatly increased, not only as between Australia's three broad classes of wage-earners, profit-receivers and exporters, but also within the wage-earning class itself, and as between the young and the old, and the urban and the rural. Bitterness is added to by the uncertainty and anxiety that pervade the everyday actions of the great majority of citizens, combined with an irresistible incentive to dishonest behaviour that is built into lending and borrowing institutions during inflation. By the last point I mean that people take it as a matter of course that it is prudent to borrow in inflationary situations, knowing full well that as contracts are made in terms of money, this inevitably implies robbery by one group from another (unless interest rates are adjusted accordingly). Moreoever, both the ability and incentive to make rational decisions about productive investment and employment are greatly reduced in a world in which the basic monetary unit is no longer stable or dependable.

POLICY SUGGESTIONS: WHAT IS TO BE DONE?

I take it that the usual measures suggested for controlling inflation are well known, as well as their advantages, limitations, deficiencies and difficulties. Thus, in order to tackle excess demand, overall planned expenditure needs to be cut, either directly by reducing government expenditure or indirectly by raising rates of income and indirect taxes, by raising interest rates and/or reducing loans, in order to reduce the private sector's ability to spend. The efficacy of these measures depends upon whether the groups most directly affected believe the measures are permanent or temporary, and on whether the spending functions of the groups are as stable and predictable as orthodox economic theory, designed for other worlds and situations, has assumed. Moreover, the latter set of measures have cost-push consequences that are almost certainly undesirable (witness the reasoning behind Snedden's proposed income tax cuts in the recent election campaign, the validity of which as an anti-inflationary measure rested on these consequences applying). I myself have always opposed the use of cuts (or increases) in government expenditure primarily as demand management tools. The public-private sector split in the use of resources, it seems to me, ought to reflect the basic philosophy of the government in power and the longer-run social and economic developments of the economy, rather than be directed to the shorter-run problems of demand management. True Keynesian theory leads inexorably to a plea for some form of incomes policy emphasising, as it does, the crucial strategic importance of the money–wage rate in determining the stability or instability of capitalist economies. But as Joan Robinson has remarked (she herself has advocated the need for an incomes policy since the mid-1930s), how can one reasonably expect the unions to co-operate in such a policy when they are repeatedly faced, especially in the present speculative and unsettled time, with examples of 'the unpleasant and unacceptable face of capitalism', to quote Mr Heath's immortal phrase? Finally, we have seen in recent years an upsurge of monetarist measures, the guiding star of which is Professor Milton Friedman of Chicago, which take a long (and uncertain) time to work, and the relative impact of which on the price level and activity is still uncertain, even in theory, as presented by the monetarists. We have also seen use of the exchange rate and tariff cuts, courageous measures which hurt sectional interests but seem to have the approval of many academic economists: witness the 130:4 in support of the Labour governments's measures during the recent election campaign.

I want, though, to concentrate on another policy proposal; namely, the suggested reintroduction of automatic quarterly cost-of-living adjustments for all money wages and pensions, i.e. indexation. This has been advocated by both the government and a number of academic economists; for example, Trevor Swan, Eric Russell, Alan Hall, John Nevile, Barry Hughes and (immodestly) me. On the face of it, such a proposal sounds paradoxical, guaranteed, almost certainly, to accelerate the rate of inflation and it has been criticised on just these grounds. (My former colleague, Professor Donald Whitehead of La Trobe, set me up on this one and described the proposal as 'the silliest way to fight inflation': so much for honour amongst thieves.) But I think that good economic sense *can* be made of the proposal though it must be said at the outset that it is as yet a case of 'non proven' and that the proof of the pudding will be in the eating.

The argument in outline (there are, of course, many modifications and qualifications) goes as follows. As we have seen, one factor causing the present rate of inflation is the anxiety associated with widely-held expectations of *continuing* increases in prices. This leads wage-earners to attempt to obtain increases in money wages that not only restore their real purchasing power but also offer some insurance against its expected erosion in the future. Because, in a mixed capitalist economy such as Australia, money-wage bargains are not made simultaneously across the board but by various groups of wage-earners and employers, either by collective bargaining procedures or before arbitration commissions, it must be expected that each group, quite rightly, will put its own interests first. Yet it is the collective outcome of all the bargains struck which is relevant for the *overall* rate of increase of money wages, itself an important factor in the overall rate of increase of prices. In order to influence this collective outcome and especially to so reduce the overall rate of increase of money wages that it is consistent with a single figure rather than the present double-figure rate of increase of prices, it is surely desirable to remove the anxiety that is associated with this erosion of the absolute real income of wage-earners. This the proposed cost-of-living adjustments would do. It might then be hoped that the money-wage bargains which were struck and which, individually, reflect the bargaining power of groups in, and the prosperity of, each industry, would collectively be associated with significantly lower overall rates of increase of money wages than otherwise would have occurred.

Put succinctly, then, the argument is that the removal of one major source of uncertainty in the general process of setting individual money wages—namely, that associated with erosion of absolute real income—coupled with widely held expectations of continuing, indeed increasing, price inflation, could lead to an 'otherwise situation' in which the overall increase of money wages would be substantially lower.

Turning now to details: should indexation be applied to a minimum wage (and the same *absolute* amount added to all) or, at a proportionate rate, to *all*? (The latter would tend to leave relatives unaffected.) My own preference is for the former. I think there is a lot to be said for regarding the wage bundle conceptually as divisible into two segments—'necessaries' and the wage-earning class's share of the surplus. (This distinction has its roots in classical political economy and has been revived in recent years by Piero Sraffa.) It would be the object of quarterly cost-of-living adjustments to protect the former portion. Relative bargaining strengths, levels of activity and conditions in individual industries and firms should be the factors which (in a capitalist economy with efficiently functioning markets, something we are, of course, far from achieving) determine the latter. This calculation would also provide a guide for the indexation of pensions as well. In an open economy like Australia, some adjustments would need to be made for the impact of overseas prices and there remains the vexed question of what is the appropriate index of prices of wage goods to use. But it does not seem beyond the wit of man both to design one and to get general acceptance from the groups concerned, or, at least, if it is, it suggests that class conflicts have bitten so deep in our society that we should perhaps be thinking of designing a new set of institutions anyway. In order to minimise the impact of seasonal and chance influences on prices, especially of foodstuffs, there would be much to be said for designing an index that incorporates a moving average of prices.

We could note in passing that indexation serves to secure the same objectives as the scheme originally proposed by Professors Weintraub and Wallich (see, for example, Sidney Weintraub, *Keynes and the Monetarists*, Rutgers University Press, New Jersey, 1973, Ch. 6) and given some prominence here by Professor Ronald Henderson in his 1971 Joseph Fisher Lecture (*Australian Economic Papers*, June 1972), essentially because much the same true Keynesian analysis has been made, especially concerning the strategic importance of the money–wage level. Both the Weintraub-Wallich and the Henderson schemes are variations on the theme that penal rates of business taxation should be levied on those firms that pay increases in money wages above certain standard 'norms' set by the authorities with certain upper limits to the rate of increase of prices in mind. The object is to give strong incentives to employers on their side of the bargaining process to keep down the rate of increase of money wages to levels consistent with relatively low rates of price inflation. All these suggestions are essentially those of people who either through conviction or a sense of realism, at least in the short period, take existing institutions and market structures and social and power groupings as they find them, and attempt to design policies which have reasonable chances of success within these constraints. In practice, they may be disappointed.

The last area that I wish to discuss concerns the protection of people's saving for retirement. I have long advocated a national superannuation scheme whereby, in effect, the productive during *their* active productive lives support the retired or ill or widowed by current tax provisions (preferably raised by progressive rates), in return for support themselves by the *then* active when they have retired, or become ill, or are otherwise out of action. In a sense, this is what the proposed abolition of the means test implies, and there is much to be said for it if you accept the philosophy that all citizens should have a pension as a right merely by virtue of being citizens and usually because of the contributions that they have made to the revenue during their productive lives. It does mean, of course, giving a bonus to the well-off (who may be so either because of their own efforts, or because of inheritance, or scarcity rents in their earnings while active, or appreciation of the value of their assets) in order to provide for the otherwise destitute. But this may well be a cost worth paying in an affluent society, in order to achieve social benefits by creating a sense of equity and fairness. There would, of course, be room for private superannuation schemes whereby saving could gain people a pension over and above a state one. There would be much to be said for the funds so made available being invested in long-lived development projects, the returns to which would be expected to keep up with any inflationary tendencies.

Finally, I cannot resist putting in a plug for a negative income tax,[2] the break-even point of which would be indexed. This seems to me to be a logical policy measure to be implemented by a government nominally dubbed 'socialist' but which in reality seems more appropriately to have Milton Friedman or even Adam Smith as its patron saint rather than Karl Marx or even, alas, Keir Hardie or Ben Chifley.

POSTSCRIPT: AUGUST 1974

I have left the address as it was originally written in May (and given in August). However, events have moved swiftly over even this short time, so it seems appropriate to add a postscript, especially as three colleagues (Eric Russell, Barry

Hughes and Phillip Bentley) and I have become associated, between May and August, with a package deal set of proposals known as the Adelaide Plan. (The name is rather inept for the principles underlying it, and the measures themselves, broadly conceived, are coming to represent a consensus of opinion amongst non-Treasury economists.) An integral part of the proposals is a variant of indexation, one which stresses proportionality, at least up to quite high income levels, rather than flat-rate adjustments to most incomes (themselves determined by proportionate adjustments for the lowest paid). It is proposed that this scheme be commenced in the early months of the first quarter of 1975 and that the line be held, more or less, on money wages in the meantime. (This is to allow the recent increases in money wages and those already in the pipeline, most of which are very large, to feed through into prices by the end of the year.)

Whatever the equity merits of the flat-rate version (in my view, they are considerable), in the present situation of badly ruptured relativities, the effects of introducing such a scheme could be disastrous as an anti-inflation measure. Since the present situation is extraordinarily serious—unchecked, we could be experiencing rates of inflation of the order of 30 per cent per annum or more by the end of 1974—equity (and efficiency) considerations must take back seats, at least for the time being.

Allied with the indexation scheme are proposals that company profits and the prices of companies' products be controlled through the tax system. It is suggested that (with obvious exceptions for new companies, or those that recently made losses) profits be such as to not exceed the average of the net profit to sales ratio of (say) the last three years. Any excess over this would be taxed away completely, that is, we are proposing a 100 per cent excess profits tax. Also any money wage increases (measured per hour and including the value of fringe benefits and other factors that add directly to costs) in excess of those allowed by indexation and a mild (say three per cent per annum) adjustment for relativities would not be allowable as a cost for tax purposes; their consequent inclusion in *taxable* profits would bear a 100 per cent tax rate also. In this way profit margins per unit would be controlled (larger profits could still be made by selling larger volumes) and there would also be a considerable incentive for businessmen not to acquiesce in wage payments in excess of the norms established for the emergency period, that is, sweetheart agreements would be out. The accounting profession in their capacity as auditors would be a vital link in this scheme of things. For they would have to certify that the net profit to sales ratios and wage payments had not exceeded the allowable limits. (In this regard, it was most heartening to find at the Whyalla Convention that the accounting profession, as evidenced by the resolution passed by a resounding majority, were favourably disposed towards playing their proposed indispensable role.)

The three per cent annum increase allowed for relativities is necessary both because of gross departures from established norms in the recent leap-frog movements in money wages and also to make sure that trade union officials have worthwhile jobs — indexation by itself is tantamount to voting them out of a job, something neither they nor their union members would wear. In some cases, with really badly out-of-line relativities, the adjustments may have to take a number of years. The self-employed would be subject to a similar system of excess income control, by using the personal income tax system. Promotions, and so on, could be handled by a version of Keynes's deferred pay system whereby excess income over the average increase indicated by indexation plus (mild) adjustments for relativities would be deferred for (say) two years, a modest rate of interest being paid on these amounts in the meantime.

By itself, indexation in this scheme would only serve to stabilize the rate of increase of prices, not to bring it down. (Even the former would, of course, be a major achievement.) To bring it down we must look for 'dampeners' in the C.O.L. index in the form of reduced food prices (at the farm gate), increases in productivity (here the threat of a recession is a real worry as productivity tends to fall or even to become negative with the onset of a recession) and State and Australian Government behaviour with regard to charges, direct and indirect taxes. Thus, it is vital that the Australian Government put the State Governments in such financial positions that they do *not* have to raise charges or introduce State taxes; indirect and direct tax cuts would also be desirable, if the macroeconomic situation warrants it. Here the recession might be a blessing in disguise, as far as the cost-push elements of the inflation are concerned, for tax cuts would be needed for demand management purposes. Given *very* favourable circumstances, we estimate that inflation rates *could* be down to single figures (high ones, alas) by the first quarter of 1976.

We take the view that the present inflation, whatever its initial causes, is now predominantly wage-price and wage-wage, that is to say, it has a life of its own in terms of these elements. We therefore are opposed to measures which imply a sharp rise in unemployment which is sustained for a considerable period of time, because they are inhumane and inappropriate. We feel that some package deal such as ours, the strands of which are not original but borrowed freely, *could* secure wide community consensus and, conceivably, just might work. The alternatives are a move towards hyper-inflation (prices rising at 50 per cent annum or more), with all its attendant and undesirable political and social consequences and anxieties, including, as an outside chance, the destruction of our democratic institutions themselves; a wholesale and widespread freeze of wages and prices; or the deliberate creation of unemployment, at least three per cent of the work force, in order to shock the system and break through the expectations barrier. We feel that the last would be the worst of all possible worlds, enough to create a great deal of unnecessary misery and loss of employment and output, not enough to have a significant effect on money wage increases, unless it is held for an intolerably long time, certainly over a year. We note that up until now (early August) the Government has shown every sign of adopting such an evaluation and that its measures to date (in the second half of 1974) are tragically wrong, if our diagnosis is correct. We stress that we are faced with a serious inflationary situation, to which must be added the possibility of a world-wide slump, in which the whole capitalist world is moving in unison, all parts of which faced with inflation and tackling it by reducing demand. Prospects are bleak but we stress that these are the alternatives before us and that our proposals, unpalatable as they may be in the short run, are relatively the least unpalatable of them all.

NOTES

1. Reprinted from the *Australian Accountant*, October 1974, pp. 520–8.
2. This concept is due to Milton Friedman. Basically, if a taxpayer's income is less than that at which, at present, no tax is paid, the taxpayer would receive a subsidy (i.e. a negative income tax) equal to some proportion of his negative income for tax purposes. In this way, a flow below which no person's net income could fall is created.

10 Making Socialism in your own Country[1]

I am delighted to accept the invitation to give the John Curtin Memorial Lecture. When I was a youth in Melbourne I grew up in the heart of Barry Humphries' land, 24 Faircroft Avenue, Glen Iris, SE6 (as it then was) and my parents, who were loving and kind people, nevertheless were very right wing, and so people like John Curtin and Ben Chifley, and particularly Dr Evatt, were used as bogey-men to send me to sleep. When first I went to the University of Melbourne I still reflected the views of my parents—but only for the first six months. For during those first six months I found out that not all the world was like 24 Faircroft Avenue. This converted me to socialism. This was in the early 1950s (in fact, it was 1950). In those days we used to worry about two things, well *at least* two things (it is customary in economics these days to use inequalities): what political stance we should take and whether God existed. Having made up my mind on political matters in those first six months principally as a result of the Economic Geography lectures of Molly Bain and Bob Wilson, I settled down for the next three and a half years to decide whether God existed.

Unlike the present generation, I decided that He did. Indeed, I now know that *She* is alive and well, but in those days I was more conventional and so for many years I have been the only Jewish Methodist in Adelaide. I cannot claim to be even that now, because like all declining companies, the Protestant Churches have merged and they now call themselves the Uniting Church. (One of the tragedies of modern Christianity and its Churches is that just when they have become relevant there is nobody in them). I therefore present myself to you as a very old-fashioned creature, to wit, a Christian socialist who has belonged to the Australian Labor Party when I have lived in Australia and to the British Labour Party when I have lived in Britain and sometimes with an overlap in the sense that I voted in both places at the same time. One of our children was born in Britain and was recorded in both places—so if I could muck up the demography statistics I do not see why I could not follow the old Labor Party adage, especially in Victoria, 'vote early and vote often'.

The talk that I want to give tonight is called 'Making Socialism in Your Own Country', and I want to try to follow at least one maxim of a great socialist and a very fine Australian, Hugh Stretton. John Langmore quoted in his recent paper in the *Journal of Australian Political Economy*[2] a typical Stretton maxim—that the Left 'has to supply simple visions, complicated programmes and competent performance'. I see my role tonight as at least trying to provide some simple visions. Complicated programmes have never been one of my strengths—I grew up in Victoria and played far too long on the back line where the instruction was: 'you go straight, you don't go round, you don't hand ball and you kick long', and therefore to make up a complicated programme is not something that I wish to do, though I shall mention some outlines of programmes. As for competent performance, I tried to follow at dinner tonight my usual adage in all manner of activities: to drink enough to stifle the inhibitions but not to ruin the performance. (Thanks very much, it is always good to have some students around.)

To clear the way for what comes later, which mainly will be about economic theory and economic policy, I first want to take an unequivocal stand on nuclear energy and nuclear weapons. Since it is fashionable in Australia to criticise anyone who does not agree with you as being seditious and a traitor and even other unmentionable things—this is a particularly good ploy followed by the Country Party, or the National Country Party as it is now called—I have been a traitor all my adult life to the National Country Party, except once when I suggested during the Whitlam era that if we did not do something about inflation it might approach 30 per cent per annum, whereupon Mr Anthony quoted me. I want now to quote what a well-known 'Lefty' had to say about nuclear weapons just before he was killed by the IRA, namely, Earl Mountbatten. I think that this may be familiar to some people in the audience, but it may not be familiar to others. For example, I was talking to a reporter from News Limited today—now that Rupert has given up on getting his knighthood, he talks to people like me—and the reporter had not heard of this particular quote. I would like to quote his words to you because as far as I know he has never been regarded as unacceptable by either the CIA or the English equivalent of ASIO. He said:

> I repeat in all sincerity as a military man I can see no use for any nuclear weapons which would not end in escalation, with consequences that no-one can conceive.
>
> And nuclear devastation is not science fiction, it is a matter of fact...We remember the tens of thousands who were killed instantly [at Hiroshima] or worse still those who suffered a slow painful death from the effects of the burns—we forget that many are still dying horribly from the delayed effects of radiation. To this knowledge must be added the fact that we now have a missile a thousand times as dreadful.

And he added:

> I repeat a thousand times as horrible.
>
> A new World War can hardly fail to involve the all-out use of nuclear weapons. Such a war would not drag on for years. It could all be over in the matter of a day.
>
> And when it was all over, what will the world be like? Our fine great buildings, our homes will exist no more. The thousands of years it took to develop our civilisation will have been in vain. Our works of art will be lost. Radio, television, newspapers, will disappear. There will be no hospitals. No help can be expected for the few mutilated survivors in any town to be sent from a neighbouring town—there will be no neighbouring towns left, no neighbours, there will be no help, there will be no hope.
>
> As a military man who has given more than half a century in active service I say in all sincerity that the nuclear arms race has no military purpose. Wars cannot be fought with nuclear weapons. Their existence only adds to our perils because of the illusions which they have generated.
>
> There are powerful voices around the world that still give credence to the old Roman precept—if you desire peace, prepare for war. This is absolute nuclear nonsense and I repeat—it is a disastrous misconception to believe that by increasing the total uncertainty one increases one's own certainty.[3]

So having stated, as any good modern economist would, the necessary condition for discussing our topic tonight, I now move on to sufficient conditions. What I want to do is to relate some recent developments in modern economic theory and economic policy to the thinking that a progressive government would need to make when deciding on its economic policy when it comes into office. I had a sort of go at this when I was serving on the Committee that the Labor Party set up in 1978/79 to find out why it had done so badly in 1975 and 1977, apart from the fact that it had alienated the old, the young, women, the poor, the workers, the business people, the ethnics and the blacks. As part of our work, we wrote Discussion Paper No. 6, which was on economic policy and the future of Australia. When the paper was published we were accorded an editorial in *The Canberra Times* which bore the heading 'An Unreal Proposal'. (I notice that Neil Blewitt is in the audience and he will share my painful remembrance of this fact.) The reason why the editorial writer thought it was an unreal proposal was that towards the end of our paper we mentioned that, possibly, nationalisation was something that ought to be discussed, from which the editorial writer concluded that we had concluded that nationalisation was the cure-all for every possible economic ill of which the modern world could possibly conceive, which was somewhat a distortion of our argument. But I am pleased to be able to report—and I always say this at any lecture or seminar I give in case there are questions afterwards, which I understand there will be, just to let you know who is on my side—as I said, I am glad to be able to report that the very next day the editorial writer was struck down with a painful disease in a private part of his anatomy. This led me to speculate that while in the old days the Lord sent thunderbolts to punish the guilty and innocent alike, these days, His, or should I say, Her, aim is much improved. I leave that story with you when you are phrasing your questions.

It is my contention that since the mid-1970s in the Western world in general and in Australia in particular, we have seen, if not the death, at least the illness in ruling circles of some of the more admirable human virtues; namely, compassion, altruism, charity and tolerance. Their place has been taken by the worship of ruthlessness and selfishness under the guise that in this different environment that they are attempting to create, enterprise and initiative would the better flourish.

One of the things that I think a progressive government has to take seriously into account is how do you create institutions in a society like ours—a small open, mixed capitalist economy—in which the more desirable and positive virtues of human nature may be given a go. That is one of the problems which I hope to discuss during the talk. I do not think I will be able to provide necessarily persuasive or simple answers, but it is something to which I think it is very necessary for us to address ourselves.

We could do a lot worse than following what Hugh Stretton said about simple visions and go back to another person who had visions which inspired generations; namely, Bertrand Russell. Bertrand Russell had a vision of:

> the world that we must seek, [a world] in which the creative spirit is alive, in which life is an adventure full of joy and hope based rather upon the impulse to construct than upon the desire to retain what we possess or to seize what is possessed by others. It must be a world in which affection has free play, in which love is purged of the instinct for domination, in which cruelty and envy have been dispelled by happiness and the unfettered development of all the instincts that build up life and fill it with mental delights.

I think that this is an extraordinarily useful starting point for Hugh Stretton's 'simple vision'. Russell added: 'Such a world is possible; it waits only for men to wish to create it.[4]

But when we come down to brass tacks, we start way behind scratch because we have witnessed over at least the last seven years some very disturbing events in our society which may have unfortunate long-run consequences. By this I mean that we have seen an increasing tendency for politicians to make short-run political gains without regard for the long-run consequences that they have for the tacit understandings and arrangements which are necessary in a society like ours in order to make it function effectively, with some hope of bringing about social justice and harmony between the different interest groups in society. I think that some of our leading politicians (it has to be said on both sides of the fence) have been very clever at seeing the short-run moves that they can make for their own political advantage but have not been so clever, indeed sometimes they have been very dense, in working out what the long-run consequences of those particular moves could be. I think that this was given a start by the way in which the Whitlam government was brought down, and it has been continued by events which have occurred since then. We are particularly unfortunate in Australia to have such a short time constitutionally between elections, especially given the complicated nature of economic processes that are at work in our society in these days; but, of course, we have made this a lot worse by insisting on having elections at much shorter intervals than the constitutional requirements stipulate.

In a way it was nice recently to see a letter in the Adelaide *Advertiser* commenting on Des Corcoran's abortive attempt to have an early election. The writer said that Des woke up one night and his wife said to him, 'Des, if you wish to be loved you'll have to have an election first', and before he had worked out he had not heard aright, he had called one. I say this to the Adelaide people in the audience because if they have lived long enough to know what *The Advertiser* used to be like, they will know that ten years ago you could not have read *that* in its pages. There is a political moral to the story as well.

The point I want to make, however, is that when we think about economic policies, one of the legacies of Keynesianism —not so much Keynes's own writing but of the way in which Keynes has come down into the textbooks—has been, I believe, an excessive preoccupation with the short run. Partly a rather superficial reading of Keynes is to blame for this, partly Keynes himself is to blame for it, but more importantly, I think it is the way in which his message has been disseminated in the textbooks—with one notable exception, I have to say, looking at one of my co-authors in the audience. What I mean is the following: if we look back over the long haul of how political economy developed from the Physiocrats and Adam Smith on, one of the principal concepts that the original writers wrote about (and Marx wrote about them also) was what Smith called the 'centres of gravitation of the system'; namely, those fulcrums or magnets of the system which were brought about by sustained and dominant forces. Adam Smith himself used to distinguish between what he called 'natural prices', which were centres of gravitation, and market prices, which were the actual prices that were observed but which often departed from, in fact *usually* departed from, equality with the natural prices because they were affected by transitory and once-for-all factors like temporary gluts or temporary shortages in harvests. The point about these centres of gravitation was that they were exactly what they are called, centres of gravitation, positions towards which the economy would tend to go, and if there were departures from them, it was believed that there would be forces at work in the economy which would drive the economy back towards these particular positions. When Keynes came to write *The General Theory*, the particular centre of gravitation that he had in mind was one which he said had vanished from the consideration of economists for about a hundred years prior to the time of him writing. He said that if you looked in the writings of economists after the end of the debates between Malthus and Ricardo, you could not find an explicit theory of the level of activity and the level of employment as a whole, that in fact, an account of the forces which determined the level of activity and the level of employment as a whole was missing, and so it was his particular role (he was never a modest man) to provide what had been missing for over a hundred years.

Keynes argued that in a capitalist economy there was a centre of gravitation of employment and output as a whole, that it was not necessarily a full employment one, and therefore there was a case, as we know, for intervention in order to raise the level of output and employment. *The General Theory* revolves around this central idea. In writing it as he did, he laid great stress on the fact that the capital accumulation, the investment expenditure of business people, would not only be one of the most volatile factors in the capitalist economy but also would tend to fluctuate round an average level, its own centre of gravitation, which itself usually was not sufficient to provide full employment for all those wishing to work and for the stock of capital goods in the economy as a whole. Therefore there was a role for intervention at the public level in order to try to do something about this. This has usually descended into the textbooks as being a theoretical argument for using government deficits and government spending, but if we look at what Keynes actually said, he also stressed that it might well be the role of government not so much to spend on its own accord as to try to influence the level and composition of spending by business people on investment goods, because he regarded the way in which we decide on both the level and the composition of our stock of capital goods as not one of the greatest success stories, to put it mildly, of the way in which a capitalist economy functions. Indeed, he has a very entertaining chapter (based no doubt on his own experiences on the stock exchange) describing the irrationalities of using a stock exchange where speculation dominated enterprise as the means to decide how the savings of the community are to be used. He suggested that we should try to get business people to do it right, but if they did not, then perhaps the government itself should think about the socialisation of investment decisions. This is not Lenin, this is not Stalin, it is not even some of our well-known Labor politicians, this is Keynes in 1936. The principal thrust of his book though was that there was a tendency to a deficiency of effective demand in the economy.

The wheel now has come full circle in discussions of economic theory and economic policy due to the influence of, first of all, Milton Friedman, who is the head of what James Tobin calls 'monetarism wave one' or 'mark one', and who has been succeeded by some of his own pupils and followers and colleagues, those whom Tobin calls 'monetarism mark two'[5] and who are known in the trade as 'the rational expectations school'. Now Friedman's argument, put very briefly, is that in the long run a capitalist economy *is* self-correcting; or, at least, even if it is not, it self-corrects quicker than if you try to do something about it other than provide institutions which make it behave *as if* it were a competitive economy, and which allow the money supply to advance at a steady rate in order to cater for the growth in productivity. But he said it was an empirical question whether or not this came about. The rational expectations school has taken the argument one step further and has argued that not only is the natural resting place of a capitalist economy one where people are in their preferred positions but, on the whole, these are positions which are reached very quickly indeed. So the best model of our sort of an economy is to suppose that people have voluntarily reached a position which, given the constraints under which they operate, is one in which they find optimal and therefore stabilisation policy (but not policies like cutting minimum wages, or deregulating or increasing information, or retraining or relocating schemes; all these are part of their platform) is likely to do more harm than good because they believe that stabilisation policies are likely to take people away from their preferred positions.

Indeed, we have had a recent article by two members of this school on unemployment in Britain during the inter-war years where in a footnote (at least they had the grace to put it in a footnote) they say that because of the level of unemployment benefits in Britain in the inter-war years employers did the young of Britain a favour by giving them the sack so that they could take out the dole and that it was a voluntarily position which the unemployed took up.[6]

It is one of the ironies of modern economic theory that in the city of Liverpool in England where unemployment is on average somewhere up near 20 per cent and amongst black youths some extraordinarily higher figure, that the chief proponent of rational expectations in the UK, who stresses that if people are unemployed it is because of voluntary decisions, is the Professor of Economics at the University of Liverpool. All I can say is that it speaks volumes for the legendary tolerance of the British Isles that he has been allowed to lecture without someone coming in and at least throwing a blackboard duster at him. (That happened to me when I was at Melbourne University. I used to teach religious instruction at University High on behalf of the SCM. I threw a blackboard duster at a young man, and when I turned back to the board he threw it back at me. A lesser person would have been rather upset about this but I took both blackboard dusters, I gave one to him, I took the other one myself and I said, 'Now when I count to three, we will fire'. Of course, being young and inexperienced, he threw wildly as soon as 'three' was up—and missed. I, knowing that I had my reputation as a teacher in my hands, took very careful aim and hit him right behind the ear—not a very hard blow, of course, but nevertheless right behind the ear. That would have been a very successful ploy if only I'd been able to observe that the headmaster was watching the lot through the window.) As I say, it says much for the youth of Liverpool that they have not been in to take this professor on.

What comes out of the argument about the natural resting place of a capitalist economy is that there is a dividing line between those who believe something can be done about overall economic performance and those who think that if you do something, you can only make matters worse. Nevertheless, the second group do teach us a very important lesson, one which Maddock and Carter stress, and which is also stressed by another economist who is not favourable to Keynes's way of looking at things (Meltzer), which is that often economic processes take an enormous amount of time to work themselves out. In particular, it is very difficult to turn round habits which have taken a number of periods to form. Therefore, one should not expect miracles from economic policies; rather, one should frame policies which have a long period to run, with which people may become famliar. Indeed, policy should be made explicit so that people do become familiar with what it is that you are trying to do, and then you should hold onto these policies by and large, only making marginal changes as unexpected circumstances occur. Robert Eisner, who has courageously carried on the Keynesian debate against overwhelming odds on the American scene, has argued that if there is, as he believes, this long-run tendency to a lack of effective demand in the capitalist economy, then fiscal policies and monetary policies should not be designed for fine tuning, as it used to be fashionable to call it, but should be designed in such a way that over the long haul they give expansionary help to the level of activity and the rate of growth of the economy. This is a message which I think a progressive government should take to heart and one which I think we on the whole failed to learn in the hectic three years of the Whitlam government.

Now it was true that the Whitlam government was an extraordinarily unlucky government, because when it came in it tried first of all to restructure the economy. At the same time it was faced with the turn around, at the end of the long boom, in levels of activity of major parts of the economy as well as by the oil-price shock and the aftermath of the Vietnam war and its effect on the world money supply. Nevertheless, the essential message which we get from these speculations is one of designing policies which do have sustained effects and which slowly change people's attitudes and habits rather than hoping to bring them about in a twinkling of an eye or, at least, over night. This is reinforced by the fact that when I said that one of the by-products of Keynes's message was excessive preoccupation with the short run, there is also another thing which I think is a by-product of Keynesianism, which we have not completely ground out of our way of thinking about the economy now. We have taken over from Keynes (and from the way in which Chicago economists think about the economy) an inappropriate model of the nature of price formation in our economy.

Keynes himself put into *The General Theory* a very simple Marshallian model of price formation by the impersonal forces of the market, using supply and demand curves, because I think he did not want to fight two revolutions at the same time. He was quite content to let the orthodox have their old-fashioned way of looking at price formation in order that he could tackle the problem of getting rid of massive unemployment. Increasingly, we have become aware that this is a model which will not do for modern capitalist economies—that there are large parts of them where discretion about the prices which you charge for your products and the prices which are charged for the services which people provide are not brought about by the impersonal forces of the market but are to a very considerable extent within the power of the people who are either providing the products or the services. The person who has stressed this in a most thorough way is the late Arthur Okun, who, sadly died far too young at the age fifty-one a couple of years ago. In his last book, *Prices and Quantities*[7] his major preoccupation was with the implications for economic policy of the fact that there are these segments of the economy where considerable discretion holds sway—where there are long-run norms which have been formed and which guide the setting of prices of either products or services. And he has argued, quite rightly, that the by-product of this is that if you use blunt and crude weapons like contractionary monetary and fiscal policies to try and tackle things like inflation, you are going to have a very considerable impact on the employment of labour and of capital goods but only a very minor and very much spread-out impact on the rates of change of prices and wages. This is a lesson which we are learning only too painfully from the last seven years of the Australian scene, of the British scene, and of the American scene as well. What this left open for us to argue was, I think quite rightly, that we must supplement our conventional fiscal and monetary policies with the appropriate form of prices and incomes policy for the economy under consideration. There will be horses for courses.[8]

I was interested to see that Paddy McGuiness has at last come round to arguing that something like an incomes policy is necessary in the present setting if we are ever to make any progress in moving ourselves out of our present levels of unemployment and sluggish levels of activity. With typical Paddy panache, he has rubbished every incomes and prices policy that has ever been tried before and has put his money, as a good betting man, on the most theoretically logical but practically impossible one, the one that has been advocated by Abba Lerner.

Lerner exploits the notion that you want the monetary value of the gross national product to grow, such that all the growth is in output and none is in prices. You know that particular industries are going to grow faster than the average because they have good prospects and other industries are going to decline and therefore you give people chips which they can buy and sell according to what they believe their output and sales prospects are going to be. If they are believed to be profitable, they will buy them from people who do not believe that their prospects are likely to be profitable, the market will set the price and the end result will be the money gross national product expanding at a rate which provides for full employment. You will not be imposing a controlled prices and incomes policy, you will be using the carrot and stick incentives of market forces and market incentives in order to persuade people to act in a socially desirable way. Now, as I say, whether that is practical or not is a matter that has not yet been tried. There have been variants of these schemes suggested by various American economists including Tobin, Solow, Okun, and especially by Sidney Weintraub and Henry Wallich, whereby you give people incentives not to charge higher prices and not to acquiesce in higher increases in money wages than are consistent with the overall rate of inflation which you think, given your current exchange rate, will still allow you to be competitive and maintain full employment.

These sorts of ideas ought to get a hearing and ought to be given a chance. It is very heartening to see that the Labor Party, in thinking its way through to the sort of economic policy that it is going to have, has made the restoration of full employment a primary plank, and also, at the same time, has accepted the notion of using an incomes and prices policy to have an effect on the prices and wages which are set by the discretionary sectors of our economy. These are to be coupled with the stimulus of fiscal and monetary policy which is intended to take us steadily but relatively slowly towards a fully employed position. This is a very sensible and realistic stance to take—and a courageous one because it is very difficult for a progressive party ever to talk about using any sort of wage restraint because people, especially wage-earners, understandably, immediately get up in arms about it, and they forget the distinction between money wages, on the one hand, and real wages, on the other. Whenever I have talked about the need for wage restraint, I have always had in mind money-wage restraint in order that we could run the economy at a level of economic activity and at a rate of growth which allows at least for the maintenance of real wages and preferably and in most circumstances for a steady rate of increase in real wages.

But unless we can do this, the chance of getting back to full employment, particularly when we live in a world where we have contractionary policies being advocated and implemented, is a very remote one indeed. It still is an extraordinarily difficult problem to move out of step with the rest of the world, because when you are a small open economy you have the problem of what are you going to do about the balance of payments? People have addressed themselves to this problem; it is part of the tariff debate, and there are arguments in the community that we should be moving steadily towards reduction in our tariff levels. Interestingly enough, this is not only the province of the 'dries' in the Liberal and National Country Parties. It has been argued recently by a left-wing economist in the last issue of the *Journal of Australian Political Economy*[9] that raising tariffs and imposing import controls are not, on the whole, in the interest of the people they are supposed to help; namely, wage-earning groups who might otherwise be unemployed. It is argued in this recent article that tariffs mainly serve to preserve the profits of the industries which are most protected and at the same time to encourage the installation of machinery and methods of production which affect adversely the employment of labour. My own view has been that one should not go, at least in the short run, and particularly in a period of unemployment, for tariff cuts. What you should do is to sustain your existing level and take a leaf out of the experiences of our near neighbours, who, having kept their tariff structures, went all out for export drives, tailor-made exports for the countries who were to become their partners.

This case has been argued convincingly by Clive Edwards and it seems to me it is a very sensible political economy solution. It is sensible because it signals to Australian business people that they should not waste their efforts and their initiative and their ideas in trying to lobby in Canberra for higher tariffs or higher quotas because they are not going to be forthcoming—you have signalled that you are not going to cut tariffs but you are certainly not going to raise them. Rather what they should be doing (and what business people ought to be given the signal to do) is to go out and find where the most profitable markets are and to construct the products which are most acceptable in those particular markets. That seems to me to be a reasonable political solution, at least at the moment, to the problem of what to do about the tariffs. If in years to come we are successful in getting back to full employment and a reasonable rate of growth, we may be able to consider in a much more favourable climate the long-run advantages of lowering tariffs and diffusing the benefits amongst us as consumers. I mean, the terrible trouble about tariff cuts is that we all benefit marginally as consumers as we bedeck ourselves out in shoes that have come from abroad and so on, and those benefits may give us a marginal jump in our total utility, but this is hardly enough to set against the understandable agony of the people who are thrown out of work in a particular industry in a particular centre. Especially is this so in a country like Australia, where we are the size of the USA but where our centres of industry are spread around and where relocation and retraining is a very considerable job for which we have not set up a completely comprehensive or appropriate set of institutions.

In arguing the case for moving towards not only using fiscal and monetary policy but also an incomes policy which is suitable to our own society, I am glad to be joined by other economists who have long been, as they describe themselves, 'Lib-Lab', in the sense that they like to allow people to have freedom of choice as far as many of the commodities that they buy are concerned but they really have a great hatred of the distribution of property which is thrown up by the unfettered workings of a capitalist society. I have particularly in mind James Meade, who, in his Nobel Prize Lecture,[10] suggested that we should use fiscal and monetary policies to affect the rate of growth of the money GNP and money wages to affect employment, but that the *quid pro quo* for doing this should be a much more comprehensive attack on the distribution of property that is thrown up by the market. I think that the way in which we should attempt to get acceptance of money-wage restraint by wage-earning groups in particular is through the moves that are being made at the moment towards 'the social contract'. The social contract has to include not only comprehensive spending through the public sector on things which are of benefit in particular for low-income groups but also taxes of a form which do have a considerable impact on the distribution of property.

There is, of course, a major difficulty here, for unless the Commonwealth decides to take up the problem of death duties, there is really no way that any particular state government can move—as Mr Cain, admirable though his purpose was, recently found to his cost. He, with the aid of right-thinking unions, has not given a welcome to warships but he has had to scrap a very modest suggestion for the reintroduction of death duties. If he had had James Meade as his adviser, he would not have got away with that at all, because Meade's suggestions (in, for example, his *Intelligent Radical's Guide to Economic* Policy)[11] concerning what you ought to do about gifts, and what you ought to do about property, are extraordinarily radical. Meade rightly makes the point that if you are going to have a just and equitable society, you have to stop accumulation of property in the hands of particular groups and that the way to do that is to make us all start again from scratch after the previous generation has died. I think this is an admirable sentiment; I know it is not one that is particularly popular in the Labor Party at the moment because it is thought to be its death knell, but I think it is one that nevertheless has to be thought about or we will find ourselves in a position where we are not getting the necessary environment and necessary attitudes for consensus policies to be a possibility.

One of the things that I think all people who have thought about policy in an economy such as ours—and here I think especially of my old friend, the late Eric Russell, who always stressed this—is that you do not get effective economic policies accepted in a country like Australia unless you can bring about consensus policies so that people can see not only the sacrifices that they have to make themselves but also the benefits that they are going to get. One of the tragic by-products of the bouts of confrontation policies over the last seven years or so is that we are rapidly drying up those springs of goodwill from which consensus comes. I think that is a very serious thing, and I was comforted—well I was not exactly comforted but in one sense I was—to find that Thomas Balogh in his recent book, *The Irrelevance of Traditional Economics*,[12] argued that, in the UK anyway, they have moved themselves towards such a position that they might well have only one last chance to try and build up again pragmatic, consensus-based policies, such has been the confrontationist nature of the recent experiments with Thatcherism.

I mention these things because I think that people forget

how very delicate and shallowly rooted is the plant of democracy in a country like ours and the UK and that if you go about destroying these tacit understandings, you very quickly get people hankering for a so-called strong leader. I am not saying that we would get a neo-fascist state in Australia, because on the whole I do not believe that we would. (Our cadet corps are far too inefficient to produce the necessary material—after all, I was a cadet lieutenant myself once at the school I went to, and my most celebrated feat was to march the whole of my platoon into a wall because I forgot the order for change direction left.) But I can see that in other circumstances, for example, in Italy it would be possible for the reaction to the breakdown of consensus and the use of the present policies to lead to the emergence of neo-fascist regimes, which would be a detriment to us all.

So, I think that a necessary prerequisite for making a more just and equitable society in a country like Australia is to find some way of getting ourselves back to full employment, and in order to do that we have to use not only the traditional weapons but also we have to build on the institutions that we already have and re-establish an effective prices and incomes policy. I have always advocated that we should use the Arbitration Commission and indexation procedures. I think that it is significant, not because I advocated it, but because the present government and its advisers have thought them not to be effective, that we have seen a concerted effort to downgrade their influence and to move away from using such institutions and depend instead on measures which come directly through the Treasury. Now, those sorts of measures have been described by Balogh very colourfully, but I think with a considerable element of truth, as 'the incomes policy of Karl Marx'. Why the incomes policy of Karl Marx? Well, Balogh says that by deliberately setting out to base the viability of the capitalist system on the maintenance of a large industrial reserve army, monetarists may validate Marx's analysis. I think that there is a tremendous amount of truth in that. Beneath the guise of using contractionary policies, what we have really been seeing is an attempt to redress the change in the balance of power which occurred during the twenty or twenty-five years of virtually sustained full employment and growth whereby power went much more to labour and much less to capital. What we see now is an attempt to swing that around. In the Australian case it has been not only an internal fight between the capitalist class and the wage-earning groups, it also has been an attempt to signal to overseas investors that we now have a quiescent and cowed labour force which makes Australia a good place in which to invest. It also has been a kind of incomes policy. The policy envisaged an average rate of money-wage increases which would give us a price level (and a rate of increase of the price level) which still left us competitive, while at the same time allowing money-wages in the expanding areas to go up in order to attract labour there, this to be counterbalanced by either falling or very slowly increasing money-wages in the depressed or declining industries as a result of the higher levels of unemployment.

I do not think this has been successful, because I do not think this is the way in which the Australian labour market necessarily works. I also do not think it has been successful, because it ignores one of the basic questions which I mentioned at the start of my lecture; namely, that not only one of the most volatile forces at work in the economy but also one which tends to run on average at a level which is not sufficient to maintain full employment, is the level of capital accumulation by private business people. There is nothing like years of sustained failure of sales to dampen what Keynes called the animal spirits of business people. While they may be slowly having an effect on the rate of increase of money-wages, you are simultaneously having a disastrous effect on the confidence and the ability of business people to invest at a rate which not only raises productivity but also gives a level of activity which is a satisfactory one in a capitalist economy.

If we decide that either as a result of what we have done in the past, or for policy reasons, a progressive government ought to have something much more to say about both the rate and the composition of accumulation of capital goods, this immediately brings into focus whether we should put nationalisation back on the agenda. When I go back to my first year at Melbourne University, one of the things that really led me towards thinking about socialism was a description of how oil wells were developed on the Californian oilfields by unfettered private enterprise. The wells were put down so close to one another that they let the gas out and so, much oil which otherwise could have been taken out, was lost forever just because the wells were too close together. It seemed to me that this was a very irrational way both to use and to start developing resources which were meant to be used, not only by this generation but by future generations as well. In other words, the horizon for the rational use of oil seemed to me to be much longer than the horizon of any one particular person developing it, and therefore it seemed to me that we ought to develop institutions which allow us to take much longer horizons in planning the development of resources which are vital to the community as a whole, not only the current generation but future generations as well. Now, of course, one of the things that has come out of our experience with nationalised industries is that they also are subject to the whims of politicians, if not to the whims of business people, and that politicians themselves have short-run constraints imposed on them by the distances that they have between elections. Therefore their horizons often may be even shorter than those of the private business people who were thinking about developing the resources, and this is one of the things which has led, I think, to disillusionment with using the public sector and to a movement back to using the market and market signals as the means for developing our resources.

I have to admit at least the partial validity of such an argument, so I now would argue that if we are considering bringing nationalisation back for key industries in our economy, supposing for a moment the constitutional puzzle to be solvable, we would have to do so within a context of at least two major reforms. One is that their managers would have to be given instructions about the time horizon that they were to bear in mind and also about the overall pattern of development of the economy that the government explicitly had set out. The other thing is (and this is an aspect of our experience of the industrial relations of nationalised industries) that there is no point nationalising industries and leaving intact the same hierarchical internal structures as those which traditionally have been used in private enterprise. We now know that the wage-earners become just as browned off with socialised managers as they are with private ones. So if nationalisation is to be put back on the agenda, it will have to be coupled with reforms of the hierarchical structures that are contained within the management structure. I do not pretend to have any profound or wise words on the details, but I do put this forward as a general principle which would have to be considered.

The final major point that I would like to make and which I think interventionists such as myself seriously have to try to think about, has to do with the hierarchical structures of modern civil services. It seems to me that they are such that while we can always ensure that highly intelligent people get to the top in the key decision-making positions, we cannot always be sure that the people who do that also have other desirable characteristics such as altruism and compassion and tolerance. This is not meant to be a criticism of any particular individuals, it is a criticism of the structure of the system; indeed, it is one of the problems of bureaucratic structures, whether they be in the public sector or in the private sector. Therefore, one of the major things which a progressive government will have to look at is how *do* you overcome this puzzle so that when you come in with coherent explicit plans of your own, you can make sure that they are implemented at key points without being frustrated by people who think that they are not necessarily practical or workable—or desirable. This is a major problem and I think it is one of the reasons why there has been considerable disillusionment with the role of the public sector and the revolt against big government, both of which have been features of modern capitalist economies in the last five to ten years. It is a major puzzle and a major problem.

I entitled this lecture 'Making Socialism in Your Own Country' and I am afraid that I have had to spend a lot of time talking about the things that I suppose relatively I know best; that is, about economic theory and economic policy. Nevertheless, I want to say in conclusion that I have tried to keep in mind that vision of a new world which I quoted from

Bertrand Russell. While I have at times been disillusioned and distressed about the possibility of bringing about a better society, yet I think that one always has to keep on going, and I do not think that people who call themselves socialists should be ashamed of it; they should not allow 'socialism' to be treated as a dirty word, which is the custom in the media and in the more conservative parts of Australian politics. I personally like to keep in mind—because I think it links onto the vision that Russell put before us—a memory from the days of anti-war protests during the Vietnam war. I remember that we had a march through Adelaide one evening (there is nothing like being an anti-war protestor to get to know your city, particularly the byways and highways when you are trying to get away). This particular march had been busted up, but we had regrouped on the steps of Parliament House. There, we had the long-playing record of Woodstock, itself a quite exceptional happening, noted for some very memorable songs. As the twilight came down in Adelaide, there was a group of women dressed in the long flowing dresses that they wore in those days, dancing to the music of Woodstock in front of the pillars of Parliament House in Adelaide. And I thought as I watched those women dancing that here at least was a generation who would not accept the tired old jingoistic statements that we have been brought up on, who would really believe in making a better and more noble and greater world than we ourselves had experienced. Well, I suppose that was at the beginning of the 1970s when people still had hope, and I suppose after the reaction and the outburst of jingoism in the UK during the recent Falklands war, for example, one might, perhaps, discount some of one's hope for the future. Nevertheless, I take comfort in at least two things. One is that those particular people are still around, they have kept their ideals and have tried to implement them in practice. Second, the Archbishop of Canterbury preached at the end of the Falklands war one of few really Christian sermons—for which he was bucketted in no uncertain terms by both the British Prime Minister and the Tory politicians and Tory press. Well, that is as it should be—Archbishops of Canterbury ought to be bucketted by such groups—I mean the terrible thing is that they have not been more often. Yet all he did was to say that war was a confession of failure and that in the aftermath of war we should remember the parents, the spouses and the friends of all the soldiers on both sides who had fallen. I thought that was a pretty sensible and inspiring thing to say, and indeed I wrote him a letter which said in part that I would be proud to live in a country which had him as the spiritual leader. Joan thinks that MI5 will open it and that when Mrs Thatcher comes to renew my twelve-months work-permit this time next year I may well be asked to leave. If I am, I can see at least two Vice-Chancellors[13] in the audience and since I am the risk-taker while I am away, I hope that there at least will be a job of picking up leaves round the ANU campus for me to take on.

Thank you very much.

NOTES

1. The twelfth annual John Curtin Memorial Lecture given at the Australian National University, Canberra, Australia, in August 1982. The lecture was delivered from notes, then tape-recorded and typed. I have left it much as it came out, except that I have removed some repetitions and made some sentences shorter. I am also much indebted to Terry O'Shaughnessy for his thorough sub-editorial work on the manuscript.
2. John Langmore, 'An Economic Strategy for a Labor Government', *Journal of Australian Political Economy*, nos. 12–13 (June 1982), 37.
3. As quoted by Joan Robinson in her splendid 1981 Tanner Lectures 'The Arms Race', in Sterling M. McMurrin (ed.), *The Tanner Lectures on Human Values* III, 1982 (University of Utah Press, Cambridge University Press, 1982).
4. Bertrand Russell, *Roads to Freedom: Anarchism and Syndicalism* (London: Allen & Unwin, 1919), p. 210, quoted in Noam Chomsky, *Problems of Knowledge and Freedom*, The Russell Lectures, 1971 (London: Fontana, 1972), pp. 10–11.
5. Rodney Maddock and Michael Carter recently immortalised them, fortunately and unfortunately—I mean, fortunately for Maddock and Carter and unfortunately for the others—in their recent paper 'A Child's Guide to Rational Expectations', *Journal of Economic Literature* XX (Mar. 1982), 39–51.
6. Daniel K. Benjamin and Levis A. Kochin, 'Unemployment and Unemployment Benefits in Twentieth-Century Britain: A Reply to Our Critics', *Journal of Political Economy* 90, no. 4 (Apr. 1982), 412–13.

7. Arthur M. Okun, *Prices and Quantities: A Macroeconomic Analysis* (Oxford: Basil Blackwell, 1981).
8. I do not need to explain to an Australian audience what a horse for a course is, but I have had terrible trouble with Italian audiences on this, because they are not as keen on horses as we are, or on the races. I nearly was lynched once when interpreting this phrase, because I was explaining how at Randwick the horses went round one way and at Flemington they went round the other way, and I got them mixed up. You know, I had Randwick going round the wrong way and Flemington going round the wrong way. There were some Australians in the audience, and I was lucky to escape with my life. So I'm not so willing to say which way they go round; I will just say that you have to use horses for courses policies for the various economies with which you are dealing.
9. David Peetz, 'Protection and the Labor Movement', *Journal of Australian Political Economy*, no. 12/13 (June 1982).
10. James Meade, 'The Meaning of "Internal Balance"', *Economic Journal* 88 (Sept. 1978), 423–35.
11. James Meade, *The Intelligent Radical's Guide to Economic Policy: The Mixed Economy* (London: Allen & Unwin, 1975).
12. Thomas Balogh, *The Irrelevance of Conventional Economics* (London: Weidenfeld & Nicolson, 1982).
13. There were in fact three!

11 Notes on the Social Limits to Growth[1]

These notes are intended to pose more questions than they provide answers to. They are prompted by an important book, the *Social Limits to Growth* [2], published by a lifelong socialist, Fred Hirsch (1977) the year before he died; and they draw on three stimulating and challenging reviews of Hirsch's work: the first by Robin Matthews [4]; the second by Anthony Clunies Ross in a review article of Hirsch's book and Hugh Stretton's *Capitalism, Socialism and the Environment* [7]; and the third by Don Lamberton [3]. As I have said, Hirsch was always a socialist; moreover, he knew an incredible amount about the detailed workings of the financial institutions of modern capitalist economies. I believe that his views should be accorded respect and that they are of great relevance to those of us who are thinking about the nature of economic growth and the role it has to play in the transition to a more just and equitable society.

Hirsch himself poses three main questions ([2], p. 1):

(1) 'Why has economic advance become and remained so compelling a goal to all of us as individuals, even though it yields—he asserts, then argues—disappointing fruits when most ... achieve it?' He calls this the *paradox of affluence*.
(2) 'Why [are we so concerned] ... with the division of the pie ... when it is clear that the great majority of people can raise their living standards only through production of a larger pie?' That is, why do we suffer from *distributional compulsion*?
(3) 'Why [have we witnessed in] the twentieth century an increasingly predominant trend toward *collective* provision and state regulation in economic areas ... when *individual* freedom of action is especially extolled,

> [indeed] given unprecedented rein in noneconomic areas—aesthetic and sexual standards, [for example]?' (The emphases are mine) This is the phenomenon of *reluctant collectivism*.

Hirsch's basic answer depends on his classification of goods into *material goods* and *positional goods*. Access to material goods is a function of *real* income, so that both for society as a whole, and for individuals, growth may be expected to bring greater quantities of them. With positional goods, however, access is a function of *relative income*, and general growth does not necessarily, or even usually, increase their availability, not least because many of them are in fixed supply. In a sense, Hirsch's distinction is related to the Ricardian distinction between 'commodities, the value of which is determined by scarcity alone' and those 'commodities only as can be increased in quantity by the exertion of human industry'. Ricardo, of course, thought that in maturing capitalism the latter would dominate the former, at least until the stationary state was reached. Hirsch is examining the consequences in modern economies of the former tending to reach parity with the latter.

In Hirsch's view material goods are those which serve to satisfy our biological needs. We leave aside for the moment the question whether this is a tenable definition. Since there are limits to these biological needs, growth increasingly must satisfy them and so expenditure on positional goods figures more and more prominently in our individual expenditure patterns, and in national expenditure as a whole. This implies in turn that to an increasing extent the goods that people want cannot be provided—'delivered by growth'. Positional goods are 'like places in a race. Only one person can come first. More efficient methods of running will not increase the number who can get first prizes' ([6], p. 180). More prosaically, supply is limited, the rise in demand paradoxically both raises the price *and* diminishes the ultimate satisfactions. What I get, you must miss out on because there is only a limited stock of what we both want. Examples are leadership of a (once great?) political party; general manager of the largest company; 1890s bluestone houses in Adelaide;

accessibility and seclusion—what was country for me as a child in Victoria is now an inner Melbourne suburb.

The most serious example, as far as this self-defeating process is involved, relates, in my opinion, to education and educational qualifications. It is serious because it leads to frustration and disillusionment, and these in turn may lead to the destruction of valuable institutions and to undesirable uses (or non-uses) of the community's resources. While educational qualifications may open the door to a higher income as well as to a more satisfying occupation and life-style for any one person, provided that they are available to them alone, *all* attempting to attain educational qualifications means often only that the qualifications demanded for access to the limited supply of such jobs are raised. Educational qualifications are then a sifting device rather than ends in themselves.

These are just specific examples of a general proposition: the standing on tip-toe paradox. The trouble is that the market system does not give the correct signals to warn us that if we *all* attempt to stand on tip-toes, *none* of us will be better off. Externalities, far from being an exception in a world of mainly material goods, become the rule in a world increasingly dominated by positional goods. 'The benefits ... claimed for the competitive system are ... reduced, even by its own standards ... [To] an increasing extent the goods that people want are not capable of being delivered by growth ... concealed by national accounting definitions, which too often count means as ends' ([4], p. 574): hence the distributional compulsion and the reluctant collectivism, because of increasing market failures inevitably associated with the very nature of positional goods.

Because we are reluctant to adopt, and begrudging about, collectivism, and quickly disillusioned with it—witness the backlash to the Whitlam years, modest and timid though much of the programme was, now so successfully exploited by Fraser[2]—a new source of instability may be diagnosed in our society. Its source goes back a long way. Redistribution and collectivism are responses to aspects of the process of growth which bring in their train disillusionment and dissension. We have glorified self-interest, made capitalism institutionalised selfishness, as Milton Friedman proudly tells us, drawing on the socially beneficial by-products of Adam Smith's 'invisible hand' for justification. (Joan Robinson, however, recently has reminded us that, in Smith's day the invisible hand related to the case against protection ([5], p. 62). Now, though, it has been generalised to much wider applications than that.) What the champions of vulgar Smithism forget to tell us is that Smith was also the author of *The Theory of Moral Sentiments*, in which it is argued that there are altruistic, compassionate and tolerant attributes in human beings which also can be harnessed by suitable institutions. It is the neglect of these, and of the provision of appropriate institutions to accommodate and foster them, together with the fostering of greedy and selfish outlooks, institutions and behaviour, which is the new source of instability that the spread of externalities brings to the fore. Capitalism may have been saved from itself so far, not so much because of the beneficial nature of the invisible hand, nor the predominance of material goods in its earlier stages, itself a debatable hypothesis, but because of the hangover of the moral presuppositions and constraints of a pre-capitalist age. 'Adam Smith believed in a natural order of morality [, that man] was endowed with the moral sentiments which would make society possible ... [The] second part of his doctrine ... has succeeded in undermining those sentiments to a very considerable extent ... putting in their places the doctrine that the pursuit of profit is a substitute for morality' ([5], p. 64). As Matthews says ([4], p. 576), Smith never intended that 'the model of man is and ought to be that of a gangster'.

Hirsch himself sums it up ([2], p. 12): 'the principle of self-interest is incomplete as a social organizing device'—who controls the controllers? Why expect them to act other than in accordance with *their* self-interest? In another context, the (so-called) failure of Keynesianism is placed at the door of Keynes's belief that public servants, in particular, and indirectly, the politicians that they advise, would operate within the constraints imposed by 'the presuppositions of Harvey Road':[3] that the fundamental political and economic policy decisions would continue always to be made by a small group of enlightened and rational people who had the interests of society as a *whole* continually before them. Such a belief, it is argued, is completely at variance with the true nature of the sources of power and decision-making in our society. Kalecki's political trade cycle is much closer to the mark as a description of the operation of modern-day capitalism. Again, Australian experience in recent years offers confirmation of these fears.

Thus it is becoming increasingly apparent that the hierarchical and promotional structures of modern bureaucracies are not designed to ensure that altruistic and disinterested (as well as intelligent) people necessarily will emerge in key positions. There is little doubt that intelligence will win out but, too often, it is accompanied by ruthlessness and coldness, a lack of compassion which is not necessarily compensated for by great ambition and drive. All this was borne in on me when I read, a couple of years ago, a series of profiles of the heads of the main public service departments in Australia. On the whole it was not pleasant reading. Yet the people themselves are not entirely to be blamed; it is the system within which they have to operate, especially interdepartmental jealousies and rivalries, together with the often random or irrelevant allocations of their political chiefs to each ministry, which are to be held mainly responsible. It is not surprising, therefore, that we have witnessed in recent years a reaction against, indeed, abhorrence of, 'Big Government'. Those of us who nevertheless remain interventionists will have to come to grips with this phenomenon.

One of Hirsch's conclusions is that if we are to restore stability to our social life, we are going to need to re-establish Adam Smith's moral sentiments (with a dash of the presuppositions of Harvey Road—for all). We need to establish 'a consensus on certain aspects of social ethics and on the proper distribution of income and wealth'. Since the process of growth turns us inevitably towards distributional compulsion and reluctant collectivism, this should be accompanied by explicit discussion and explanation of why it is so. Redistribution and collectivism have been unsatisfactory policies just because, as Matthews say, we suffer from 'the illusion that the privileges of the haves could be maintained *and* made available to the have-nots'([4], p. 578).

Another aspect of Hirsch's thesis which Clunies Ross

homes in on is the increasing commercialisation of the provision of services which detracts from the very satisfactions they are meant to bring. Hirsch himself illustrates this by bought sex. 'Orgasm as a consumer's right rather rules it out as an ethereal experience' ([6], p. 101). More generally, '[as] cash income becomes increasingly dominant in governing consumption activities and attainment of social and economic position, so it must increasingly dominate productive activities... [Growing] more dependent on money for our life and leisure, we...grow more dependent on money earnings...the internal logic in the process of...commercialization' ([6], p. 104). Nor is this phenomenon confined to the private sector. We have already referred to the disappointments and frustrations associated with educational expenditure. The same point may be made about highway expenditures. These, too, are examples of the central issues of Hirsch's book, the 'adding-up problem: what individuals want and what individually they can get, society cannot get; and society has to find some means for determining how the difference should be reconciled' ([2], p. 106). It is the 'competitive system [that] produces an excessive and increasing *bias* towards *commercialization*, conducting the business of life by means of self-interested one-off transactions at arm's length [instead of] on the basis of friendship and mutual trust' ([4], p. 576).

What then are we to do? The first point to make is that the concept of biological needs is *not* a viable one, if it is meant in a strict sense. Even for such basic needs as food, clothing and shelter there are historical and social determinants involved so that the material/positional distinction is blurred. Second, it is *not* obvious that satiation of desire for material goods has been reached, only that with the existing distribution of incomes and property it may often be thought necessary to titillate jaded middle-class appetites to raise demand for them. There is, therefore, still a strong case on both humanitarian and Keynesian effective-demand grounds for a more egalitarian structure to our income distribution and, especially, to the distribution of wealth. This argument shades over into the positional one as well, in that if it is, for example, non-pecuniary attributes which make many occupations attractive, there is no need to have the positive correlation between attractive jobs and real incomes that is characteristic of our income distributions today. Clunies Ross thinks straight away of university teachers in this regard. Hugh Stretton has consistently argued for an income range which does not exceed 3 : 1. Hirsch's book adds further good reasons. A cut in monetary rewards would reduce the 'total demands for such jobs by shedding potential applicants for whom the pay advantage is dominant' ([2], p. 183). For example, universities are now paying for their greed of the 1960s when the going was good. The public then was both excited about and favourable towards education as an end in itself. University staff took advantage of this climate more to secure large incomes than to ensure that they created conditions whereby creative and productive scholarship would be ensured. Due to the, probably necessary, phenomena of tenure, their huge salary bills are now akin to fixed costs, and for many of the tenured staff, their salaries bear a close resemblence to sinecures. This means that younger scholars, research facilities, study-leave schemes and the students themselves have to bear the painful brunt of the major restructuring and retrenchment which is occurring at the moment, all over the world. Yet, if tenured scholars were altruistic enough to forgo increases in their real incomes, for say, a five-year period, it would be possible to create a sustained number of new positions for their younger colleagues, which would be beneficial not only for them but also for students in particular (who would continue to be taught, at least in part, by the brightest and the best, those still on the frontiers) and for scholarship in general. Externalities are nowhere more to be found than in great educational institutions—benefits and costs which rarely can be caught or counted by penny-pinching bureaucrats and antagonistic politicians, trying merely to balance the books of our educational institutions.

Another, rather nebulous, conclusion is that we should always explain what it is that we are doing, and why, and what the costs (and benefits) will be for particular groups and for society as a whole. In the light of the experience of the Whitlam years this *should* be a lesson that is easily absorbed.

We need to devise means whereby people are encouraged to act 'as if' they were altruistic. '[People] must recognize[, for example,] that they ought to pay for their taxes, because although it would be in their interest not to, it would [even more] not be in their interest to have a system in which no one did' ([4], p. 577). Matthews points out that getting such a moral code accepted has great practical difficulties associated with it. Obviously, it would be impossible to precede every major proposed economic change by a discussion of the 'general-equilibrium analysis of what would happen if everyone acted on the same principles'! So we must settle instead for some rules of thumb; but they in practice too often turn out to be silly.

What are the practical implications of all this for democratic socialist parties such as the Australian Labor Party, both in opposition and in power? The first is that we now have a compelling new set of arguments with which to attack the back-to-the market, get-out-of-the public sector attitudes of the current conservative government. Second, social democrats as well as democratic socialists may reaffirm their belief in an egalitarian distribution of income and wealth and in the need to take measures to secure them. Third, and in the long run the most important, it establishes the need for thoroughgoing discussions of major economic and social changes before they are enacted. In particular, people always need to be made aware of the costs and benefits involved, especially when the former are often concentrated and local, while the latter are widely diffused, but nonetheless real and important for that. In saying this I am not meaning to overlook either Hirsch's own warnings nor Don Lamberton's, that information is both very costly and, while partly positional in character, is mainly an *intermediate good*, 'a necessary social cost', so that the 'information sector may grow while the product dwindles' ([3], p. 66).

NOTES

1. Reprinted from *Economic Forum*, Summer 1981, pp. 1–8. This paper was presented to the Conference of Labor Economists, Brisbane, Australia, May 1978.

2. Gough Whitlam, head of the Australian Labor Party, was Prime Minister of Australia from 1972 to 1975; Macolm Fraser, head of the coalition of the Liberal and Country Parties, was Prime Minister from 1975 to the present.
3. *See* Buchanan, Burton and Wagner [1].

REFERENCES

[1] Buchanan, J. M., Burton, John and Wagner, R. E. *The Consequences of Mr Keynes*. London, Institute of Economic Affairs, 1978
[2] Hirsch, Fred. *Social Limits to Growth*. London and Henley, Routledge and Kegan Paul, 1977
[3] Lamberton, Don 'Review of *Social Limits to Growth*'. *Economic Analysis and Policy* (Mar. 1977)
[4] Matthews, Robin. 'Review of *Social Limits to Growth*'. *Economic Journal* (Sept. 1977), 574–8
[5] Robinson, Joan. 'Morality and Economics', *Challenge* (Mar./Apr. 1978), 62–4
[6] Ross, Anthony Clunies. 'Review of *Social Limits to Growth*'. *J. Econ. Stud.* (Nov. 1977), 4.
[7] Stretton, Hugh. *Capitalism, Socialism and the Environment*. Cambridge, Cambridge Univ. Press, 1976

Acknowledgements

We are grateful to the editors and publishers of the following journals and books for permission to reproduce the articles which appear in this volume: Duke University Press for the article 'Reflections on the Development of Economics as a Discipline' from *History of Political Economy* 16/4 (Winter 1984); M. E. Sharpe Inc. for the articles 'A Man for all Systems: Talking to Kenneth Boulding' (1983) and 'A Twentieth Century Eclectic: Richard Goodwin' (1985) from *Journal of Post Keynesian Economics*; the Frederick May Foundation of Italian Studies, University of Sidney for the article 'On Piero Sraffa's Contributions to Economics' from P. D. Groenewegen and J. Halevi (eds.), *Altro Polo. Italian Economics Past and Future* (1983); Cambridge University Press for the article 'On the Contributions of Joan Robinson and Piero Sraffa to Economic Theory' from the *Economic Journal* (Supplement) March 1986; McGraw Hill Book Co. for the article 'Investment-Decision Criteria, Capital-Intensity and the Choice of Techniques' from John T. Dunlop and Nikolay P. Federenko (eds.), *Planning and Markets* (1969); American Economic Society for the article 'Some Cambridge Controversies in the Theory of Capital' from the *Journal of Economic Literature* (1969); The University of Chicago Press for the article 'The Rate of Profits in Equilibrium Growth Models' from the *Journal of Political Economy* 81, no. 5 (September 1973); the Australian Society of Accountants for the article 'The Social Consequences of Inflation' from the *Australian Accountant* (October 1974); the Australian National University for the article 'Making Socialism in your own Country' given as the Twelfth Annual John Curtin Memorial Lecture (1982); and Utah University Press for the article 'Notes on the Social Limits to Growth' from *Economic Forum* (Summer 1981). The letter from John Maynard Keynes to Joan Robinson in Essay 5 is quoted with permission from Lord Kahn.

Index